Law, Language and Change

Legal History Library

VOLUME 42

The titles published in this series are listed at *brill.com/lhl*

Law, Language and Change

A Diachronic Semantic Analysis of *Consideration* in the Common Law

By

Caroline I.B. Laske

BRILL
NIJHOFF

LEIDEN | BOSTON

Cover illustration: Wren Library of Trinity College in Cambridge, drawing by Jean-Philippe Brondel.

The Library of Congress Cataloging-in-Publication Data is available online at http://catalog.loc.gov
LC record available at http://lccn.loc.gov/2020028818

Typeface for the Latin, Greek, and Cyrillic scripts: "Brill". See and download: brill.com/brill-typeface.

ISSN 1874-1793
ISBN 978-90-04-42848-5 (hardback)
ISBN 978-90-04-43616-9 (e-book)

This book is printed on acid-free paper and produced in a sustainable manner.

Dedicated to Pia, Noé, Simon and Félix

"When I use a word," Humpty Dumpty said in rather a scornful tone,
"it means just what I choose it to mean – neither more nor less."

"The question is," said Alice, "whether you *can*
make words mean so many different things."

"The question is," said Humpty Dumpty,
"which is to be master – that's all."

LEWIS CARROLL

Contents

Preface

Innovative research can only see the light if the researcher is lucky enough to be surrounded by people who believe in her project. I had the privilege to be in this position. When I first discussed my research idea of combining and adapting linguistic methodologies to the study of law with Mark Van Hoecke, he immediately saw the potential of this project. It underwent a number of changes, and was carried out, at times, against all odds of family and health issues. But Mark never wavered and I will forever be grateful to him for his unfaltering support. Bart Defrancq and Dirk Heirbaut were two further unshakable pillars on this journey. No words can sufficiently acknowledge my appreciation of their encouragements and the many hours of time they offered so generously to advise me and discuss the many issues that the research raised. Paul Brand has also been very kind to make many helpful suggestions.

A special vote of thanks goes to my friends and colleagues for helping me so diligently with the proof-reading of the text and for making creative suggestions for improvements, in particular Stephen Engelhard and Toby Robinson who also offered tremendous help with the statistics and graphs. Wendel Scholma and Jorik Groen from Brill have been patient and supportive and two anonymous Brill readers greatly encouraged me with their enthusiastic endorsement for my work.

Last but not least, I owe enormous gratitude to my family, in particular to Jean-Philippe for the beautiful cover page design, and to my four wonderful children who have supported and assisted me every step of the way whether in form of discussion, practical help, morale boosting or their wonderful unconditional love. This book would not have seen the light without their encouragements. I dedicate it to them and to the intellectual curiosity of their generation.

Illustrations and Tables

Figures

Charts

Tables

CHAPTER 1

Introduction

> Law in particular becomes then only a rational study, when it is traced historically, from its first rudiments among savages, through successive changes, to its highest improvements in a civilised society. And yet the study is seldom conducted in this manner. Law, like geography, is taught as if it were a collection of facts merely: the memory is employed to the full, rarely the judgment.[1]

∵

Lord Kames, like so many of his contemporaries, embodied interdisciplinarity and, despite having enjoyed no university education, wrote with equal erudition about law, history, philosophy, religion, aesthetics, literary criticism and agricultural improvements. In the above extract from the introduction to his *Historical Law Tracts*, Kames not only shows himself as the staunch defender of the study of legal history that he was, but he also deplores what we would describe in today's jargon as the compartmentalised autonomy of the study of law: seeing 'facts' in isolation with limited concern for contexts. Whilst the study and profound knowledge of autonomous 'facts' are no doubt essential, the contribution to scholarship is only truly informative and fascinating if context is created by taking a step back from the conditions of autonomy and adding dimension by comprehending the issues from a broader angle. The present research was born from such thinking and considerations.

Its aim was to trace the advent and early use of the concept of consideration in English contract law, by studying the doctrinal development in parallel with the corresponding terminological evolution. It was essential to adopt a two-track, interdisciplinary approach to the research and to mark out a research field beyond the mere content analysis of the case law and legal writings. On the one hand, the enquiry of the legal historian revealed the historical process of the legal thought that initiated this concept. On the other hand, the pragmatic and empirical angle of studying the language in its context by the linguist showed how legal thought was encoded in linguistic expressions and meanings. This allowed for a better understanding of the continuous

1 H. Home (Lord Kames) (1761) *Historical Law Tracts*, 2nd edition, Edinburgh: Kincaid, ii–iv.

 | DOI:10.1163/9789004436169_002

interaction between the way legal thought creates meaning in language and language creates realities in law.

Interdisciplinarity is, as the term indicates, an approach that brings together two or more academic disciplines. It allows for thinking to make links between different fields of ideas and areas of study. Crossing disciplinary boundaries in this way liberates the creative thinker from restrictive perceptions and practices associated with one or the other discipline. But it comes with the price of having to define an *inter*-disciplinary space linking the different subjects, in which the research is to be carried out. The majority of scholars find it a challenge to think and 'feel' across disciplinary categories. It is comparable to the phenomenon that few people are truly bi- or multilingual. And as counting, dreaming, swearing still tends to be in the same 'first' language for multilinguists, researchers also relate intuitively to the theoretical and methodological paradigms of their 'first' discipline, which can become a stumbling block for interdisciplinary work. It is indeed possible that representatives from all the different disciplines involved in a given research initiative will be dissatisfied with the process and results because they are likely to be missing a paradigm that is familiar to them, while being confronted with a way of thinking and proceeding that is not.

This very point has been one of the main challenges for the present research. It felt at all times to be a fine balancing act between requirements established by the legal scholar, the historian or the linguist. Maybe, the best observation is to acknowledge that the balancing act was only possible to the extent that the *inter*-disciplinary space was defined in relation to the specificities of this particular research initiative, rather than on an absolute level. The research was then carried out in relation to the parameters of that specific 'third' space, which comes with all the imperfections of only including certain aspects of the theory and methodology from each discipline involved.

Legal history is, in itself, an interdisciplinary undertaking. Law is not totally independent of context but enjoys some autonomy and the historical approach takes law out of its semi-autonomous position to place it within its historical context. In this research, a further dimension was added, namely the study of language and terminology. However, the various disciplines are not brought together in equal measure. This is primarily an enquiry into the diachronic evolution of legal thinking in relation to a particular issue, and the study of the relevant language is a *tool* in this enquiry. The novelty of the approach in relation to legal texts lies in the use of corpus linguistics methodologies[2] as models

2 Corpus linguistics studies language based on large collections of computerised texts using linguistic software, which retrieves alphabetically or otherwise sorted lists of linguistic data from the corpus.

for a better understanding of the development of legal thinking beyond the mere content approach that legal research usually practices.

But the tension of combining the study of law and that of language remained. The linguist studies terms and how these are used, while the legal historian is concerned with the legal concepts that the terms denote and how these can be ordered in a system throughout time. This enduring tension goes back to the clash between the humanists of the Renaissance who understood Roman law by examining the context in which legal terms were used, and their scholastic predecessors, who wanted to understand the meaning that the terms must have if law is to be orderly and systematic.

Matilla describes it as follows (my emphasis):

> Legal science is mainly interested in abstract entities – concepts – that are to be found in the background of terms, that is, in the meanings of terms. This science systematises the legal order through legal concepts. Terms are designations of concepts, necessary to legal science. However, the primary interest of this science *does not have bearing on legal terms but on the concepts themselves*. By contrast, in legal linguistics it is the *terms as such* that constitute the primary object of research.[3]

The present study has attempted to bring together the two 'sciences' in an *inter*-disciplinary space that makes linguistics a means for studying legal concepts.

For the linguistic community, the methodology and conclusions are of interest in relation to the use of specialists' language and terminology – language for special purposes or LSP. From the linguistic study of the concept of consideration, we observe the opposite of what has so far been described in the area of LSP, namely a semantic shift from everyday vocabulary and the general register of ordinary life via repeated use in a legal context with increasing legal connotations to a highly specialised, incomprehensible and by now sometimes archaic register. This semantic development moved in the opposite direction from what is usually associated with LSP studies.

However, the diachronic corpus linguistics approach does not result in a full, general and statistical linguistic analysis of the language of law reporting between the 14th and 18th centuries. Such an approach, typical for the linguistic research community, was not imported into the *inter*-disciplinary space. The use of linguistics methodologies was restricted to revealing a specific

3 H. Mattila (2013) *Comparative Legal Linguistics. Language of Law, Latin and Modern Lingua Francas*, Surrey: Ashgate, 15.

development of legal thinking and doctrine. It is the study of how legal concepts materialise, evolve and are translated into the letter of the law that stands at the centre of the *inter*-disciplinary space created for this research.

•••

From our 21st century view, we often perceive long-standing, well-established legal concepts and the language used to express them as having been carved in stone as far back as the legal mind can remember. And yet, this is somewhat a post-rationalisation by legal historians, who want to see a linear development of the law, presupposing that the shape legal concepts were to take at the end was aimed at from the start. The customary law set-up of the late Middle Ages mirrored to some extent everyday circumstances and allowed more readily for the intellectual and doctrinal process involved in the development of a concept to be revealed. The language used is frequently less set and settled in comparison to that of dogmatic writing or statute law. Studying this language and terminology reveals how legal concepts materialise, evolve and translate into the letter of the law. This is the underlying interest of the present research.

The object to be examined is the common law concept of consideration, its historical development and how its terminology and the semantic/lexical fields changed and shifted throughout this evolution. In today's perception, the doctrine of consideration, as a central element to contract formation, appears so well anchored in contract law and in our legal minds, that we may find it difficult to imagine its development took a tortuous and at times haphazard path, stretching over several centuries. The forerunners of consideration arose in a medieval legal world of archaic procedures and complex technicalities, and where the need was increasingly felt for the development of a tool that could meet the rising commercial needs in terms of contracts and quasi-contracts. But various strands from different legal issues came together in the idea that informal promises should be enforceable. The evolution was somewhat haphazard because the facts in case law tended to appeal to different established legal actions. It was largely a question of constructing arguments to win a court case. Milsom[4] described this as "the only reality before the court was the dispute, and the only need was to settle it". Every decision related to specific facts and was then extrapolated onto wider issues but it was not devised as part of an overall doctrine of contract law. Indeed, there was no general

4 S.F.C. Milsom (1985) *Studies in the History of the Common Law*, London: The Hambledon Press, at 187.

common law theory of contract at the time – that would be initiated only in the 18th century by Blackstone and his treatise-writing contemporaries. Today's contract law doctrine of offer and acceptance as the moment when a promise becomes binding was unknown then; there was no requirement, as there is in modern contract law, for the plaintiff to show that a contract had been made. Instead, it had to be demonstrated that a promise had been made for good consideration but had not been honoured.

To retrace the development along this path was the ambition of this study, and the approach, akin to *Begriffsgeschichte*, was to go beyond looking at the mere content of the historical material. The texts need to be placed within their diachronic context, so as to reveal the conceptual shifts in thoughts and meanings. Law is not a collection of physically verifiable 'natural facts'.[5] Rather, it is a phenomenon created by man, without existing as such in the material world and the language used to describe this phenomenon is intrinsically linked to its specific reality. To that extent the study of language used in the 'making' of the concept of consideration was at the heart of the research question. Language as an act of communication encodes meanings in accordance with the socio-political, cultural and historical contexts in which they are uttered. Similarly, the language used in particular in legal proceedings is the product and a reliable indicator of these contexts and of how laws are created, practiced and interpreted. There is a continuous interaction between the way laws create meaning in language and how language creates realities in law.[6] Consequently, studying the language means gaining a better understanding of the contexts and the realities of the law, including the intertextuality of prior legal-discursive traditions.

The function of language that is of particular interest is its representational aspect, as it encodes our experience of the world and thus conveys a picture of reality. Researching that representational aspect informs us about the concordance between the historical and conceptual development of 'consideration' and the way the relevant terms and vocabulary have been used, changed and shifted throughout this evolution, most notably the increased abstraction of both the legal concept and the language. For example, considering the vocabulary used in relation to the concept of making informal agreements enforceable by looking beyond the traditional grammar classification (verbs, nouns,

---

5 D.N. MacCormick, O. Weinberger (1986) *An Institutional Theory of Law*, Dordrecht: Kluwer, Chapter 3.

6 M. Van Hoecke, M. Warrington (2010) Legal Cultures, Legal Paradigms and Legal Doctrine: Towards a New Model for Comparative Law, first published 1998, reprinted in M. Del Mar, W. Twinning, M. Giudice (eds.) *Legal Theory and the Legal Academy*, The Library of Essays in Contemporary Legal Theory, vol. III, Farnham: Ashgate, 291–332, at 305.

adjectives etc.) of the words in question and considering instead the function (ideational, interpersonal, textual) they play, we can get a more complete and in-depth picture of the evolution of that vocabulary.

The methodology adopted to reveal how language and the evolution of legal concepts interact is to examine the language in question in its textual context. The use of corpus linguistics methods and linguistics/concordance software is ideal for this sort of empirical approach, as it allows for systematic diachronic analysis of authentic evidence of large scale electronically held corpora.

But it was the application of corpus linguistics and the interpretations of the results that revealed some of the main methodological challenges, mainly because (common law) lawyers and linguists have different views and methodologies for the evaluation of textual evidence. In law based on legal precedents, some shifts in legal thinking can, at times, originate in a few short sentences (maybe even in a mere subordinate clause) that can be found in a discussion, legal argument, decision or mere *dictum.* Essential for common law thinking is that some of these points, however fleetingly touched upon in a legal action, form the basis (precedent) for taking the law into specific directions. In other words, the textual evidence for such shifts in legal thinking/decision may be very slim at times. A linguist, on the other hand, works on the basis of a lot of textual evidence, which forms the support for an empirical approach of analysing language-in-use rather than mere content analysis. This paradox was not easy to resolve in the *inter*-disciplinary space and it may well be a contentious issue that satisfies neither discipline. But, as mentioned above, the linguistics methodologies were used as *tools* to indicate *tendencies* in legal thinking. The purpose was not to make a full analysis of the language in the Year Books and Law Reports.

The results confirmed tendencies sufficiently definite to show a concordance between the hesitant and at times confused development of the concept of consideration and the terminology used in discussions of the issue in the case law. It also revealed the many proposals and attempts that were made before legal thinking settled on the terminology as we know it today. The study showed how, from the 16th century, the use of the word 'consideration' rose exponentially, coupled with a semantic shift towards a technical legal sense and denoting an abstract concept. The research demonstrated how a prepositional expression denoting a causal relationship (*en consideration de*) gave rise to a fully-fledged legal term crystallising the new concept which had hitherto only been expressed through paraphrase. This is a good illustration of how neologisms develop. Of particular interest is the observation that while certain aspects of the new legal action were already established and confirmed in subsequent cases, the terminology still lingered behind and remained on well-trodden paths. So for example, the promissory notions increasingly present in informal agreements were not necessarily expressed by the use of the term 'promise'. Instead the repeated references to 'covenant', 'bargain' and 'debt', all notions emanating from older actions, point to proprietary rather than promissory concepts. With today's hindsight, we understand that promise was actually already at the heart of the new legal thinking, but the terminology continued to refer to prior discursive elements of proprietary notions. While the legal mind was progressing along a path of new ideas, the language expressing such innovations remained conservative. The uncertainty in the use of terms is a witness to the hesitancy in the legal thinking. As the idea that consideration should be a central element necessary to make informal agreements enforceable, so did its position as an autonomous concept. This was reflected in the use of the term 'consideration', no longer solely in the context of a causal connector but as a stand-alone noun and cover-term for the conceptual thinking of how to make informal agreements enforceable.

This book will take us on a journey retracing the evolution of the concept of consideration from the legal as well as the linguistic angle. The next chapter discusses the notion of legal concepts and their relation to language and specialised terminology. The method of combining the two areas of study in an approach akin to *Begriffsgeschichte* will be outlined briefly. Chapter 3 describes the view this research took of language, how language encodes meanings and how it interacts with law and legal thought. It also includes an explanation of the corpus linguistics methodologies that were used. In Chapter 4, we travel back in time to the 14th century and consider the legal language that dominated England for three hundred years and how this Anglo-Norman import intermingled and interacted with the local vernacular until it was abolished in the early 18th century. Chapter 5 takes us on a similar journey, though this time through the intricacies of the common law concept of consideration. Having thus become acquainted with the cultural and linguistic landscape of multilingual England and its specific situation of medieval legal text production, as well as with the origins and historical evolution of the legal concept of consideration, Chapter 6 describes in detail the corpus linguistic analysis that was carried out in order to highlight the concordance between the development of the concept of consideration and the terminology used in the discussions of the issue in the case law. This includes an explanation of how the different corpora of texts taken from the Year Books and Law Reports were constituted, as well as a detailed description of the methodology applied. The last chapter summarises the observations and conclusions that can be drawn from the research.

The legal sources and case law used for this study were drawn from the Year Books, the Selden Society (Annual) series, the Ames Foundation publications or the English Reports, Full Reprint. All documents can be accessed electronically through www.heinonline.org and are described in detail in Annex 2. A table of cases discussed specifically can be found in Annex 3.

CHAPTER 2

Legal Concepts and Terminology

In this discussion of legal concepts, the temptation has been resisted to define the concept of law itself. Many eminent legal scholars, throughout the centuries, have offered such definitions, some of which were incidentally modified by the rise of supra-national legal systems such as international law, EU law etc. On a general level, law in this study is not to be understood as a mere collection of rules, but as a full system to include authoritative texts, institutions, decision-making actors, communities and patterns and modes of thought, as described by Gerber.[1] Law is a man-made phenomenon, it does not exist as such in the material world and is not a set of 'natural facts'.[2] Rather it is more akin to an interpretive reality that invests material reality with special significance. Drawing on MacCormick and Van Hoecke,[3] John Bell explains the phenomenon of law as a system of rules in terms of how "the legal community creates the institutional reality, which individuals can then use legal concepts to explain. But the institutional system and practices precede the ideas".[4]

Pivotal in this construct is the use of language, as it is the linguistic expression of this man-made phenomenon that cannot be verified as such in physical facts but evolves in interpretive realities. Our specific experience of the world in the form of these realities are encoded in the representational aspect of the legal language. Studying the language will, therefore, inform us on how meanings are encoded within that specific phenomenon.

In the present study, the concept of consideration was examined in its evolution from a collection of piecemeal legal rules established in the case law and for pragmatic requirements, to a fully-fledged doctrine that still dominates today's contract formation in the common law. The underlying question to ask relates to the stage in this development at which this array of piecemeal rules began to be considered a legal concept. In other words, the object of the research is the *process* of bundling together a collection of rules into a legal

1 D.J. Gerber (1998) System Dynamics: Towards a Language of Comparative Law?, in: 46 *American Journal of Comparative Law* 719–734, at 730.

2 D.N. MacCormick, O. Weinberger (1986) *An Institutional Theory of Law*, Dordrecht: Kluwer, Chapter 3, by analogy to Searle's conception of law as 'institutional fact' (J.R. Searle (1995) *The Social Construction of Reality*, London: Allen Lane, at 46).

3 M. Van Hoecke (2002) *Law as Communication*, Oxford: Hart Publishing.

4 J. Bell (2014) The Importance of Institutions, M. Adams, D. Heirbaut (eds.) *The Method and Culture of Comparative Law*, Oxford: Hart Publishing, 207–219, at 210.

 | DOI:10.1163/9789004436169_003

concept, and the approach was to study the language as an indicator for this process.

To track the advent and early use of the concept of consideration in English contract law and to trace the historical process of legal thought that constituted this concept required a wider ambit than just the description and analysis of the content of the case law and legal writings. Though these are essential units of analysis, they must be placed within their diachronic contexts for the conceptual shifts in thought and meaning to be revealed.

This approach is akin to the *Begriffsgeschichte* work undertaken in German-speaking academia, in particular by scholars such as Brunner, Conze, Koselleck and Meier who worked on the encyclopaedia *Geschichtliche Grundbegriffe*.[5] This monumental work is a historical study of the concepts and semantic fields that constitute the language of social and political thought and economic structures, and provides insights into the meanings and uses of words and concepts in classical, medieval and modern languages.[6] The aim of the *Geschichtliche Grundbegriffe* project was to test the hypothesis that the main concepts used in German political and social language were transformed during what Kosselleck, one of the principal editors, called the *Sattelzeit* – the period between approximately 1750 to 1850, a century of crisis and transition, during which conceptual change led to transformations in political, social and economic structures.[7]

One of the methodological principles applied by the editors of the *Geschichtliche Grundbegriffe*, was to analyse the semantic fields of political and social language, because language offers a reliable indicator of the thinking and contexts in which concepts are established and are shifting in meaning. Methodologies imported from linguistics sciences, such as philology, historical semantics and structural linguistics are essential tools for *Begriffsgeschichte* research.[8] In the *Geschichtliche Grundbegriffe*, these were used for the

5 O. Brunner, W. Conze, R. Koselleck (2004) *Geschichtliche Grundbegriffe. Historisches Lexikon zur Politisch-sozialen Sprache in Deutschland*, Stuttgart: Klett-Cotta, 9 volumes.

6 There were other similarly important German works: J. Ritter, K. Gründer, G. Gabriel (1971–2007) *Historisches Wörterbuch der Philosophie*, Basel: Schwabe, mainly concerned with the history of philosophical concepts; R. Reichardt, E. Schmitt, H.J. Lüsebrink, J. Leonard (1985-) *Handbuch politisch-sozialer Grundbegriffe in Frankreich 1680–1820*, München: Oldenbourg Wissenschaftverlag.

7 R. Koselleck (1979) Begriffsgeschichte und Sozialgeschichte, in: *Vergangene Zukunft. Zur Semantik geschichtlicher Zeiten*, Frankfurt am Main: Suhrkamp, 107–129.

8 R. Koselleck (2006) *Begriffsgeschichten*, Frankfurt am Main: Suhrkamp, 32–55.

> purpose of charting both continuities and discontinuities in the use of concepts. Concerned to identify persisting meanings in concepts transmitted from the classical or medieval thought, it also studies decisive shifts of meaning in concepts that continue to be designated by the same word. Finally, it seeks to identify neologisms.[9]

The application of linguistics methodologies to the analysis of concepts historically was related to the shifts in their meanings throughout the period of structural, political, social and economic transformations. In other words, the study of the language used to discuss society, politics and economics was combined with the identification of the transformations in the structures during the *Sattelzeit*.

This particular aspect of the *Begriffsgeschichte* approach guided the present research of tracing the historical process of legal thought that constituted the advent and early use of the concept of consideration in English contract law. Linguistic means of expression are central to law and legal texts are endowed, besides the informative and communicative purposes, with prescriptive and/or performative functions, which make, for example, their translation into another language or socio-political and cultural context particularly complex.[10] The study of law is, among others, an enquiry into the abstract entities that make up a legal order. Law is a phenomenon entirely created by man, it does not exist as such in the physical world. Consequently, the language used to describe this phenomenon is intrinsically linked to its specific reality. This contrasts with the natural sciences, which represent to a certain degree an objective reality and where the language used to describe it cannot change that physical reality, though admittedly conceptual systems in natural sciences and the language to express them are also conditioned and influenced by the societal and cultural contexts. The legal reality of a legal system exists through the linguistic means of expression.

A concept, according to a general definition as, for example, in the Oxford English Dictionary, is a general idea or notion, a universal; a mental representation of the essential or typical properties of something, considered without regard to the peculiar properties of any specific instance or example. In other words, concepts are constituents of thought, abstract representations created by the human mind on the basis of features specific to a thing or matter.

9 M. Richter (1987) *Begriffsgeschichte* and the History of Ideas, in: *Journal of the History of Ideas*, vol. 48(2), 247–263, at 261.

10 C. Laske (2012) Translating the Law, in: *Rechtgeleerd Magazijn Themis*, 267–278, at 270.

A 'term' is the verbal expression of a concept and is usually a part of the conceptual system of a specialised language or language for special propose (LSP).

In law, a clear dividing line is not always drawn between legal conceptions and non-legal conceptions. According to Hohfeld,[11] this is because of a failure to differentiate between purely legal relations and the physical and mental facts that create such relations. He believes there are two reasons for this confusion. First of all, in a specific issue, the ideas associated with each set of relations can be very similar, leading to a blending of legal and non-legal quantities. For example, the early action of debt in medieval common law was applicable to real contracts where a *res* had passed between the parties.[12] It was based on the proprietary notion of possessing a corporeal entity. Rights could be transferred if they were embodied in a physical thing, the premise being that the defendant had received something (a *res*) from the plaintiff and, hence, there had been a *quid pro quo*. In other words, the action of debt was based on a proprietary notion (physical/mental facts leading to a legal relation) rather than promissory one (legal relation) and it evolved around the fiction that the lender was claiming what belonged to him, rather than what the object of a promise was. Historically, in the example of debt, there was no differentiation between the physical and mental facts that constitute the legal relation and the actual legal relation itself.

This was emphasised by a general ambiguity in the legal terminology, which is the second reason for the confusion between legal conceptions and non-legal conceptions. Hohfeld discusses the term 'property' as one example for such looseness of the terminology:

> Sometimes it is employed to indicate the physical object to which various legal rights, privileges, etc. relate; then again – with far greater discrimination and accuracy – the word is used to denote the legal interest (or aggregate of legal relations) appertaining to such physical object. Frequently there is a rapid and fallacious shift from the one meaning to the other. At times, also, the term is used in such a 'blended' sense as to convey no definite meaning whatever.[13]

11 W.N. Hohfeld (1913–1914) Some Fundamental Legal Conceptions as Applied in Judicial Reasoning, in: 23 *Yale Law Journal*, 16–59, at 20.

12 The action of debt also applied to formal contracts under seal specifying a sum.

13 W.N. Hohfeld (1913–1914) at 21–22.

Hohfeld also cites Mr. Justice Smith in the leading case of *Eaton v Boston Concord & Montreal Rail Road Co*:[14]

> In a strict legal sense, land is not 'property', but the subject of property. The term 'property', although in common parlance frequently applied to a tract of land or chattel, in its legal signification means only the rights of the owner in relation to it. It denotes a right over a determinate thing.

In the example of 'property', we can observe how the term is being used in relation to corporeal and incorporeal entities alike, hereby further obscuring the differentiation between legal and non-legal conceptions. In the case of legal relations, the term is used figuratively. One of the reasons for this 'looseness' of legal terminology is that although certain terms refer to highly complex legal concepts, the actual language is imported from general language registers and many terms refer to everyday physical things, while actually describing an abstract legal concept. Pollock and Maitland described this as follows:

> Few, if any, of the terms in our vocabulary have always been technical terms. The license that the man of science can allow himself of coining new words is one which by the nature of the case is denied to lawyers. They have to take their terms out of popular speech; gradually the words so taken are defined; sometimes a word continues to have both a technical meaning for lawyers and a different and vaguer meaning for laymen; sometimes the word that lawyers have adopted is abandoned by the laity.[15]

This demonstrates perfectly the difference between the notion of concept as a cognitive category (constituents of thought) on the one hand, and as a linguistic category (semantic meaning) on the other.[16] To understand the fundamental nature of legal language, it is important to make that distinction. But it also shows the intrinsic link between the two and the inevitable confusion that can be created when they come together.

---

14 (1872) 51 N.H., 504, at 511.

15 F. Pollock, F.W. Maitland (1895/1968) *The History of English Law before the Time of Edward I*, vol. II, Cambridge: CUP, at 31.

16 "Der Begriff ist eine erkenntnistheoretische Kategorie, die Bedeutung eine linguistische". in: H. Felber (2001) *Allgemeine Terminologielehre, Wissenslehre und Wissenstechnik. Theoretische Grundlagen und philosophische Betrachtungen*, Wien: Termnet, at 58–59; also: H. Mattila (2012) Legal Vocabulary, in: P. Tiersma, L. Solan (eds.) *The Oxford Handbook of Language and Law*, 27–51, at 27–28.

Legal terminology, as Pollock and Maitland have pointed out, has often migrated from general language into the specialised legal register. A lot of it is the result of linguistic short-cuts, adapting the ordinary language to serve the functional needs of practising lawyers.[17] Ordinary language terms are given specialised meanings by each legal system. This specialised meaning is conceptually related to the core meaning of the word in common speech. 'Offer and acceptance' is one such example: these words reflect the core idea that was taken up by contract law doctrine, yet the ambit of the semantic field of those words in law is different and much wider than in the ordinary language. Similarly the collocation 'in consideration of' and even more so the term 'consideration' have been subject to this kind of semantic shift, as this study is demonstrating. Malinowski[18] goes so far as to write that a general language term which has not undergone this semantic shift cannot be treated as a law term. It goes without saying that there are many other types of legal terms, such as for example technical terms in a stricter sense, that relate to institutions and concepts, which do not exist outside the legal field. A legal term can be formed in a variety of ways. Apart from terms migrating from general language to specialised legal terminology, a term can also be borrowed from a foreign legal language or new terms or neologisms may be created.

As mentioned in the previous chapter, lawyers and linguists approach (legal) language from a different view point. Lawyers tend to adopt a deterministic view of legal terms,[19] while for the linguist the legal terms are in their nature mainly polysemic, their intended meaning being dependent on the context in which they occur.[20] As legal systems are in a constant state of evolution

17 L.M. Friedman (1964) Law and its Language, in: *33 George Washington Law Review*, 563–579, at 565.

18 A. Malinowski (2006) *Polski jezyk prawny. Wybrane zagadnienia*, Warszawa: Wydawnictwo Prawnicze LexisNexis, at 154.

19 H.L.A. Hart (1961) Positivism and the separation of law and morals, in: *Harvard Law Review* 71/4, 593–629; H. Kelsen (1967) *The Pure Theory of Law*, Berkeley: University of California Press; D.N. MacCormick (1974) Law as Institutional Fact, in: *Law Quarterly Review* 90, 102–129.

20 For example: G. Cornu (2005) *Linguistique Juridique*, Paris: Montchrestien; G. Cornu (2007) *Vocabulaire juridique*, Paris: PUF; J-C. Gémar (1995) *Traduire ou l'art d'interpréter, Langue, droit et société: éléments de jurilinguistique*, tome 2: *Application – Traduire le texte juridique*, Saint-Nicolas: Presses de l'Université du Québec; J.E. Joseph (1995) Indeterminacy, Translation and the Law, in: M. Morris (ed.) *Translation and the Law*, Amsterdam/Philadelphia: John Benjamins Publishing Company, 13–36; S. Roszkowski (1999) The language of law as sublanguage, in: J. Tomaszczyk (ed.) *Aspects of Legal Language and Legal Translation*, Lodz: Lodz University Press, 7–16.

and change, are not isolated but influence each other in both time and space, we can observe a high frequency of polysemy in legal terminology.[21] This polysemy together with the fact that legal discourse dealing with everyday problems or phenomena is often addressed to society at large, can create the illusion of comprehension by the lay person. But even among lawyers, polysemy causes confusion in legal interpretation and translation. In legal translation, the difficulties of transferring legal concepts from one legal culture/language to another can be addressed by combining conceptual analysis and cognitive linguistics. This allows us to determine the set of characteristics brought together in a particular concept, and the relation between a characteristic and the concepts it describes.

Before turning to the question of retracing the *making* of a concept and the concurring shift in meanings of the terminology, the next chapter discusses the angle from which language was considered for this research.

21 H. Mattila (2012) Legal Vocabulary, in: P. Tiersma, L. Solan (eds.) *The Oxford Handbook of Language and Law*, 27–51, at 30.

CHAPTER 3

Language, Functional Linguistics and Corpus Linguistics

1 Language: The Theory of Functional Linguistics

Starting with the angle on language, we first need to outline the way language is considered in this book, how language is used to encode meanings and how it interacts with law and legal thought.[1] According to the Oxford English Dictionary, language has a multitude of meanings. These can relate to the concept of language, to specific linguistic systems, or systems of communication, including non-verbal, signal or gestural communication or expression in music and art, to computing, to manner/style of expression or specific jargon, to a community of people or a nation etc. In this research, we are not concerned with language as a mental faculty nor with the human capacity for language as universal and altogether innate and as a unique development of the human brain.[2] Nor will this research explore the structuralist view of language as a system of symbols and as a closed system in which elements are held in balance and are assembled according to specific (grammatical) rules. In the structuralist approach, meaning is not given in advance but is created with the formation of the sign itself and it is not rooted in some universal logic but is the result of entirely arbitrary decision on the part of each linguistic community. Consequently, if two communities construct different meanings for the same thing, there is no objective basis for deciding which meaning is better or right.[3]

The premise on which this research is based, is that of language as an act of communication. It is a pragmatic view which stresses the function, notably the social function, of the use of language when people interact with each other. This approach has been adopted mainly in the context of socio-linguistics and

1 See also C. Laske (2013) Translators and Legal Comparatists as Objective Mediators between Cultures? in: J. Husa, M. Van Hoecke (eds.) *Objectivity in Law and Legal Reasoning*, Oxford: Hart Publishing, 213–227.

2 Chomsky's Universal Grammar is a prominent exponent of this school of thought, see e.g. N. Chomsky (1965) *Aspects of the Theory of Syntax*. MIT Press; N. Chomsky (2000) *The Architecture of Language*, New Delhi: OUP (India); N. Chomsky (2007) Approaching UG from Below, in: H-M. Gärtner, U. Sauerland (eds.) *Interfaces + Recursion = Language? Chomsky's Minimalism and the View from Syntax-Semantics*. Studies in Generative Grammar. Berlin: Mouton de Gruyter.

3 F. de Saussure (1916/2005) *Cours de linguistique générale*, Paris: Payot & Rivages.

 DOI:10.1163/9789004436169_004

linguistic anthropology. In the context of examining the use of legal language, the approach which emphasises usage, communicative function and social context of language seems the most appropriate to adopt. The theory of language to be discussed here is generally known as systemic functional linguistics, or systemic functional grammar or systemic linguistics and was first adopted by Michael Halliday in the 1980s.[4]

It offers an account of language as it is used in actual social situations and is, in this sense, always concerned with the meaning, communicative functionality and rhetorical purposes of language. At the heart of systemic linguistics is the understanding of the communicative properties of written and spoken texts of all types (why a text means what it does and why it is valued as it is), as well as the understanding of the relation between language, on the one hand, and culture, community, social grouping and ideology, on the other.[5]

For functional linguists, language appears to have developed and is used for three purposes, which Halliday has called metafunctions:

i. *Ideational metafunction*, encodes meanings of experience which realise field of discourse ('experiential meanings'). It refers to the use of language to represent experience and construct a view of reality with the various categories language offers to talk about real-world happenings. There are three main constituents: processes (typically expressed as verbs identifying entities and states of affairs), participants (typically expressed as nouns identifying entities), and circumstances (typically expressed as adverbs or prepositional phrases acting to provide some context to the first two elements).

   An example of the simplest clause constituent structure in the experiential function would be:

The train	departs
(PARTICIPANT)	(PROCESS)
The dog	barked
(PARTICIPANT)	(PROCESS)

   This becomes more elaborate when other participants are added:

My uncle	missed	the train
(PARTICIPANT)	(PROCESS)	(PARTICIPANT)

4 The standard reference work for systemic theory is M. Halliday (1985/1994) *An Introduction to Functional Grammar*, London: Edward Arnold.

5 M. Halliday (1985/1994) at xxi.

Or circumstance is added:

The train	departs	at six o'clock	
(PARTICIPANT)	(PROCESS)	(CIRCUMSTANCE)	
My uncle	missed	the train	by five minutes
(PARTICIPANT)	(PROCESS)	(PARTICIPANT)	(CIRCUMSTANCE)

ii. *Interpersonal metafunction*, encodes meanings of attitudes and relationships which realise tenor of discourse ('interpersonal meanings'). It refers to the use of language to represent interaction between speakers, the way they construct and fill social roles, adopt and/or express attitudes/points of views, form relationships and alliances and so on. A speaker can adopt four basic interpersonal positions (which can be complicated, qualified and extended): declarative (offering information), interrogative (demanding information), imperative (commands in relation to action or response rather than information) and offer (willingness to supply action and response).

There are many elements that indicate interpersonal meanings and it is not possible to go into any detail. For a better understanding, here are a few examples:

- mood (order, apologise, invite, reject, describe, etc.): *Sit down!*, *Please be seated.*
- modal auxiliary: *will* (inclination/futurity), *can* (ability/possibility), *should* or *have to* (obligation); e.g. *I will collect her, I could go and collect her after work, You should go to the station now!*
- use of pronouns: *I, you, we, our, your*; e.g. *Before we begin, I would like to set out the main stages of our trip together.*

iii. *Textual metafunction*, encodes meanings of text development which realise mode of discourse ('textual meanings'). It refers to the use of language to organise the experiential and interpersonal meanings into a coherent, connected and unified entity. The most prominent textual function in this context is what has been termed the 'theme' which indicates the angle or the point of departure adopted by the speaker. Themes can be subdivided into simple, multiple, topical, interpersonal or textual themes. The rest of the clause is called 'rheme'.

The following example illustrates how the organisation of a text informs the textual meaning:

THEME	RHEME
My dog	chased the cat all around the garden.
The cat	was chased all around the garden by my dog.
All around the garden,	the cat was chased by my dog.

From the simple examples above, we can see how meanings are encoded in what linguists call 'text' which is a piece of language in use that can be of any length and in either written or spoken form. It is "language that is functional".[6] A text, in this sense, is a coherent collection of meanings appropriate to its context. The way the text's meanings are combined gives the text its texture and the text's structure rests on the mandatory structural elements used in the combination of these meanings. Encoding the meaning depends on two surrounding contexts on extralinguistic levels and as illustrated in Figure 1 below. The context of culture refers to the general outer cultural environment in which a text occurs. It includes elements such as conventions of address, politeness, discourse etc., which shape meanings within a particular culture. It

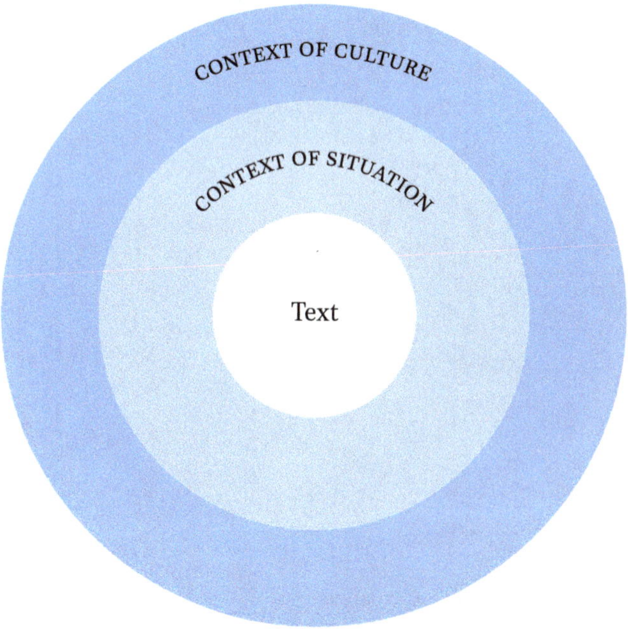

FIGURE 1 Text in context

6 M Halliday, R Hasan, eds. (1985) *Language, context and texts: Aspects of language in a social semiotic perspective*, Geelong: Deakin University Press.

has been described "as the sum of all the meanings it is possible to mean in that particular culture".[7]

Within that general context of culture, there is an inner context, which functional linguists have named the 'context of situation' and which refers, as the term indicates, to the specific situation in which a text occurs and in which meanings are formed. It includes "the things going on in the world outside the text that make the text what it is".[8] Linguists have identified three basic parameters of the situational differences within context of situation, namely field, tenor and mode. Field relates to experimental meanings, tenor to interpersonal meanings and mode to textual meanings, as described above in relation to the metafunctions of language (also illustrated in Figure 2 below).

The study of language developed by linguists who consider language as an act of communication, and who show how meanings are encoded by examining the extra-linguistic levels of context of culture and of situation, will stress

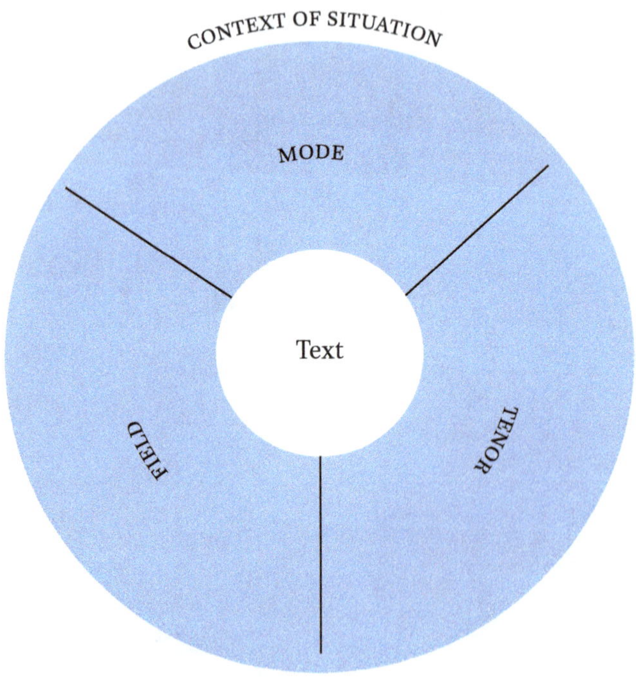

FIGURE 2 Parameters of context of situation

7 D. Butt, R. Fahey, S. Feez, S. Spinks, C. Yallop, eds. (2000) *Using Functional Grammar. An Explorer's Guide*, Sydney: Macquarie University, at 3.

8 D. Butt, R. Fahey, S. Feez, S. Spinks, C. Yallop, eds. (2000) at 4.

the function, notably the social function, of the use of language when people interact with each other. On the linguistic levels, the analysis of semantics and lexico-grammar considers the elements in the language by describing how it functions. This approach has been adopted in the present research. The semantic and lexical-grammatical patterning surrounding key terms, such as 'consideration', 'assumpsit' or 'promise' were examined in relation to their functional purposes, which has revealed the extent of the abstraction and technicality of the legal language.

Moving beyond traditional grammar classification of words and considering the function they play, we can shine a very different light onto the meanings and realities they represent. In our quest to understand the evolution of the use of 'consideration' in the context of developing the concept of consideration in contract law, we can examine diachronically the experiential function and meanings encoded from the experience that conveys a picture of reality. As illustrated in the Figure 3 below, the experiential function of language is to be understood by proceeding from the centre outwards from PROCESS, realised by the verbal group, interacting with the PARTICIPANTS, realised by the mainly nominal groups and placed into context by the CIRCUMSTANCE(S) of

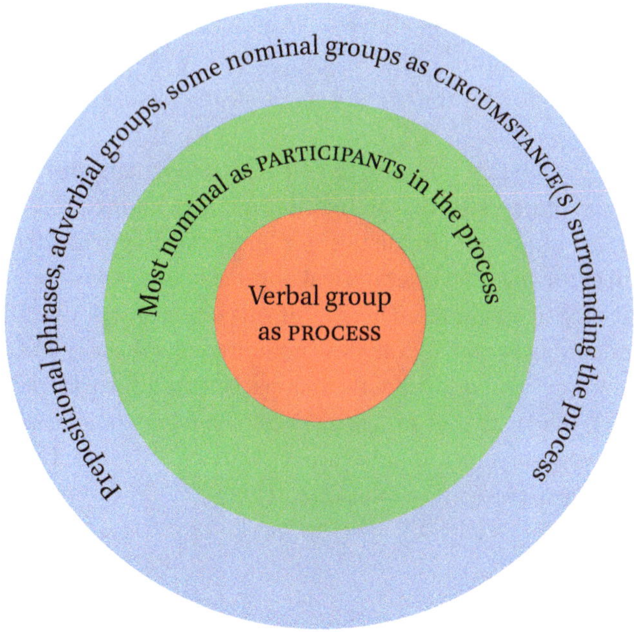

FIGURE 3 Patterns of experience in the clause

human experience, expressed by adverbial groups, prepositions phrases and sometimes nominal groups acting as if they were adverbs.

In the case of, for example, the phrase 'in consideration of', we are on the outer layer of the experience:

- something is (done) = PROCESS
- in relation to something or someone = PARTICIPANTS
- in consideration of = CIRCUMSTANCES

For example:

> Such a promise might be made in consideration of delivering up a letter.[9]

In contrast, when studying the experiential function of the word consideration in its technical and abstract uses, we find ourselves in the middle layer of the functional constituents represented by the three rings in Figure 3 above, namely that of the participants in the process, most commonly realised by nominal groups.

For example:

> Such a consideration appears not to be sustainable.[10]

Or adapting the example given above:

> The consideration for the promise consists in delivering the letter.

The methodology most appropriate to reveal how language and the evolution of legal concepts interact, is to examine the language in question in its textual context. The use of corpus linguistics methods and linguistics/concordance software is ideal for this sort of empirical approach, as it allows for systematic analysis of authentic evidence. The rest of this chapter will describe corpus-based and concordance methodologies, including how these relate specifically to the research question and historic sources selected for this research. Also discussed will be the way that sampling decisions were taken, revised and adjusted, and the way corpora and sub-corpora were constituted. The specifically technical details will be dealt with in Chapter 6.

---

9 *Haigh v Brooks* (1839) 10 Ad. & E. 309 or 113 Eng. Rep. 119.

10 *Meyer v Haworth* (1838) 8 Ad. & E. 467, or 112 Eng. Rep. 916.

2 Corpus Linguistics

Corpus and concordance work as a method of exegesis on the basis of detailed searches of words and phrases in multiple contexts and among large amount of texts, goes back as far as the Middle Ages, when biblical scholars manually indexed the words of the Holy Scriptures.[11] Subsequently, it has also been practised by literary scholars[12] and lexicographers.[13] The first computer-generated concordance tools appeared in the 1950s, when it took twenty-four hours to process 60,000 words and used punched-card technology for storage! Modern corpus work, as we know it today, emerged in the 1980s and 1990s.

Corpus linguistic methodologies have been used in a number of domains[14] ranging from language teaching[15] and translation,[16] to literary criticism[17] and media language/discourse analysis,[18] just to name a few. Enquiries using

---

11 M. Albaric (2004) Hugues de Saint-Cher et les concordances bibliques latines (XIII–XVIII siècles), in: L-J. Bataillon, G. Dahan, P-M Gy (eds.) *Hugues de Saint-Cher (†1263), bibliste et théologien: Etudes réunies*, 467–479.

12 e.g.: A. Becket (1787) *Concordance to Shakespeare*, London: G.G.J. and J. Robinson.

13 e.g.: S. Johnson (1755) *Dictionary of the English Language: in which The Words are deduced from their Originals, and Illustrated in their Different Significations by Examples from the best Writers*; Ancestor of the OED (first published in 1884 as unbound fascicles) *A New English Dictionary on Historical Principles; Founded Mainly on the Materials Collected by The Philological Society.*

14 For an overview, see e.g. E. Tognini-Bonelli (2001) *Corpus Linguistics at Work*, Amsterdam and Philadelphia: John Benjamins.

15 See e.g.: S. Hunston, G. Francis (1998) Verbs Observed: A Corpus-driven Pedagogic Grammar, in *Applied Linguistics*, 19/1, 45–72; E. Tognini-Bonelli (2001), at 14–46.

16 See e.g.: M. Baker (1993) Corpus Linguistics and Translation Studies: Implication and Applications, in: M. Baker, G. Francis, E. Tognini-Bonelli (eds.) *Text and Technology: in Honour of John Sinclair*, Amsterdam and Philadelphia: John Benjamins, 233–250; S. Laviosa (1998) The corpus-based approach: a new paradigm in translation studies, in: *Meta* XLIII, 4, 478–479; J. Munday (1998) A computer-assisted approach to the analysis of translation studies, in: *Meta* XLIII, 4, 542–556; M. Tymoczko (1998) Computerized corpora and the future of translation studies, in: *Meta* XLIII, 4, 652–660; E. Tognini-Bonelli (2001), at 131–156.

17 See e.g.: B. Louw (1997) The Role of Corpora in Critical Literary Appreciation, in: A. Wichmann, S. Fligelstone, T. McEnery, G. Knowles (eds.) *Teaching and Language Corpora*, London and New York: Longman, 240–251.

18 See e.g.: P. Chang (2002) Who's behind the personal pronouns in talk radio? Cartalk: a case study, in: A. Sanchez-Macarro (ed.) *Widows on the World: Media Discourse in English*, Valencia: University of Valencia Press; A. O'Keeffe (2006) *Investigating Media Discourse*, London: Routledge; K. O'Halloran (2010) How to use corpus linguistics in the study of media discourse, in: A. O'Keeffe, M. McCarthy (eds.) *The Routledge Handbook of Corpus Linguistics*, London: Routledge, 563–576.

digitally held corpora allow for access to large bodies of texts of naturally occurring language, that can be searched electronically, according to given criteria with a few mouse clicks, providing information on the data that is both quantitative and qualitative, and is empirical rather than intuitive. Our own intuition of the relative frequency of words, phrases and structures can be little more than vague and general. And while we may be conscious about the frequency of lexis, it is highly unlikely that we have any precise intuitions about the frequency of grammatical categories. Corpus linguistics methodologies can be purely descriptive and ideologically neutral, but can also be used in discourse analysis and coupled with critical approaches.[19] This is best done by undertaking a diachronic linguistic and semantic analysis using corpus linguistics methodologies. Besides providing an empirical basis for studying language in use, corpus work also has a heuristic function to the extent that the analysis of the material systematized in a corpus generates new knowledge. By using algorithm-based analytical tools, the researcher may find him/herself confronted with results that were unexpected.

Besides statistical information, linguistic concordance tools allow for search terms to be placed within their textual context (KWIC[20] lines), which in turn reveals the patterns associated with particular uses of the search term. If we start from the premise of communicative functionality of language, it may be more productive to look at patterns first, rather than at meaning in an isolated fashion. If a word has several meanings or its meaning has shifted throughout time, we will find a tendency for each meaning to be associated most frequently with different patterns, consequently words which share a pattern also tend to share aspects of meaning.[21] This approach dismantles the traditional distinction between grammar and lexis.[22] Sinclair argues that the two do not operate independently, as separate systems, but together, as a single system: lexical items cannot be described without reference to their grammatical patterning, meaning is dependent upon grammar and vice-versa, all grammar patterning is dependent upon lexical choice. Sinclair reverses the common

19 K. O'Halloran (2011) Critical discourse analysis, in: J. Simpson (ed.) *The Routledge Handbook of Applied Linguistics*, London and New York: Routledge, 109–125.

20 Key Word In Context.

21 Examples of this are given in S. Hunston, G. Francis (1998) Verbs Observed: A Corpus-driven Pedagogic Grammar, in: *Applied Linguistics*, 19/1, 45–72.

22 Of the traditional split between 'grammar' and 'lexis', Sinclair wrote: "*In the explicit theoretical statement of linguistics, grammatical and lexical patterns vary independently of each other. In most grammars, it is an assumption that is obviously taken for granted ... Equally, it is rare for a dictionary to note the common syntactic patterns of a word in a particular sense*". in: J. Sinclair (1991) *Corpus Concordance Collocation*, Oxford: OUP, at 103.

(Chomskyan) assumption that grammatical generalisation arises from an underlying rule and believes such generalisations to be derived from the observation and extrapolation of experience:

> The new evidence suggests that grammatical generalizations do not rest on a rigid foundation, but are the accumulation of the patterns of hundreds of individual words and phrases. The language looks rather different when you look at a lot of it at once.[23]

Work on electronically held corpora and with linguistics software obviously offers the perfect basis for observations of language in use.

The type of corpus constituted for this research is diachronic in nature, which means we are dealing with a collection of texts that vary along the parameter of time. Strictly speaking most linguistic corpora are constructed in this way, but what makes a corpus diachronic is for the corpus compiler to divide it into successive periods according to self-determined criteria.[24] Quantitative analytical methods have been applied to the growing field of corpus-based socio-linguistics[25] investigating, for example, parameters such as gender, dialect and genre in grammatical change. But standards of how to interpret statistically the frequency changes in diachronic data are still debated.[26] The

23 J. Sinclair (1991) *Corpus Concordance Collocation*, Oxford: OUP, at 100.

24 M. Hilbert, S. Gries (2009) Assessing frequency changes in multistage diachronic corpora: Applications for historical corpus linguistics and the study of language acquisition, in: *Literary and Linguistic Computing*, vol 24, No. 4, 385–401, at 386.

25 T. Nevalainen, H. Raumolin-Brunberg, (1996) *Sociolinguistics and Language History. Studies based on Corpus of Early English Correspondence*, Amsterdam: Rodopi; D. Biber, J. Burges (2000) Historical change in the language use of women and men. Gender differences in dramatic dialogue, in: *Journal of English Linguistics*, 28(1), 21–37; T. Nevalainen (2000) Gender differences in the evolution of standard English. Evidence from the corpus of the early English correspondence; in: *Journal of English Linguistics*, 28(1), 38–59; T. Nevalainen, R. Reppen, S. Fitzmaurice, D. Biber (2002) *Using Corpora to Explore Linguistic Variation*, Amsterdam: Benjamins; H. Raumolin-Brunberg (2003) *Historical Socio-Linguistics: Language Change in Tudor and Stuart England*, London: Pearson Education; M. Hilpert (2006) Distinctive collexeme analysis and diachrony; in: *Corpus Linguistics and Linguistic Theory*, 2(2): 243–257; A. Hinneburg, H. Mannila, S. Kaislaniemi, T. Nevalainen, H. Raumolin-Brunberg (2007) How to handle small samples: bootstrap and Bayesian methods in the analysis of linguistic change, in: *Literary and Linguistic Computing*, 22: 137–150; S. Gries, M. Hilpert (2008) The identification of stages in diachronic data: variability-based neighbour clustering; in: *Corpora*, 1: 59–81.

26 M. Hilbert, S. Gries (2009).

present research is less concerned with purely sociolinguistic premises but uses corpus linguistics methods for the purposes of illustration. Yet, it is essential to strike the appropriate balance in the interactive relation between human processing (human analyst), computer processing (software) and corpus data (database), which largely depends on the extent the human analyst delegates the responsibility for analysis to the computer.[27] In the corpus work carried out for this research, the linguistic software is a tool for sorting and counting data but the analysis, evaluation and interpretation of the data provided by the software is done by a human researcher providing the necessary linguistic, legal and historical insights. The aim of the present analysis is not to provide a full statistical linguistic analysis, as corpus-based socio-linguists would do, but rather to reveal trends in the use of language and semantic contents to retrace the concordance between the evolution of a new legal concept and that of the language used to describe it.

Apart from socio-linguistics, the diachronic approach to corpus work is relevant to terminological studies, as it provides essential insights for the sort of terminological work, akin to *Begriffsgeschichte,* adopted in this research. 'Terms' are usually defined as words, compound words or phrases used in a definite or precise sense in some particular subject, expressing a notion or concept, or denoting an object of thought.[28] It has been argued that a diachronic approach to terminology questions the traditional opposition between words and terms. Instead it may be:

> more appropriate to consider terms as lexical entities which transcends the boundaries of expert language and can also be used by the general public in non-specialised communication.[29]

This has been described as a process of de-terminologization.[30] However, the linear terminological evolution studied in this research takes, in fact, the opposite path. Rather than moving from the specific to the general, it shifts from general language usages of specific words and phrases to a highly technical and abstract legal use of the very same words and phrases. Corpus-work on a diachronic corpus divided into successive periods, is an essential tool to reveal

27 G. Leech (1991) The state of the art in corpus linguistics; in: K. Aijmer, B. Altenberg (eds.) *English Corpus Linguistics*, London: Longman, 8–29.

28 Oxford English Dictionary definitions 13 a & b.

29 P. Dury (2005) Terminology and Specialized Translation: the Relevance of the Diachronic Approach, in: *LSP & Professional Communication*, vol. 5, nr. 1, 31–40, at 38.

30 I. Meyer, K. Macintosh (2000) When Terms Move into our Everyday Lives: An Overview of De-terminologization, in *Terminology* 6(1), 111–118, at 112.

this process, in particular because it allows for the relevant words/phrases to be placed in their context and as they appear in the texts under consideration. In this way, we can study the terminological evolution and various transitional situations of general usages via usage in legal contexts to abstract usage of an autonomous legal concept.

2.1 *Constituting a Corpus – Representativeness*

A corpus is usually defined as a systematic collection of naturally[31] occurring texts of both written and spoken language that has been computerised. It offers the empirical basis for carrying out systematic linguistic investigations on authentic evidence. The fact that it is held digitally and searchable electronically offers possibilities that are not otherwise available. Yet, the corpus linguistics methodologies only make sense if a corpus is designed in such a way that it forms a representative basis for making generalisations about a language as a whole or as defined by the underlying premises of the research. The overall corpus design is conditioned by the methods of text sampling and sampling decisions made by the researcher whether conscious or (in part) unconscious. Only a well-defined conception of what the sample is intended to represent will subsequently allow for choices to be evaluated as to the adequacy or representativeness of the corpus. It is less a question of sample *size* and more one of being representative for the range of text types in the target population (the latter of which has to be defined in turn) and for the range of linguistics distribution in the population.

Biber[32] has developed a very comprehensive set of principles for achieving 'representativeness' in corpus design, which will not be repeated here. His main message is that corpus design is cyclical, the bottom-line being:

> that the parameters of a fully representative corpus cannot be determined at the outset.[33]

He has represented this process schematically as presented in Figure 4. This process of continuously revising the design of the corpus following empirical research carried out on the initial pilot corpus in order to adjust the design parameters, has been an important part of the process of constituting a corpus

31 Natural language, as opposed to artificial or constructed language devised for international communications, computer programming or mathematical purposes, is language that has evolved naturally, is hereditary and in extended use (see definition in the OED).

32 D. Biber (1993) Representativeness in Corpus Design, in: *Literary and Linguistic Computing*, Vol. 8, No. 4, 243–257.

33 D. Biber (1993) at 256.

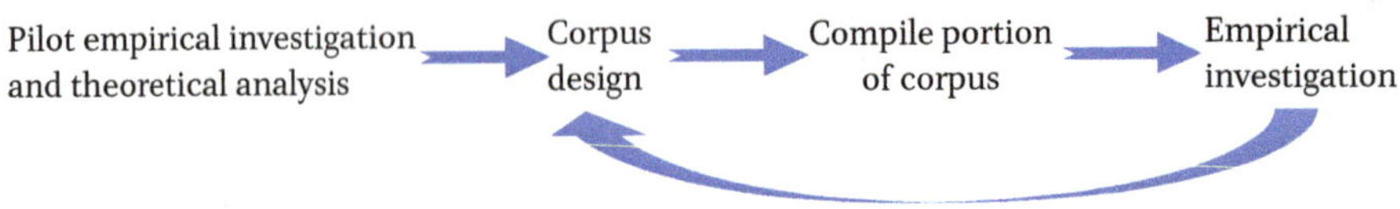

FIGURE 4 Biber's cyclical process to achieve 'representativeness' in corpus design

for this research. This was particularly relevant in view of the complexity of working with medieval texts of a specialised but not very uniform register. It has meant that the standard corpus-based strategies of extracting data could not be applied as such but had to be adjusted to the specificities of the medieval Year Books and Tudor/early Stuart Law Reports. It was precisely the cyclical process of revising the corpus design in response to further empirical investigation that allowed for adjusting and refining the constitution of the corpus, including the creation of new sub-corpora. The way that sampling decisions were taken, revised and adjusted, and the way corpora and sub-corpora were constituted in relation to diachronic aspects and on the basis of the search terms, are described in the next Section (2.2). The technical details are further discussed in Chapter 6.

2.2 *Corpus for This Research – Sampling Decisions*

The initial sampling decisions for constituting the present corpus were fairly straightforward but evolved cyclically, both in relation to the time span of the selected documents and in relation to the types of cases that were selected for inclusion in the corpus. It was thought that the most representative naturally occurring language in relation to the evolution of the concept of consideration would be found in the reports of cases that lawyers were extracting as early as the 1220s from the plea rolls. While plea rolls remained the most authoritative source of precedents their formulaic Latin language and the use of phrases instead of detailed assertions, the omission of the evidence, the arguments of counsel and the reasons for judgments, meant that debates and arguments were less prominent in those records. But precisely these elements would be more likely to reveal the dynamic process of the evolving conceptual thinking on a particular legal issue. A mere record of the formalised results of a legal case is a weaker reflection of the legal and conceptual thinking involved in the decisions. These could not be captured in set formulae.

The Year Books and early Law Reports did not supplement the rolls for official purposes. There is no evidence of appointments or payments of official reporters, and the Year Books were not preserved with the records and office-books of the courts. Their "purpose must have been to record the intellectual aspect of litigation".[34] In that sense, discrepancies between the earliest reports must not be seen as lacking historical authenticity as precedents, but rather as a way of teasing out specific ideas and suggestions in a case by adapting the facts. For these reasons and for the purposes of this research, these sources allow for plenty of insights into the development of thought on the enforceability of informal agreements.

Yet, their use is not without challenges, as they are neither systematic nor official, nor standardised, but scant, personal and erroneous in matters of factual details at times.[35] This was particularly the case up to the early Tudor period, at which point the reports began to change in character as a result of developments in the legal systems during the renaissance period. From the late 15th century, the reports dealt more with the discussion of substantive law and less with the type of tentative pleading that could be found in the earlier Year Books.

Moreover, the texts from which the corpus was constituted, are reports and notes in varying registers, different structures and styles. The texts were written in Anglo-French, except for three (later) documents[36] which are in Middle English. The facts of the case are sketched briefly and the arguments described succinctly. Some entries appear as scant as a note that may have been scribbled on a spare piece of parchment. Frequently, official records are paraphrased in Latin, but these Latin texts were not taken into account for constituting the corpus. The diversity in register that can be found throughout the texts under consideration, is not only due to the different format of reporting and the long time span during which they were written, but also because the reported cases were heard in differing circumstances. For example, reports of cases that came before the King's Council and Star Chamber[37] contain a lot of formal language addressed to the King in forms of praise, pleas, requests or prayers etc.

34 J.H. Baker (2007) *An Introduction to English Legal History*, Oxford: OUP, at 179.

35 The Year Books have been compared to the (early) *Lois de Lille*, see D. Heirbaut (2012) The spokesmen in medieval courts: the unknown leading judges of the customary law and makers of the first continental law reports, in: P. Brand, J. Getzler (eds.) *Judges and judging in the history of the common law and civil law: from antiquity to modern times*, Cambridge: CUP, 192–208.

36 Select Cases in the Council of Henry VII (1485–1509) (75 Selden Society); Select Cases Before The King's Council in The Star Chamber, vol. I, A.D. 1477–1509 (16 Selden Society); Select Cases Before The King's Council in The Star Chamber, vol. II, A.D. 1509–1544 (25 Selden Society).

37 Select Cases before the King's Council, 1243–1482 (35 Selden Society); Select Cases in the Council of Henry VII (1485–1509) (75 Selden Society); Select Cases Before The King's Council in The Star Chamber, vol. I, A.D. 1477–1509 (16 Selden Society); Select Cases Before The King's Council in The Star Chamber, vol. II, A.D. 1509–1544 (25 Selden Society).

An interesting feature, to be found in particular in the Year Books, is the paraphrasing of direct speech. Changes and shifts in language are generally considered to take place in the spoken form first, before materialising in the written one.[38] But it is only the relatively recent technical means of sound recording that can offer genuine empirical proof for such developments. For the late Middle Ages and early Renaissance period under consideration here, we have to rely on written records that are produced albeit by and for the small elite of literate people in a generally illiterate society. This raises the so-called 'bad data' problem[39] that the written record does not reliably reflect the linguistic changes in the spoken language. While paraphrasing direct speech is nowhere near as good evidence as a sound recording may be, it does offer some limited glimpses of the spoken interaction in court hearings. Ingham has used these documents in comparison with the legal register written-mode origin texts in the Parliament Rolls of the same period, to investigate the language change in Anglo-Norman.[40] While such a purely linguistic approach is not the object of this research, the use of paraphrased, admittedly selected, direct speech offers insights into the evolution of the legal mind.

The size of the Year Books and Law Reports sources, in terms of word tokens,[41] was not ascertainable as the HeinOnline database does not offer the possibility of counting the word tokens. Nevertheless, once the corpus with its subcorpora were constituted, it was possible to produce a word count.

Standard corpus linguistics requires that decisions be made about the target population that the sample is supposed to represent. This includes considerations of the boundaries and hierarchical organisation of the target population. In order to evaluate the adequacy and representativeness of a corpus, it is essential to decide which texts are included and excluded from the population, what text categories are to be included and what are their definitions.[42] In the present research, the possibilities of sampling decisions are much conditioned by the relative scarcity of readily available electronically accessible original language documents. A well-defined conception of what the sample is intended to represent could be drawn up but not necessarily applied in detail due to

38 M.S. MacMahon (1994) *Understanding Language Change*, Cambridge: CUP, e.g. at 8.

39 U. Weinreich, W. Labov, M. Herzog (1968) Empirical foundations for a theory of language change, in: W.P. Lehmann, Y. Malkiel (eds.) *Directions for Historical Linguistics: A Symposium*, Austin: University of Texas Press, 95–195.

40 R. Ingham (2016) Investigating language change using Anglo-Norman spoken and written data, in: *Linguistics*, 54(2), 381–410.

41 Word tokens are the total number of words in a text.

42 D. Biber (1993) Representativeness in Corpus Design, in: *Literary and Linguistic Computing*, Vol. 8, No. 4, at 243.

the limitation of available sources. This has meant that texts of different styles, formats and registers, as described above, were all included, as long as it was believed the texts could reveal the legal thinking relevant to the development of the concept of consideration. Whatever their diversities, the texts' commonalities lie in the fact that they are the results of lawyers listening to arguments discussed in court. The target population is lawyers (in the generic sense) who communicate about legal court cases because it was recognised that opinion of the courts and serjeants[43] were good indicators for the law and for accepted practice. This dynamic process was best captured in the abstracting and annotating of legal texts and case notes that were a part of the legal self-education in the rapidly evolving common law system. In addition to excluding the rolls and official court documents for the reasons mentioned above, the sources that can be found at the Inns of Court were not considered for lack of available time.

Sampling was ring-fenced by the time span chosen as most appropriate to reveal the intellectual evolution relating to the research question. The concept of consideration materialised in the 16th century. But to have concentrated solely on that century would have precluded any investigation of the origins of the new action and how it subsequently evolved. To understand the intellectual development that lead to the rise of the new concept, it was necessary to go back in time and examine its forerunners, namely trespass on the case and the action of assumpsit. Both are evidence for the emerging idea, during the 14th century,[44] that it was necessary to enable certain informal undertakings and promises to become legally enforceable. The resulting diachronic corpus was subject to the cyclical readjustment and refinement described earlier, and divided into sub-corpora of successive periods. This has led to the initial 16th century corpus being supplemented by further corpora constituted from available documents from the late 14th to 15th and 17th to 19th centuries.

So much for the methods of how sampling decisions were taken, revised and adjusted, and the way corpora and sub-corpora were constituted in relation to diachronic aspects and on the basis of the search terms. The technical details are discussed further in Chapter 6.

43 Serjeants at (the) law or serjeants of (the) law are members of a superior order of barristers at the English bar, from which, until 1873, the common law judges were chosen. Formally created under Henry II, the order was abolished by the Judicature Act 1873. The etymology of the term can be found in the Latin *serviens ad legem* (one who serves [the king] in matters of law).

44 The first trespass on the case actions were reported in the second half of the 14th century. Actions of assumpsit emerged in the 15th century.

CHAPTER 4

Legal Language in England from the 14th to the 18th Centuries

As discussed in the previous chapter, law cannot be imagined without the use of language and, in particular, without the use of written language for the common law. The way meanings are encoded in spoken or written form depends on the context of culture, on the one hand, and on the context of situation, on the other. Medieval text production is never truly monolingual and the linguistic landscape of multilingual England was particularly diverse. As in other parts of Europe, besides the vernacular, Latin was the language of the learned, the church, the administration and the law. Specific to England was that the invading Normans imported their Norman-French language. This paved the way for future language contact opportunities, as well as for the import of French culture (literature etc.) and certain legal concepts, such as feudal law.

Boundaries between the three languages were porous and language contact phenomena such as, code-switching and calque[1] meant there were continuous interplay and lexical borrowings, in particular, between continental (Parisian-basin) French, Norman-French, insular French specific to England and Middle English on English soil. Rothwell provides us with examples which clearly show that, at times, the French of England went its own semantic way irrespective of developments in continental French dialects.[2] So, Anglo-French and the absorption of French words into Middle English were the results of language contacts on *English soil*. In other words, Anglo-French was a contact variety of

1 Code-switching and calque are common phenomena among multi-linguals. Code-switching in linguistic terms is the practice of alternating in conversation between two or more languages or language varieties, using them in a way consistent with the phonology and syntax of each language. Calque, also called loan translation, occurs when a phrase or word is borrowed from another language by literal translation and introduced in the target language as a new lexeme. It is a very common type of word-formation in a multi-lingual environment. See G. Miller (2002) The Death of French in Medieval England, in: C. Wiltshire, J. Camps (eds.) *Romance Phonology and Variation,* Amsterdam/Philadelphia: John Benjamins Publishing, 145–160, at 149; W. Rothwell (1998) Arrivals and Departures: The Adoption of French Terminology into Middle English, in: 79 *English Studies*, 144–165.

2 W. Rothwell (1993a) From Latin to Anglo-French and Middle English: the Role of the Multilingual Gloss, in: 88 *Modern Language Review*, 582–599, at p. 584; W. Rothwell (1998) at 156.

 | DOI:10.1163/9789004436169_005

French in its own right and should be considered as a part of the medieval French dialect continuum.[3] To that extent, the French language in England both influenced English and was influenced by it.

It is, however, important to stress that the linguistic situation in England was multilingual rather than diglossic. In his ground-breaking article of 1959, Ferguson[4] defines diglossia as:

> ...a relatively stable language situation in which, in addition to the primary dialects of the language (which may include a standard or regional standards), there is a very divergent, highly codified (often grammatically more complex) superposed variety, the vehicle of a large and respected body of written literature, either of an earlier period or in another speech community, which is learned largely by formal education and is used for most written and formal spoken purposes but is not used by any section of the community for ordinary conversation.

This was subsequently extended by Fishman[5] to include the use of unrelated languages beyond mere dialectical variations. The linguistic situation of medieval England was somewhat different to the ones Ferguson[6] had in mind when he formulated his concept, mainly because of the inherently unstable situation of the languages in question. The Middle Ages was an era when texts interchanged their languages both in terms of phraseology as well as lexis, responding to constantly changing socio-cultural and (geo-) political circumstances. Language contact models were therefore extremely complex with:

> deeply interwoven lexical borrowings back and forth from English to French and from French to English that makes the boundaries of our modern dictionaries of 'Middle English' and 'Anglo-Norman' themselves problematic.[7]

3 D. Trotter (2003) Not as eccentric as it looks: Anglo-French and French French, in: *Forum for Modern Language Studies* 39, 427–428.

4 C. Ferguson (1959) Diglossia, in: *Word* 15, 325–340.

5 J. Fishman (1967) Bilingualism with and without diglossia; diglossia with and without bilingualism, in: *Journal of Social Issues* 23 (2), 29–38.

6 Greece: the alternation of Katharevusa and Demotic,
Switzerland: the alternation of Swiss German and German,
Arabic-speaking countries: the coexistence of literary and dialectal Arabic,
Haiti: the alternation of Creole and French.

7 J. Wogan-Browne (2009) General Introduction: What's in a Name: The 'French' of 'England', in: Wogan-Browne (ed.), *Language and Culture in Medieval Britain*, York: York Medieval Press, 1–13, at 6.

The "relatively stable language situation" of Ferguson's diglossia definition does not correspond to the realities of medieval text production, at least not during the period when both Middle English and the French of England were in constant mutation. From the period of early modern or Tudor English, when English had gained the upper hand and ousted French in all but a few sectors, Law French showed characteristics of being a "very divergent, superposed variety" as defined by Ferguson. If the concept of diglossia could be used it may be in relation to that period. Yet, the hierarchical notion of H(igher) (the prestigious, codified varieties used in education) and L(ower) varieties is not necessarily applicable. Law French was not highly codified but in a gradual process of degeneration and it never underwent the kind of successive cycles of renaissance that, for example, Latin experienced. Yet the use of French in the law continued because it had developed appropriate vocabulary for expressing legal concepts. This vocabulary was in the process of being totally absorbed into the English language during the Tudor era.

It has traditionally been argued that the regular use of French was abandoned from the mid-13th and especially 14th centuries in favour of English, and that French declined into a corrupt language. It was described as "mauvais français [...] en Angleterre"[8] and "gradually became a dead language that [...] always had to be taught".[9] Price[10] describes it as "a language in advanced state of decline". He adds that:

> grammatically it was often little more than 'bad French' [...] Late Anglo-Norman is characterised by so many and such marked deviations from any other kind of French at the time as to lead one to the view that what we have before is not just another authentic speaker French but incorrect French written by people for whom it was foreign language and whose command of it was inadequate.

The key lies in the notion of deviation from any other kind of French: as long as the French of England is being compared to Continental French, it will appear as an imperfectly learned second language on the path to serious degeneration. If the insular French was indeed in such decline, it appears difficult to

8 P. Meyer, L. Toulmin-Smith (1889) *Les contes moralisés de Nicole Bonzon*; Paris: Société des anciens textes français.

9 M. Pope (1934) *From Latin to Modern French*, Manchester: Manchester University Press; at 424.

10 G. Price (1984) Anglo-Norman, in G. Price (ed.) *The Languages of Britain*, London: Edward Arnold; at 224.

explain why this language was still being used for legal education and legal writing.

More recent research – a lot more work is still required in this field – has suggested the French of England as a contact variety of French in its own right.[11] And it is this very language contact that has put the insular French on a different path from the Continental French, in relation to lexis or morphology, for example. Ingham shows how supposedly deviant grammatical features, such as chaotic gender-marking on articles and modifiers, or the lack of a tonic/atonic object personal pronoun distinction, or the extension of the *-er* ending of the first conjugation to other classes can be explained with a view to the wider historical contexts of language contact influences and a general medieval dialect continuum. In other words, we are not dealing with divergence due to imperfect second language acquisition, but with disparity between first language dialects.

1 French in Medieval England

The story of French in medieval England[12] started with the advent of Norman rule over a realm that included England from 1066, consolidated by centuries of Plantagenet rule, vast estate holdings in France and feudal alliances to the French crown. In England the door was opened to the French and their language and diverse dialects. But the exact impact of the French language and culture on the English medieval linguistic and cultural landscape is still subject to considerable debate. A lot of the thinking, at least until the middle of the 20th century, about the linguistic situation in medieval England was skewed by the fact that linguists and historians alike relied for decades on writings that appear to have misinterpreted or ignored historical sources, common linguistic experience and actual Anglo-Norman-French material.[13] The view

11 R. Ingham (2010) Later Anglo-Norman as a Contact Variety of French?, 3–25; and: The Transmission of Later Anglo-Norman: Some Syntactic Evidence, 164–182, both in: R. Ingham (ed.) *The Anglo-Norman Language and its Contexts*, York: York Medieval Press; O. Jespersen, (1955 reprint/1935) *Growth and Structure of the English Language*, Garden City: Doubleday; see also W. Rothwell (1992) The Problem of Law French, in: *French Studies*, XLVI, 3, 259–271.

12 For an overview of the phenomenon of Law French between the 13th and 18th century, see C. Laske (2016) Losing touch with the common tongues – the story of Law French, in: *International Journal of Legal Discourse*, 1(1) 169–192.

13 R. Wilson (1943) English and French in England 1100–1300, in: *History*, 28, 107, 37–60. Rothwell made this point in several articles, especially in: W. Rothwell (1975) The Role of French in Thirteenth-Century England, in: 58 *Bulletin, John Rylands Library*, 445–466;

that French had first been brought over by the conquering Normans, imposed on the English, then used as a vernacular in a bilingual setting and ultimately adopted as an official language in the second half of the 13th century, was held by a number of writers[14] on Anglo-Norman-French. It has since been questioned by academics,[15] based on more recent empirical research using modern linguistic methodologies. The impact and influence of French on the linguistic landscape of medieval England is much more subtle than has been argued hitherto.

Long before the Norman conquest, the Anglo-Saxons had used the vernacular to set down their laws in writing, unlike the Germanic tribes in continental Europe who used Latin.[16] Old English had been more mature than the Norman-French of William I's time, which was still developing from its Latin origins. And according to Woodbine, this is the reason why the Norman kings did not use Norman-French in their documents, though (besides mainly Latin) they did use English.[17] In other words, English was not a *lingua rustica* incapable of literary culture and inadequate for official use. There can be no doubt that the invading Normans brought with them their Norman language and dialects, yet the extent to which it became a widely spoken language imposed in England, let alone a vernacular, is far less clear.

First of all, the English were no strangers to the Norman language. There had been numerous contacts between the two cultures in the past. Aethelred, King

---

W. Rothwell (1998) Arrivals and Departures: The Adoption of French Terminology into Middle English, 79 *English Studies*, 144–165.

14 for example: K. Lambley (1920) *The teaching and cultivation of the French language in England*, Manchester: The University Press; J. Vising (1923) *Anglo-Norman language & literature*, London: OUP; M. Pope (1934) *From Latin to Modern French*, Manchester: Manchester University Press; J. Orr (1948) *The Impact of French on English*, The Taylorian Lecture, Oxford: Clarendon Press; M. Legge (1963) *Anglo-Norman Literature and Its Background*, Oxford: Clarendon Press; H. Suggett (1949/1968) The Use of French in England in the Late Middle Ages, in: R. Southern, *Essays in Medieval History: selected from the transactions of the Royal Historical Society on the occasion of its centenary*, London: Macmillan, 213–239.

15 for example: G. Woodbine (1943) *The Language of English Law*, in: 18 Speculum 395–436; W. Rothwell (1975) The Role of French in Thirteenth-Century England, in: 58 *Bulletin, John Rylands Library*, 445–466; W. Rothwell (1991) The missing link in English etymology: Anglo-Norman, in: *Medium Ævum* LX, 173–196; W. Rothwell (1993b) Language and government in medieval England, in: 93 *Zeitschrift für französische Sprache und Literatur*, 258–270; W. Rothwell (1998) Arrivals and Departures: The Adoption of French Terminology into Middle English, in: 79 *English Studies*, 144–165; W. Rothwell (2001) English and French in England after 1362, in: *English Studies* 82, 539–559.

16 H. Brunner (1907) The Sources of English Law, Committee of the Association of American Law Schools, in: *Select Essays in Anglo-American Legal History*, vol. 2. at 8.

17 G. Woodbine (1943) *The Language of English Law*, in: 18 Speculum 395–436, at 404 fn. 3.

of the English from 978 to 1013 and again from 1014 to 1016, married Emma of Normandy (985–1052) with the intention of pacifying Normandy and uniting against the invading Vikings who frequently used Normandy as their base to raid England. Aethelred, Emma and their children took refuge in Normandy during the two years that King Sweyn Forkbeard of Denmark had conquered England. When Cnut of Denmark became King of England in 1016, Aethelred's son Edward (later Edward the Confessor), who subsequently ruled England between 1042 and 1066, went into exile for two decades, probably mainly in Normandy. Edward brought back a number of Norman customs, such as the sealing of documents, and the seal-keeper and document secretary was described with the Norman-French term of *canceler*.[18] Emma also took refuge in Flanders for a short period between 1036 and 1040, where she was joined by her son Harthacnut. In 1051, William, later the Conqueror, visited England as mentioned in the Anglo-Saxon Chronicles,[19] although in view of the fact that this was only reported in one of the manuscripts, it has become a moot point whether the visit actually took place.[20] But there is no doubt that the Normans and the English were, at least on the level of their ruling class, no strangers to each other before 1066.

Secondly, the long held view that the conquerors tried to oust the English language when they landed on the southern shores, is a misinterpretation of the historical evidence. William saw himself as the rightful successor to the English throne, not as a conqueror. He tried (unsuccessfully) to learn English and was acclaimed King in French by the Normans and in English by the local population[21] at his coronation in 1066. He vowed to the French and English of London to uphold the law as it had been under Edward the Confessor.[22] He was, in other words, not set on dismantling the structures of English society,

18 D. Mellinkoff (1963) *The Language of the Law*, Boston: Little, Brown & Co., at 60.

19 *The Worcester Manuscript*, British Library MS Cotton Tiberius Biv, ff.3–86, [1052].

20 D.C. Douglas (1953) 'Edward the Confessor, Duke William of Normandy, and the English succession', in: *English Historical Review* LXVIII, 526–545; T.J. Oleson (1957) 'Edward the Confessor's promise of the throne to Duke William of Normandy', in: *English Historical Review* LXXII, 221–228.

21 P. Shelly (1921) *English and French in England: 1066–1100*, Philadelphia: University of Pennsylvania, at 75, 77, 81.

22 *"Will'm kyng gret* [...] *and ealle tha burhwaru binnan Londone Frencisce and Englisce freondlice. and ic kyde eow that ic wylle that get beon eallra thaera laga weorde the gyt waeran on Eadwerdes daege kynges* [...]*"* Charter of William I to the City of London, in: W. Stubbs (1913) *Select charters and other illustrations of English constitutional history*, Oxford: The Clarendon Press, at 82–83.

but rather to operate through them if appropriate.[23] This also holds true for the tale that the use of French in the law was attributed directly to the Norman conquest and seen as a hallmark of Norman tyranny.[24] This line of thinking goes back to some anonymous historical writings that have since been revealed as a 14th century forgery.[25] But its narrative continued to live in the writings of prominent authors such as Fortescue (15th century) or Selden (17th century). As there was no one at Pevensey with a tape recorder in 1066 to greet the disembarking invaders, the nature of the speech they used must remain a matter of conjecture, but it is most unlikely that it could be adequately described in terms of any all-embracing formula such as 'Norman dialect'.[26] In fact, the irretrievable loss of any substantial evidence of the *spoken* language output at the time of the invasion means we know very little about the overall English linguistic landscape of the 11th century.

Thirdly, the premise that, following the Norman invasion, French became the vernacular in England in a bilingual set-up is a misinterpretation of the sources. If the term 'vernacular' is used in its Oxford English Dictionary definition of a language – that it is naturally *spoken* by the people of a particular country, rather than one acquired for commercial, social or educative purposes – there appears to be no evidence that Norman-French became the spoken language of the people in England in general as a result of the Norman invasion.[27] Similarly, there can be no question of bilingualism in the Oxford English Dictionary sense of the habitual use of two languages colloquially. The English outnumbered the incoming conquering forces. Yet, Orr speaks of a "state of almost complete bilingualism",[28] and Legge states that "most people, down to the very poorest, were bilingual".[29] In view of the lack of evidence of

23 An interesting exception to this is the imposition of political feudalism by the invading Normans and with it the import of Norman-French feudal vocabulary. Susan Reynolds has argued that it could not have been the Normans who imported feudalism to England; in her opinion feudalism was a later development (*Fiefs and Vassals: The Medieval Evidence Reinterpreted*, Oxford: OUP, 1994). This is an ongoing debate!

24 The so-called 'Norman yoke'.

25 G. Woodbine (1943) *The Language of English Law*, in: 18 Speculum 395–436, at 403.

26 W. Rothwell (1998) Arrivals and Departures: The Adoption of French Terminology into Middle English, in: 79 *English Studies*, 144–165, at 150.

27 G. Woodbine (1943) at 433; W. Rothwell (1975) The Role of French in Thirteenth-Century England, in: 58 *Bulletin, John Rylands Library*, 445–466, at 449, 453.

28 J. Orr (1948) *The Impact of French on English*, The Taylorian Lecture, Oxford: Clarendon Press, at 5.

29 M. Legge (1963) *Anglo-Norman Literature and Its Background*, Oxford: Clarendon Press, at 4.

the spoken language output, as mentioned above, these writers can only have relied on written sources. But, considering the widespread illiteracy of 11th century England, one cannot infer complete bilingualism from the existence of some Anglo-Norman-French texts, to which the great majority of the population would not have had access. Suggett, unwittingly contradicts herself by calling the Anglo-Norman

> a true vernacular whose roots had penetrated deeply into all classes of English society who could read and write.[30]

As we have seen from the Oxford English Dictionary definition, vernacular refers to spoken, not written language, and if Suggett refers to the classes who could read and write she actually excludes the bulk of the population. So, neither at the time of the Norman conquest, nor for the century that followed, can there be any question of French as a vernacular tongue outside the Norman elite, neither in the true sense of the word, nor in quantitative terms.

Nevertheless, it can be said that medieval England was multilingual to the extent that these languages were in use, but the distribution of that use was by no means uniform.[31] Within a century, as a result of intermarriage, it was no longer possible to distinguish who was of Norman and who of English birth among the freemen.[32] The language the Normans had brought with them blended into the English linguistic landscape and was evolving fast along its own insular path. From the 12th century, the French of the Parisian basin was becoming a more accepted standard for written texts in a large part of Northern France, yet the different local languages with their diverse dialectical features continued to co-exist. In a parallel movement, the French of England, despite its specific insular features, became a recognised standard intelligible beyond dialectical restrictions, which was a major advantage over English.[33]

30 H. Suggett (1949/1968) The Use of French in England in the Late Middle Ages, in: R. Southern, *Essays in Medieval History: selected from the transactions of the Royal Historical Society on the occasion of its centenary*, London: Macmillan, 213–239, at 235.

31 B. Crespo (2000) Historical Background of Multilingualism and its Impact on English, in: D. Trotter (ed.) *Multilingualism in Later Medieval Britain*, Cambridge: Brewer, 23–35 at 24 Table 1.

32 *"Set iam cohabitantibus Anglicis et Normannis et alterutrum uxores ducentibus vel nubentibus, sic permixte sunt nationes ut vix decerni possit hodie, de liberis loquor, quis Anglicus quis Normannus sit genere".* written in 1179 by Richard FitzNeale *Dialogus de Scaccario*, cited by W. Rothwell (1975) The Role of French in Thirteenth-Century England, in: 58 *Bulletin, John Rylands Library*, 445–466, at 449.

33 W. Rothwell (1975) at 456.

Fourthly, the invading army of 1066 was by no means a homogeneous Norman group. William had contracted many Bretons, contingents from Picardy and further up the French coast, and included those provided to him by the Count of Flanders. In addition, the social aspect of dialectical fragmentation makes it unlikely that a common speech was even shared by the Norman section of the army.

During the 13th century, on both sides of the Channel, French began to develop into a language of culture, education, science, diplomacy and administration (including the law). In other words, French was used as a vehicle for ideas, a position that hitherto had been occupied only by Latin[34] and its advantage over English was that it could be understood more widely, while English was not comprehended beyond England's shores.[35] Hence, it is less a question of French being turned into an official language during the 13th century and much more that the upward surge of French, as the main non-classical currency for creativity in the cultural and administrative spheres, offered the possibilities to handle and transmit new ideas and concepts. Woodbine argues that the increasingly generalised use of written French in medieval England was not a result of the Norman conquest (Norman-French) but due to the French literary revival (Central-French sources) during the reign of Henry II and his wife Eleanor of Aquitaine,[36] and subsequently, although this is disputed,[37] to the major influx of French officials following Henry III's marriage to Eleanor of Provence in 1236, a period dubbed 'that other French invasion'.[38] The age of French as a language of 'learning and gentility' was well under way.[39] Hence, French was becoming more dominant, not through demographic weight but in relation to cultural prestige.

Meanwhile, during the years following the Norman invasion, English[40] was neglected as a language of learning and literature, but it continued on its path of being a popular tongue and was in constant contact with the other

34 W. Rothwell (1975) at 464.

35 The great diversity of dialects in England meant that even within its own borders people did not necessarily understand each other.

36 G. Woodbine (1943) *The Language of English Law*, in: 18 Speculum 395–436, at 404 fn. 3.

37 W. Rothwell (1998) Arrivals and Departures: The Adoption of French Terminology into Middle English, in: 79 *English Studies*, 144–165, at 151–152.

38 G. Woodbine (1943) at 402.

39 D. Mellinkoff (1963) *The Language of the Law*, Boston: Little, Brown & Co., at 70.

40 This was the period of Middle English, which was in use in England between approx. 1100 and 1500, linking the Anglo-Saxon language with its Germanic influences of *Beowulf* to the early Modern English of Shakespeare. It developed out of Old English (with major changes in the grammar, pronunciation and writing) and massively incorporated chunks of Norman-French and Latin. Among its literary high points was the work of Chaucer.

languages. The evolution of clusters of words expressed new sets of related concepts, which in turn introduced shifts in conceptual thinking that was reflected in the adoption of foreign compounds, idioms, formulaic expressions and other multi-word constructions. New and foreign words came hand in hand with different patterns of sound, changes in pronunciation and ultimately new spellings.[41] Hence, Middle English was developing along non-linear lines,[42] fragmented by dialects, with no rules on grammatical structure or spelling, an unsettled alphabet, and no language dictionaries (as opposed to glossaries) nor any grammatical manuals to impose uniformity.[43] The 13th century saw a rise in feelings of English identity, starting with the loss of Normandy, the Barons' War (1258–1265), in part a reaction against foreign (French) influence, and later the hostilities with France that started the Hundred Years' War (1337–1453) during the reign of Edward III. The English Channel began to be conceptualised as a peripheral boundary marking a border, rather than a central conduit that could carry a traveller from one half of the realm to the other, as had been the case following the conquest and during the rule of the early Plantagenet/Angevin kings.

The English language played an essential role in this quest for English identity. Its use became increasingly the common currency of communication, not just among the 'lower classes'. This rise in (linguistic) English identity found its expression in the 1362 Statute of Pleading, written (ironically!) in French and attempting to oust French in favour of English. Although it is concerned with the specific use of language in court pleadings, the text of the statute provides us with interesting information about language usage in general (my emphasis):

> […] les leyes custumes & estatutz du dit realme […] sont pledez monstrez & juggez en la *lange Franceis, qest trop desconue* en dit realme; issint q les *gentz* q pledent ou sont empledez en les Courtz le Roi & les Courtz dautres, nont entendement ne conissance de ce qest dit p' eulx ne contre eulx p lour Sergeantz & auts pledours; et q resonablement les dites leyes & custumes sront le plus tost apris & conuz & mieultz entenduz en *la lange usee en dit realme*, et p tant chescun du dit realme se p'roit mieultz govner sanz faire offense a la leye […][44]

41 D. Crystal (2004) *The Stories of English*, London: Penguin Books, at 133.

42 G. Marsh (1862) *The Origin and History of the English Language*, New York: Scribner, at 380.

43 D. Mellinkoff (1963) *The Language of the Law*, Boston: Little, Brown & Co., at 84.

44 Pleading in English Act 1362 (36 Edw. III. *Stat.* 1. c. 15): "[…] the laws, customs and statutes of the said realm […] are pleaded, shewed and judged in the *French tongue, which is much unknown* in the said realm; so that the *people* who plead or are impleaded, in the king's

Three interesting facts are worth pointing out: first of all, French is described as a language '*trop desconue*', secondly pleading should be undertaken in the tongue that is generally understood (English), and thirdly this statute talks about the 'people' who come to court and 'every man' who wishes to respect the law and defend his belongings. In other words, although we are dealing with the restricted situation of a court of law, the statute describes the general linguistic landscape of every man, in which English was considered the tongue generally used and French as the one too little known. It is helpful to draw on the distinction Ormrod[45] makes between speaking a language, and merely comprehending it (fully or partially) by listening or reading. He argues that the higher echelons of the elite, such as the royal family, the members of the central administration, the senior judiciary and some of the high nobility, all knew how to speak French, whether that was its dialect of Languedoil of Northern France and the southern Low Countries, the insular Anglo-Norman French or the technical jargon of Law French. They continued to use French in oral communication until the end of the 14th century and beyond for certain purposes. However, by the end of the 13th century, the use of French among the lower ranks of the polity, the gentry and bourgeoisie was largely a mere pragmatic skill for understanding administrative, accounting and court/legal documents. That increasingly limited knowledge of French after the 13th century contributed during the 13th and 14th centuries to the development of Law French in the courts and of Anglo-Norman French as the recognised language of written communication in royal and civic governments. It is, in fact

> the employment of French as a formal and authoritative language of process actually increased in inverse proportion to its use as a language of generalised social exchange.[46]

court, and in the courts of others, have no understanding nor knowledge of that which is said for them or against them by their serjeants and other pleaders; and that reasonably the said laws and customs are learnt, known and better understood in the *tongue used in the said realm*, and so every man of the said realm can better govern himself without offending the Law [...]" (my translation and emphasis). The original text can be found on www.heinonline.org – Statutes of the Realm – 1 (1235–1377) at 375.
For a comprehensive description (including contextual information) and analysis of the 1362 Act see W.M. Ormrod (2003) The Use of English: Language, Law and Political Culture in Fourteenth-Century England, in: *Speculum* 73/3, 750–787.

45 W.M. Ormrod (2003) at 754.

46 W.M. Ormrod (2003) at 755.

A further distinction must be made between language as a spoken or written means. While the 1362 Act was a statutory abolition of Law French as the spoken language in the courts of law, it appears to have had little effect on the written language of court records – law reporting continued in French, which is, however, no proof of what language was actually spoken in court. It is likely that French continued to be used in the Inns of Court and the educational process, as much of the training centred around the elaborate forms of oral debate.[47] The fact that the statute was not scrupulously followed by lawyers, may indicate that the legislator had underestimated the influence of the bar,[48] rather than question the linguistic landscape as it had been painted in the statute.

While French was affirmed as the language of the law, its more general use was declining, restricted to the noble, wealthy and powerful.[49] Yet its standing as the language of learning meant that English speakers enhanced their language with 'high-class' foreign usage[50] or simply because, at times, they found the French vocabulary more effective. Surveys show that the period of the most extensive penetration of French words into English was 1251–1400.[51] Crystal[52] estimates that of the 27,000 words which got absorbed into the English language during that time, 22% (approx. 6000 words) were words of French origin (2,500 French words in the period 1375–1400 alone). Baugh[53] claims that during the Middle English period, about 10,000 French (including Anglo-French and continental French) words entered into the English language, of which some 7,500 are still in use today. These words were absorbed in different ways: a French word may simply replace an Anglo-Saxon one or be juxtaposed to it, expressing a new meaning, or even name something new or unknown. The generally held view is that French words were borrowed in the context of cultural life, of the nobility, of social elites, and of political and religious powers,

47 W.M. Ormrod (2003) at 765–766.

48 The reforms undertaken during the reign of Edward I (1272–1307) substantially settled the jurisdiction of the common law courts and thus professionalised the practice of the law. This resulted in a significant rise in the power of the bar and the legal profession in general.

49 D. Mellinkoff (1963) *The Language of the Law*, Boston: Little, Brown & Co., at 95–96.

50 O. Jespersen (1955 reprint/1935) *Growth and Structure of the English Language*, Garden City: Doubleday, at 47.

51 D. Mellinkoff (1963) at 97.

52 D. Crystal (2004) *The Stories of English*, London: Penguin Books, at 155.

53 A. Baugh (1935) *A History of the English Language*, New York: Appleton-Century, at 220.

while the basic vocabulary of the English language relating to semantics of daily life, popular culture and emotions remained Anglo-Saxon.[54]

The socio-linguistic take on this would be that language typically evolves when individuals diversify their social relations, and hence become mediators between their own social circle and the new one(s) they operate in. The French of the English upper classes trickled further into English society by the inevitable interaction between the lords and their servants, bailiffs and manorial stewards and the increasingly professionalised administrative classes in institutions relating to justice, administration and representation. Lawyers, royal officers and parliamentary representatives further propagated the absorption of French words into the English language in their interaction with their own circles.[55] In addition, but on a different level, literary grandees of the 14th century like Chaucer, Wycliff and Langland continued to enrich Middle English, already permeated by French vocabulary, with cultural importations from a variety of sources in several languages.

Given that medieval text production is not truly monolingual and that boundaries between languages are porous, language contacts meant there was continuous interplay and lexical borrowings between the languages. But Anglo-French was a contact variety of French in its own right and should be considered as a part of the medieval French dialect continuum.[56]

2 Law French

The linguistic landscape of medieval England was inhabited by three languages – Latin, English and French, though not in equal shares – but in continuous and subtle intermingling, in particular of the French and English languages and cultures. The role each language played, changed and evolved both in time and in terms of geographical and geo-political distribution. It is

54 S. Lusignan (2009) French Language in Contact with English: Social Context and Linguistic Change, in: J. Wogan-Browne (ed.) *Language and Culture in Medieval Britain*, York: York Medieval Press, 19–30, at 24; Rothwell had challenged this long-standing view by showing that some vulgar English terms are of Anglo-French origin: see W. Rothwell (1996) Adding Insult to Injury: The English Who Curse in Borrowed French, in: H-F. Nielsen, L. Schosler (eds.) *The Origins and Development of Emigrant Languages*, Odense: Odense University Press, 41–54.

55 S. Lusignan (2009) at 25, based on Milroy's model: J. Milroy (1992) *Linguistic Variation and Change*, Oxford: Blackwell.

56 D. Trotter (2003) Not as eccentric as it looks: Anglo-French and French French, in: *Forum for Modern Language Studies* 39, at 427–428.

precisely that intermingling/interlocking of tongues that can be so well observed in the medieval language of the English common law. Blackstone,[57] quoting Lord Bacon, wrote:

> Our laws [...] are mixed as our language: and as our language is so much the richer, the laws are the more complete.

Admittedly, Blackstone also included the entire history of the

> intermixture of adventitious nations, the Romans, the Picts, the Saxons, the Danes, and the Normans.

As mentioned earlier, the use of French in the law was previously attributed directly to the Norman conquest and seen as a hallmark of Norman tyranny. However, this contradicts William I's promise to uphold the law as it had been under Edward the Confessor, as well as the general message he wanted to promote, that he was the rightful successor to the crown. It is interesting to note that the political feudalism that was brought over and imposed by the Normans came with the vocabulary that described it. These Norman-French terms of feudal import described the relationships and functioning of feudalism, unknown as such in England before the Norman invasion. However, in general, the Normans did not use French, but Latin, in their legal documents. It is, therefore, likely that they continued to do so on arrival in England.[58] It is also important to note that the French language of Westminster and of the King's Court had evolved from the tongue brought over by the conquering Normans two centuries before (see above), into a dialect with strong Picard and Angevin influences[59] and as a part of the medieval dialect continuum.

The textual evidence of the earliest surviving plea rolls of the English royal courts from the 1190s shows the use of Latin, though it is unlikely that it was also spoken in court.[60] Writs and charters were written in Latin, but some were

57 W. Blackstone (1765) *Commentaries on the Laws of England*, Introduction, Oxford: Clarendon Press, at 64.

58 Two centuries later the Record's Commission's *Statutes of the Realm* shows the first twelve entries between 1236 and 1267 (incl. Statute of Merton 1236, Statute of Marlborough 1267) to be still all in Latin.

59 J.H. Baker (1998) The Three Languages of the Common Law, in: 43 *McGill Law Journal* 5–24, at 17.

60 P. Brand (2010) The Language of the English Legal Profession: The Emergence of a Distinctive Legal Lexicon on Insular French, in: R. Ingham (ed.) *The Anglo-Norman Language*

in English and a few in both languages.[61] It is a fact that in the second half of the 13th century,[62] French became the language used for some official documents, legal tracts, treatises and statutes (though writs, plea rolls and other official records remained in Latin) – "something happens to make Englishmen write about law in French and frame statutes in that language".[63] Though it may well be that French was introduced in the royal (common law) courts when these were established under Henry II (1154–1189) who was French-speaking though he understood English.[64]

From the textual evidence we can see that from the time of Edward I (1272–1307), French was the language used for the formal initiation and subsequent argument conducted in the courts.[65] This would, however, have been a different tongue from the Norman-French William I brought over from Normandy. Under Henry's great grandson, Edward I, major constitutional, administrative and judicial reforms were put in place. The judiciary was professionalised and began to form an organised legal body. This improved standards of professional conduct, but it also meant that the law was becoming a 'closed profession'.[66] This was emphasised by the use of a language not generally comprehensible by the ordinary man and further separated lawyers from laymen.

During that same period, court case reporting, which unlike later law reporting also included personal comments, notes, criticisms and speculations, was first compiled in the Year Books.[67] These were written in French, which

---

and its Contexts, York: York Medieval Press, 94–101, at 95; F. Pollock, F.W. Maitland (1898) *The History of English Law*, Cambridge: CUP, at 66.

61 G. Woodbine (1943) *The Language of English Law*, in: 18 *Speculum* 395–436, at 405, fn. 3 for textual sources and statistical analysis of languages used.

62 There is textual evidence that French was used in legal texts before the second half of the 13th century, see W. Rothwell (1975) The Role of French in Thirteenth-Century England, in: 58 *Bulletin, John Rylands Library*, 445–466, at 457; W. Rothwell (1993b) Language and government in medieval England, in: 93 *Zeitschrift für französische Sprache und Literatur*, 258–270, at 262.

63 G. Woodbine (1943) at 402.

64 P. Brand (2000) The Languages of the Law in Later Medieval England, in: D. Trotter (ed.) *Multilingualism in Later Medieval Britain*, Cambridge: Brewer, at 66, challenging Woodbine's view (*Speculum* 18 (1943)) that Law French was an invention of Henry III's reign.

65 G. Woodbine (1943) at 434; P. Brand (2000): French was not only used in pleadings at the royal courts but also in some county and city courts, at 75.

66 T. Plucknett (1956) *A Concise History of the Common Law*, 5th ed., Boston: Little, Brown and Co., at 217–219.

67 These run approx. from 1260–1535, unlikely to have been written by officially appointed reporters, handed down from private collections (unlike the French 'Olim'), see F.W. Maitland

does not necessarily mean it was also the language spoken in court pleadings.[68] Brand[69] has cited evidence that would suggest the use of spoken French in pleadings, but the evidence in favour of either scenario is slight. It is most likely that it was a bilingual set-up but we do not know in what proportions. French was probably used for the specifically legal parts, while proverbial phrases may well have been in English. The language of monopoly for statutes had hitherto always been Latin. In the second half of the 13th century, French began to be used, and it dominated by the 14th century.[70] Practical pleading compilations also appeared in French, e.g. *Brevia Pleidez* (1260, also known as *Brevia Placitata*), *Fat Asaver, La Court de Baron* (c.1265), *Le Ple de la Coroune*, as well as the 15th century law books, such as Littleton's *Tenures* (1481/82) and the *Statham's Abridgment of the Law* (1490s), 16th century Fitzherbert *La Graunde Abridgement* (1541) collection of Year Books cases and attempt to provide a summary of English law, Brooke *Le Graunde Abridgement* (posth. 1578) etc. French also became the language of English legal instruction[71] and for moots in the Inner Temple.[72]

A century after the 1362 Statute of Pleading, Fortescue suggested that the courts took no notice of the provisions, because lawyers could not do without the "terms which pleaders do more properly express in French than in

(1903) Of the Anglo-French Language in the Early Year Books, in: Introduction to *Year Books of Edward II*, 17 Selden Society, at p. xiii; T. Plucknett (1956) *A Concise History of the Common Law*, 5th ed., Boston: Little, Brown and Co., at 268–273.

68 T. Plucknett (1956) at 268; F. Pollock, F.W. Maitland (1898) *The History of English Law*, London: CUP, at 84–85; G. Woodbine (1943) *The Language of English Law*, 18 Speculum 395, at 426–428, 433–435.

69 P. Brand (2000) The Languages of the Law in Later Medieval England, in: D. Trotter (ed.) *Multilingualism in Later Medieval Britain*, Cambridge: Brewer, 63–76.

70 Record's Commission's *Statutes of the Realm* show the following entries: first twelve entries between 1236 and 1267 (incl. Statute of Merton 1236, Statute of Marlborough 1267) are all in Latin; 1275: first Statute of Westminster in French; then three in Latin, two in French, two in Latin, three in French etc.; 1285: Statute of Westminster is both in Latin and French; 1290: eleven entries in Latin and nine in French; Statute of Mortmain and all statutes of 1291–95 are in Latin; 1297: confirmation of Great Charter in both Latin and French; until 1307 (end of reign of Edw. I) nine statutes in Latin, seven in French; 1307–27: one in both Latin and French, six in Latin, fifteen in French; during reign of Edw. III of 55 entries 52 were in French. Data from G. Woodbine (1943) at 401, ft. 4.

71 P. Brand (2000) at 72.

72 J.H. Baker (1998) The Three Languages of the Common Law, in: 43 *McGill Law Journal* 5, at 20.

English".[73] Law reporting continued in French until the 17th century, though this is no proof for what language was actually spoken in court. But in many case reports, we find entire passages in English in the French language report. These usually referred to declarations made (in written or spoken mode) by one of the parties to the case. It is reasonable to conclude that the English passages were verbatim original language transcripts of what had been declared and were reproduced as such in the Law French reports.[74]

The intriguing question of why the use of French in the law rose and persisted, has preoccupied generations of writers and has been the subject of much speculation. Some[75] have connected the phenomenon to the contemporary major influx of French courtiers following Henry III's marriage to Eleanor of Provence in 1236. But it is likely that the Barons' War and the not-very-Francophile Edward I put a stop to this development, and yet French persisted. In all probability and given the innate conservatism of lawyers, French was the most convenient and practical language to use in the English courts. Latin, though the language of the learned, was more rigid and archaic and lent itself less well for adaptation to the new situations of an evolving society and legal system. English, on the other hand, was still fairly untried in the 13th century, especially in relation to the demands of the writ systems that required strict adherence to the prescribed form of the writ, any lapse from which would bring about a failure of an action. With Latin as the source language, it was easier to transpose more precisely into the closely related French as the target language than into the very different English. In other words, French was the most operative language at that time and it therefore played a pivotal role in that era when the foundations of the English common law systems were being laid. It was like a dual building site of two edifices that propped each other up: the law and the development of its concepts, on the one hand, and the language and the evolution of its technical, specialised vocabulary, on the other. Brand argued that the existence of a specialist legal vocabulary in insular French can be traced back to before the emergence of the legal profession and,

---

73 J. Fortescue (1741 – 2nd ed.) *De Laudibus Legum Angliae*, at 114; W.S. Holdsworth (1927 – 4th ed.) *A History of English Law*, vol. 2, London: Methuen, at 478.

74 e.g. a case dated 1560 reported by Benloe 82 in 123 Engl. Report pp. 63–65: "*Et auxy il plede ue certain bill del dit seignior W.P. per q il declare que il & le seignior Audely & seignior Russel* were pleased and also did nominate and appoint and fully agree that I Lord Bray should marry the said Anne, upon which our pleasure, nomination and assent the said marriage was solemnized *per que le dit J. Seignior Bray prist a feme le dit Anne …*" See other examples: case of 1535 in Benloe 13 or 123 Eng. Rep. at 10; case of 1586 in Savile 81 or 123 Eng. Rep. at 1024.

75 G. Woodbine (1943) *The Language of English Law*, in: 18 *Speculum*, 395–436, at 402.

while it does not as such owe its existence to that profession, its future evolutions certainly happened at the hands of the English lawyers.[76]

> The English bar and bench [...] used Anglo-French to create an entirely new legal vocabulary, the basis indeed of a new jurisprudence, by giving special meanings to ordinary words.[77]

Maitland described it as the

> elaboration of rough native material into a highly technical, but at the same time durable, scheme of terms and concepts.[78]

The continuous and highly specialised use of French within the closed ranks of lawyers resulted not only in the formation of specialised Law French but also in a separation of this professional jargon from French that was massively imported into English. The central residue was the technical part of Law French, while the everyday terminology was gradually taken over by English. What we are left with is a "lingering professional dialect, more often written than spoken".[79] But it evolved in sophistication and abstractness in parallel with the development of law it was used to describe and was like a kind of shorthand. It became

> highly technical because English lawyers had been able to make a vocabulary, to define their concepts, to think sharply as the man of science thinks.[80]

Once the upswing of the legal profession and the law in general went hand in hand with the blossoming of Law French, the two were intrinsically linked, and survived even during a period when in general terms French gave way to English. Law French was like a hyphen that kept alive the general framework of an earlier vocabulary and syntax until a time when English had become a full and

---

76 P. Brand (2010) The Language of the English Legal Profession: The Emergence of a Distinctive Legal Lexicon on Insular French, in: R. Ingham (ed.) *The Anglo-Norman Language and its Contexts*, York: York Medieval Press, at 100.

77 J.H. Baker (1990) Manual of Law French, Aldershot: Scolar Press, 2nd edition, at 4.

78 F.W. Maitland (1903) Of the Anglo-French Language in the Early Year Books, in: Introduction to *Year Books of Edward II*, 17 Selden Society, at xviii.

79 J.H. Baker (1990) at 3.

80 F.W. Maitland (1903) at xxxvi.

flexible language and had appropriated all the necessary French elements, expressions and vocabulary.[81]

Law French was not a foreign tongue, but started as the general French of Westminster Hall with all the inconsistencies in its spelling.[82] Yet, as described above, its use was more operative than the less learned English. Later, when Coke translated Littleton's *Tenure* from Law French into English, he carried over a great many terms without much change, which in itself is an indication of the extent to which technical Law French easily became a part of the English law language, e.g. the French *fee simple* became fee simple,[83] the French *fee taile* became fee tail,[84] the French *heires* became heirs.[85]

Pollock and Maitland have drawn up a (non-exhaustive) list of French words basic to the law vocabulary:[86]

action	damage	judges	pledge
agreement	debt	judgment	police
appeal	declaration	jurors	possession
arrests	defendant	justice	prisons
arson	demand	justices	property
assault	descent	larceny	purchase
attorneys	devise	lien	reprieve
battery	easement	marriage	robbery
bill	evidence	misdemeano(u)r	sentence
claim	execution	money	servant
condition	felony	note	slander
constables	gaols	obligation	suit
contract	grant	pardon	tort
counsel	guarantee	parties	treason
count	guardian	partner	trespass
court	heir	payment	verdict
covenant	indictment	plaintiff	
crime	infant	pleadings	

81 S. Stoljar (1954) A Common Lawyer's French, in: 47 *Law Library Journal*, 119–224, at 224.

82 F.W. Maitland (1903) Of the Anglo-French Language in the Early Year Books, in: Introduction to *Year Books of Edward II*, 17 Selden Society, at xxxiii, xliii.

83 E. Coke (1703 – 10th ed.) *Commentary upon Littleton*, at f.1a.

84 E. Coke (1703) f.18b.

85 E. Coke (1703) f.1a.

86 F. Pollock, F.W. Maitland (1898) *The History of English Law*, London: CUP, at 81.

More than half of these came into written English with a legal meaning by the middle of the 14th century. Today, we would recognise this list to be no longer exclusive to the field of law, nor would we think of most words as particularly foreign, they have become common currency in contemporary English. Yet, a great many terms have very specifically technical legal meanings. If we take the words 'trespass' and 'covenant', for example, it is understood by the ordinary man as a wrongdoing or transgression in the case of the former and as an agreement in the broad sense of the latter. And yet, it has very precise meanings for the common law lawyer who applies these terms to very specific circumstances. So both lawyer and non-lawyer use the same terms but still speak different languages.

Moreover, a number of Law French terms and phrases have survived in today's common law English that are distinct from both the English words of French origin and modern French:[87]

alien, in the sense of *to transfer*
cestui que trust
chose in action
de son tort
estoppel
estoppel in pais
esquire
fee simple and *fee tail*, which like *attorney general* retain the French word order
laches
metes and *bounds*
oyez
pur autre vie
quash
roll, as in *judgment roll*
save, in the sense of *except*
speciality, in the sense of *sealed contract*
voire dire

In its beginnings, the French used in the law was not as such a technical language. But with time and the general decline of French in England, Law French became a highly specialised use of that language within the closed confines of the legal profession and abstract from everyday usages. The language contact

87 D. Mellinkoff (1963) *The Language of the Law*, Boston: Little, Brown & Co., at 16.

was such that, on the one hand, the French used in the law took an independent path from the French that became widely absorbed into the English language. On the other hand, lawyers speaking native English and acquiring French, constituted the link that allowed for great quantities of French words with legal connotations to penetrate the English language.[88]

3 Protecting Privileges

During the 16th century, Law French was still used at the Inns of Court and very occasionally in the law courts. The early law reports[89] were also written in French. The legal profession hung onto this idiom that had shaped their law, legal thinking, habits and the construction of their concepts and arguments.[90] Coke described Law French as:

> *vocabula artis* [...] so apt and significant to express the true sense of the laws, and are so woven in the laws themselves, as it is in a manner impossible to change them [...]

He practiced what he preached in the sense that in some of his translations he simply transferred much of the technical Law French vocabulary straight into English.[91] In his *Commentary upon Littleton* (1628), Coke thought Law French to be "most commonly written and read, and very rarely spoken".[92] In other words, he acknowledged the use of Law French as very restricted. But when he published his *Reports* (1600–1615), he did so in French, because he contended that:

> it was not thought fit nor convenient, to publish either those or any of the statutes enacted in those days in the vulgar tongue.

88 D. Mellinkoff (1963) *The Language of the Law*, Boston: Little, Brown & Co., at 109.

89 The so-called 'old' reports first appeared during the reign of Henry VIII and ran until 1865.

90 For example: *fee simple* was *fee simple*, *fee taile* became *fee tail*, *heires* became *heirs*.

91 See fn. 83, 84, and 85 above. One of the reason Coke hung onto French may also have been his fear of unwanted interference by King James I, who had turned to Roman law with its wider powers for the king, while Coke was a staunch defender of parliamentary sovereignty. Coke also had a keen interest in ensuring that the legal profession did not lose touch with its corporate intellectual memory of English law embodied in the older body of case law and legislation in Law French.

92 E. Coke (1832 – 19th ed.) *Commentary upon Littleton*, at xxxix.

He used the language to which he was accustomed and warned at the same time that publishing his reports in English would raise the risk that:

> the unlearned by bare reading without right understanding might suck out errors, and trusting to their conceit, might endamage themselves, and sometimes fall into destruction.[93]

In other words, the reading of the law should be restricted to those who understand the tongue in which it is written. This is echoed by Bulstrode[94] in the introduction to his reports where he describes the use of French as:

> being most proper [...] and most convenient for the Professors of the law, who indeed are the only competent judges thereof. For the laws of England, do best commend themselves to them that understand them.

Later, similar charges were levelled against the use of Law French by Bentham who famously wrote that:

> a large portion of the body of the law was, by the bigotry or artifice of lawyers, locked up in an illegible character, and in a foreign tongue.[95]

It is an idiom known to the noble and wealthy classes and their sons, often educated in the law. Even from the time when English became more common, the wealthy, keen to maintain their privileges, through land law in particular, continued the use of Law French for the reasons mentioned above, but also to "lock up trade secrets in the safe of an unknown tongue".[96] John Warr[97] suggests that:

> the unknownness of the law, being in a strange tongue; whereas, when the law was in a known language, as before the Conquest, a man might be

93 3 Co. Rep. at xl.

94 E. Bulstrode (1658, reprinted 1688 – 2nd ed.) *The Reports of Edward Bulstrode of the Inner Temple. In Three Parts*, London: Lee, Pakeman and Bedell, Part II: To the Reader.

95 J. Bentham (1823) *A Fragment on Government, Or, A Comment on the Commentaries*, London: E. Wilson, at xxxv.

96 D. Mellinkoff (1963) *The Language of the Law*, Boston: Little, Brown & Co., at 101.

97 J. Warr (1650/1810) 6 *The Harleian Miscellany*, London: Dutton (new ed., this pamphlet was originally from 1649, it contains the debate leading up to the 1650 Act) at 221–223. John Warr was a Leveller and an independent reformer of law, arguing for the participatory liberty of the individual as the basis of all legal norms. Levellers and reformers like him initiated the process of establishing individual liberty at the centre stage of the political process. Later this was fully developed by Locke and the modern natural law tradition.

> his own advocate. But the hiddenness of the law, together with the fallacies and doubts thereof, render us in a posture unable to extricate ourselves; but we must have recourse to the shrine of the lawyer, whose oracle is in such request, because it pretends to resolve doubts.

There is little evidence for this being a deliberate process, but it was certainly a collateral benefit for the powerful.[98] As Mellinkoff[99] pointed out, it had been done before by the Celts who apparently perpetuated their customary law in a "learned archaic language". It is significant that the general movement of making things more accessible to the ordinary man during the Interregnum of 1649–1660, brought a major onslaught on the use of Law French, which, by that time, had become totally incomprehensible to anyone but the initiated.

4 Demise of Law French

The use of Law French made the language of the English common law increasingly technical, abstract and detached from the common tongue. Particularly rich borrowings had been made from other languages, also including remnants of Old English and Middle English, as well as many words with Scandinavian etymologies.[100] But the bulk came from Latin directly or indirectly through French or French sources. An 'addiction' to a 'grand mixture of languages', including deposits of Celtic and Norse, Latin and French has brought the warehouse of word material to overflowing, producing a number of phenomena, such as word doubling, bilingual synonyms, multiplying words etc.[101] which contributed to the language of the law being wordy, opaque and unclear. Add to this the use of court hand, abbreviations and increased condensation by the printers,[102] and it is not surprising that the reforms of the Commonwealth period included the language of the law, which had not been accessible to the ordinary literate layman for centuries and which the revolutionaries wanted to abolish in favour of a pocket book code in plain English.

---

98 W.M. Ormrod (2003) The Use of English: Language, Law and Political Culture in Fourteenth-Century England, in: *Speculum* 73, 3, 750–787, at 765.

99 D. Mellinkoff (1963) *The Language of the Law*, Boston: Little, Brown & Co., at 36.

100 The term 'law' came into Old English in about the year 1000 from the Old Norse, where in turn it had been derived from Old Icelandic words.

101 D. Mellinkoff (1963) at 120–122.

102 D. Mellinkoff (1963) at 86–88.

During the Interregnum, an Act of Parliament[103] attempted to abolish the use of any language other than English in all law writings and proceedings. It was a blanket ban and stipulated that:

> [...] Report-Books of the Resolutions of Judges, and other Books of the Law of England, shall be Translated into the English tongue [...] all Reports-Books of the Resolutions of Judges and all other Books of the Law of England, which shall be Printed, shall be in the English tongue onely [...] all Writs, Proces and Returns thereof, and all Pleadings, Rules, Orders, Indictments, Inquisitions, Certificates; and all Patents, Commissions, Records, Judgements, Statutes, Recognizances, Rolls, Entries, and Proceedings of Courts Leet, Courts Baron, and Customary Courts, and all Proceedings whatsoever in any Courts of Justice within this Commonwealth, and which concerns the Law, and Administration of Justice, shall be in the English Tongue onely, and not in Latine or French, or any other Language then English [...]

This was greeted with little enthusiasm by the legal profession, who felt deprived of their privileged position and had little patience for what they perceived as an unprofessional break with tradition. William Style (1658), who saw himself forced to make his "reports speak English" from his Law French personal notes,[104] wrote in his introduction that he had obeyed authority, but that:

> the part of the Common Law which is in English hath only occasioned the making of unquiet spirits contentiously knowing, and more apt to offend others, than to defend themselves.

Prior to the Rump Parliamant statutory reforms reportedly promoted by Bulstrode Whitelocke, only one set of printed common law reports[105] was written in English, although the equity reports from the Chancery, first printed at that time were written in English from the 1590s. During the decade of the Interregnum, ten reports were published, of which only two were originally composed in English, while the others were written in French but immediately translated into English by the publishers, as required by statute. With the Restoration,

103 *An Act for turning the Books of the Law, and all Proces and Proceedings in Courts of Justice, into English*; November 1650 Acts and Ordinances of the Interregnum, His Majesty's Stationery Office, London 1911 at 455–456.

104 W. Style (1658) *Narrationes Modernae*, London: Lee, Pakemen, Bedel, Adams, Introduction: "...taken by me in Law-french...".

105 *The Reports of that Learned Sir Henry Hobart* (1641), London.

some law reports were once again published in French and the pleading form reverted to Latin. Benloe, Jenkins and Yelverton (all in 1661), Latch (1663), Jones, Rolle and Savile (all in 1675), Palmer (1678), Siderfin (1683 84), Saunders (1686) all published their reports in French. But the clock could not be turned back. The English language had become a more integral part of the common law, e.g. Hardes (1693) reports are in English and after 1704 all reports were in that language.[106] By that time, Law French had been totally absorbed by English and its use was banned in 1731 by statute,[107] an instrument that confirmed an established situation rather than introduced a radical change. Its aim was to protect:

> those who are summoned and impleaded having no knowledge or understanding of what is alleged for or against them in the pleadings of their lawyers and attornies, who use a character not legible to any but persons practising the law: To remedy these great mischiefs, and to protect the loves and fortunes of the subjects [...] more effectually than heretofore, from the peril of being ensnared or brought in danger by forms and proceedings in courts of justice, in an unknown language, be it enacted [... that] all proceeding whatsoever in any courts of justice [...] and which concern the law and administration of justice, shall be in the English tongue and language only, and not in Latin or French, or any other tongue and language whatsoever, and shall be written in such a common legible hand and character, as the acts of parliament are usually ingrossed in, and the lines and words of the same to be written at least as close as the said acts usually are, and not in any hand commonly called courts hand, and in words at length and not abbreviated [...]

The use of Law French had come irreversibly to an end. With the 1731 Statute, the use of English was officially established in the law and all other languages banned. Yet two years later, it was necessary to enact further legislation[108] to allow for expressions such as *nisi prius, habeas corpus* etc. to be used, which had become so entrenched in the legal vocabulary that it appeared impossible to anglicise them. Moreover, the legacy of Law French is undeniable even in today's common law English. But the development of such a highly technical

106 W.S. Holdsworth (1924) *A History of English Law*, vol. VI, London: Methuen, at 552–554.

107 Proceedings in Courts of Justice Act 1730, 4 Geo II. c. 26.

108 6 Geo. II, c. 14; 6 Geo II c. 6.

and precise legal language has also meant that a certain rigidity renders it incapable of the slightest change, with the inevitable result that "both the law and the language will tend to lose touch with common life".[109] Blackstone remarked very pertinently in his Commentaries of the purpose of the reforms to make the law more comprehensible for the common people:

> I know not how well it has answered, but am apt to suspect that the people are now, after many years' experience, altogether as ignorant in matters of law as before.

The exclusive use of English for the common law from the 18th century coincided with more general developments in English law during that century, in particular in the fields of tort and contract, which moved the common law further away from its Anglo-Norman roots. English now played a similar role to the one of Law French during the times of Edward I as the linguistic vehicle for the reforms. Starting with Blackstone in the second half of the 18th century, a number of treatise writers sought to systemise the common law or certain aspects of it, using English as their language. Law French, which had once displaced Latin, had now itself been ousted by English: *sic transit gloria mundi.*

•••

Starting from the premise that the way meanings are encoded in spoken or written form depends on the contexts of culture and of situation, the present chapter has outlined these two parameters, by describing the general cultural and geo-political environment in which these texts occurred, as well as the cultural and linguistic landscape of multilingual England that are specific to medieval legal text production. Chapter 6 will describe the terminology and semantic shifts of the language in (mainly) legal reports on the concept of consideration and legal enforceability of informal agreements. The methodology used to evaluate such linguistic evolutions, was a diachronic linguistic and semantic analysis using corpus linguistics methodologies. This, in turn, informs the research on the concordance between the historical and conceptual development of consideration and the way the relevant terms have been used, changed and shifted throughout this evolution, most notably the increased abstraction of both the concept and the language. However, before going there,

---

109 W.S. Holdsworth (1923) *A History of English Law*, vol. II, London: Methuen, at 482.

the following chapter will first discuss the origin and early development of the concept of legally enforceable informal agreements, its origins in the action of trespass on the case and debt, via the action of assumpsit, to the early 17th century doctrine of consideration.

CHAPTER 5

The Origins of the Concept of Consideration

Through the centuries, the doctrine of consideration has puzzled judges, lawyers and legal scholars. Those educated in the civil law tradition find themselves confused by the basic premise of the doctrine that is both similar and different to their own thinking as embodied in the doctrine of *causa*. English law has, in particular since the accession of the United Kingdom to the then European Communities, been confronted by the insularity of this doctrine and it has been one of the stumbling blocks in the many attempts to streamline contract law at European Union level.

But legal historians are also puzzled by the diverse and sometimes contradictory historical explanations of the first ideas that consideration should be a prerequisite for the enforceability of an informal agreement and of its promotion to a fully-fledged legal doctrine central to contract law.[1] The diversity of historical theories by so many eminent scholars shows that the concept actually emanated from different distinct legal sources and it would be an oversimplification to believe that the concept evolved along a single linear path. Baker outlines what he calls a 'vexed subject' as follows:

> Was 'consideration' an unbroken development of a single idea from medieval times; or was there a break with medieval thought, and perhaps a

1 Examples of main works on consideration and its origins: A. Ames (1913) *Lectures on Legal History and Miscellaneous Legal Essays*, Cambridge: Harvard University Press, at 122–171; J. Baker (2013) Origins of the doctrine of consideration 1535–1585, in: J. Baker, *Collected Papers on English Legal History*, vol. III, Cambridge: CUP, at 1176–1201; W.T. Barbour (1914) The History of Contract in Early English Equity, in: P. Vinogradoff (ed.) *Oxford Studies in Social and Legal History*, vol. IV, Oxford: Clarendon Press, at 59–65; J.L. Barton (1969) The Early History of Consideration, in: 85 *Law Quarterly Review*, 382–383; W.S. Holdsworth (1903–1966) *A History of English Law*, London: Methuen, (1923) vol. II, at 82–87, (1923) vol. III, at 412–454, (1925) vol. VIII, at 1–98; O.W. Holmes (1885) Early English Equity, in: *Law Quarterly Review*, 162–174; E. Lorenzen (1919) Causa and consideration in the law of contracts, in: 28 *Yale Law Journal*, 621–646; S.F.C. Milsom (1981) *Historical Foundations of the Common Law*, London: Butterworth, at 356–360; Th. Plucknett (1956) *A Concise History of the Common Law*, 5th ed., Boston: Little, Brown and Co., at 627–656; F. Pollock, F.W. Maitland (1895/1968) *The History of English Law before the Time of Edward I*, vol. I & II, Cambridge: CUP, at 184–239; B. Simpson (1975a) *A History of the Common Law of Contract : The Rise of the Action of Assumpsit*, Oxford: Clarendon Press; B. Simpson (1975b) Innovation in nineteenth century contract law, in: *Law Quarterly Review*, 91, 247–278; J. Salmond (1887) The History of Contract, in: *Law Quarterly Review*, 3, 166–178.

 | DOI:10.1163/9789004436169_006

> combination of different ideas? Was it a wholly indigenous development; and, if so, was it an incidental consequence of the exigencies of the forms of action or a direct result of juristic speculation about contractual liability? Alternatively, was it something reflected or borrowed from the canon law or the Civil law? And, if so, was the influence brought to bear on the common law directly through Renaissance humanism, or indirectly by way of the canonist chancellors or ecclesiastical judges?[2]

Studying the case law, we can find evidence that various strands from different directions came together in the idea that informal promises should be enforceable. In other words, when this idea materialised, it originated from different legal issues, which is precisely why it is so complex to untangle the strands and understand the process. The case law added bits and pieces that were diverse because the facts of the various cases tended to be different: malfeasance, non-feasance, trespass, deceit, detriment, benefit/gain, forbearance etc. It was largely the result of constructing arguments to win court cases, so every decision related to specific facts and was then extrapolated onto wider issues but in the absence of any attempts at developing an overall theory of contract formation. Today's puzzlement about the historical evolution of consideration probably matches the lack of unanimous thinking among lawyers at the time when the concept materialised.

This raises interesting questions about the nature of legal development. Teubner[3] contends that the law reacts to developments of the external environment by adaptation in symbiosis and not through the incorporation of outside ideas. He compares this mode of functioning to that of biological cells, which are both self-contained but also react to modified outside conditions by undergoing internal change. Teubner's idea echoes the concept of 'path dependence' according to which complex situations are overcome by following the safe path of acting in a way that has worked before. "Each system is locked into a set of concepts, procedures and ideas from the past which are carried forward to resolve new problems".[4] Innovations will, therefore, materialise and grow within the established framework of legal rules.

Moving forward while referring back in time is also inherent in the concept of 'intertextuality' in linguistics and discourse analysis. The term was coined by

2 J. Baker (2013) Origins of the doctrine of consideration 1535–1585, in: *Collected Papers on English Legal History*, vol. III, Cambridge: CUP, at 1176.

3 G. Teubner (1993) *Law as an Autopoietic System*, Oxford: Blackwells Publishers, at 61, 95 & Ch. 3.

4 J. Bell, D. Ibbetson (2012) *European Legal Development. The Case of Tort.* Volume 9, Cambridge: CUP, at 24.

Kristeva[5] in the 1960s but based on previous work by Bakhtin, who believed that texts were 'responses' shaped by earlier texts, but which also 'anticipated' subsequent texts. Fairclough defines the concept in terms of seeing "texts historically as transforming the past – existing convention and prior texts – into the present".[6] The parallel of interest with the present context is the textual dimension of discourse and the change thereof. Fairclough describes the process as follows:

> Change leaves traces in texts [... and] in so far as a particular tendency of discursive change 'catches on' and becomes solidified into an emergent new convention, what at first are perceived by interpreters as stylistically contradictory texts come to lose their patchwork effect and be 'seamless'. Such a process of naturalization is essential to establishing new hegemonies in the sphere of discourse. [...] Producers and interpreters [of text ...] are disarticulating existing orders of discourse, and rearticulating new orders of discourse, new discursive hegemonies.[7]

We can recognise here how changes are achieved by pushing boundaries and through transgression while at the same time staying close to previously trodden paths. As discussed in this study and the present chapter, this process can be observed both on the conceptual level as well as the discursive and linguistic levels.

Changes of a more 'organic' rather than avowed nature are characteristics of the common law. According to Milsom "the common law has traced odd patterns by following its nose; but this is because it has by and large turned, however clumsily, to tasks needing to be done".[8] In the context of case law that meant court actions needed to be won, which echoed Holmes' famous words that "the life of the law has not been logic: it has been experience".[9] Growing trade and commerce meant that there was an increasing need to render informal undertakings and promises legally enforceable. The substantial body of case law shows how the new regulation in this area was achieved by nudging existing boundaries and thus reaching neighbouring premises. In his usual imaginative language, Milsom contends that "legal change under these

5 J. Kristeva (1986) Word, dialogue and novel, in: T. Moi (ed.) *The Kristeva Reader*, Oxford: Basil Blackwell, 34–61; this paper was written in 1966 but only published in 1986.

6 N. Fairclough (1992) *Discourse and Social Change*, Cambridge: Polity, at 85.

7 N. Fairclough (1992) at 97.

8 S.F.C. Milsom (1985) *Studies in the History of the Common Law,* London: The Hambledon Press, at 169.

9 O.W. Holmes (1881) *The Common Law*, www.gutenberg.org, at 1.

conditions has the appearance of a conjuring trick: out of the old hat there comes a new rabbit". But not all is as it seems because the rabbit is in fact taken from a different hat.[10] Undertakings that could not be legally enforceable for want of a sealed covenant, took a seemingly bizarre detour via trespass on the case onto neighbouring legal ideas, and the emerging rabbit had in fact primarily promissory features rather than proprietary ones.

This process is also reflected in the language and terminology used throughout the 16th century, in particular. Holdsworth contends that, as boundaries of traditional actions were being pushed and widened, it became

> obvious that some word or expression was needed to differentiate the agreements which could be enforced [...], from the agreements which could not.[11]

But the terminology settled only hesitantly, which may reflect a concordance between the complexity of the concept's evolution and the terminology used to express it. This will be discussed in the following chapter.

The forerunner of consideration – the writ[12] of assumpsit – arose in a medieval legal world that was governed by procedures, which were complex and archaic at times. Between the 13th century and the reforms of the 19th century, procedural formalities dominated the common law thinking. In its earlier stages, the common law must have been anterior to the forms, but the formulae through which justice was centralised and administered by the king's court in the 12th and 13th centuries were 'frozen' as part of the due process of law guaranteed by the charters of liberties. This immutable formulary framework gave rise to a formalistic legal culture. There were two kinds of legal complaints in the early jurisdictions: the complaint of a wrong and the demand for a right.[13] The law of obligations as we know it today has its early roots in the latter and in the writs that were in the *praecipe* form.

> It was by argument based upon this elementary difference between the kinds of possible claim, rather than by unreasoned interplay between

10 S.F.C. Milsom (1985) *Studies in the History of the Common Law*, London: The Hambledon Press, at 150 & 152.

11 W.S. Holdsworth (1925) *History of English Law* vol. VIII, London: Methuen, at 3.

12 To commence proceedings in the Common Pleas and King's Court, a plaintiff had to purchase a royal writ from the King's Chancery. This was at first exceptional and a royal favour before it became a right gradually extended to all plaintiffs.

13 S.F.C. Milsom (1981) *Historical Foundations of the Common Law*, London: Butterworth, at 243.

> 'forms of action' seen as primeval entities, that the common law of obligations was hammered out.[14]

Rights and remedies were significant to the extent that relevant procedures gave them form.[15] But by pushing persistently against the procedural limitations of the writ system, it developed into a tool that met rising commercial needs in terms of contracts and quasi-contracts. It is one of the best "illustration of the flexibility and power of self-development of the Common law"[16] because its evolution was more akin to organic shifts, than to large legislative changes; it worked within the adaptation of old rules and principles to new circumstances and needs. The present chapter will describe the story of how the action of assumpsit and the concept of consideration arose and evolved between the late 15th and 17th centuries and again in the 18th century. Much has already been written on this topic and details can be read in the abundant literature produced by many eminent scholars. This chapter outlines the history of the concept with the aim of juxtaposing it to the evolution of its language and terminology. This allows for the search for possible concordances between the two, which will reflect on the legal thinking and minds behind the court decisions.

1 Transactional Agreements – Early Notions

Before 1066, English contract law was rather rudimentary. There were Anglo-Saxon ordinances relating to trade and exchange, and local courts exercised some limited jurisdiction based on customs, administered at local fairs, markets and ports. A sale was an executed contract and it is doubtful whether there was any elaborate notion of debt. There existed some rules aimed at preventing dealings in stolen goods[17] or dealing with vendor's warranty of title[18] and quality[19] of goods sold.

The 12th century Justinian revival had a very limited impact on the development of English contract law, mainly because the way that traditional practices

14 S.F.C. Milsom (1981) at 244.

15 J. Baker (2007) *An Introduction to English Legal History*, Oxford: OUP, at 53.

16 J.A. Ames (1913) *Lectures on Legal History and Miscellaneous Legal Essays*, Cambridge: Harvard University Press, at 166.

17 IV Edgar, 6–11 (962–963).

18 II Æthelred, 8–9 (991).

19 Oaths 7 in F. Liebermann (1903) *Die Gesetze der Angelsachsen: hrsg. im Auftrage der Savigny-Stiftung*, Halle an der Saale: Niemeyer at 399.

applied by the local courts were far removed from the *ius commune* doctrines. Prior to the 16th century, the enforcement of informal contracts was left as a matter of policy to the largely non-writ jurisdiction of the non-royal courts (county courts, hundred courts and seignorial court). The jurisdiction of the King's Court, established in the latter part of the 12th century, was limited to the specific types of cases that were subject of standardised types of original writs, though causes and forms of action went on developing over the 13th and 14th centuries. Foreign influences could not easily get a foothold in the common law that "had already developed an inflexible system of procedure".[20] Glanvil knew enough about the *ius commune* to correctly describe and define the Roman classification of contract, though apparently he did not feel himself bound by these definitions.[21] The treatise that bears Bracton's name "endeavoured to express common law in Romanesque language".[22] But it was more concerned with criminal law and property law, than with principles of contract.

The two common law actions, from which the medieval law relating to transactions arose, were the action of covenant and the action of debt. There were two further contractual remedies in English law: detinue[23] and account,[24] both of which were based on real contracts. It is important to stress that the word 'contract' in the early Year Books refers to a narrower sense than is understood today. Contract was seen in terms of real contracts covering the transactions where a duty arose from the passing of a *quid pro quo*, such as a sale or a loan. The formal or speciality contracts were described as grants, obligations or covenants.[25]

20 Th. Plucknett (1956) *A Concise History of the Common Law*, London: Butterworth, at 627.

21 R. de Glanvil (1187–89) *Tractatus de legibus et consuetudinibus regni Anglie* (The treatise on the laws and customs of the realm of England commonly called Glanvil), edited and translated by G. Hall, M. Clanchy (2002), Oxford: Clarendon Press, x. 3.

22 Th. Plucknett (1956) at 627.

23 Dating back to the 12th century, detinue is one of the oldest forms of action in common law and relied upon for the recovery of personal property or their value in money from a person who refuses to give it up.

24 Dating back to the 13th century, account was less concerned with the obligation to pay a sum due (action of debt) and more with the prior obligation to enter into account in order to ascertain if and what was owed. Before 1300, it was a remedy mainly for the breach of obligations owed by fiduciaries, such as bailiffs who owed to their lord of the manor. By the early 14th century, the scope of the action was much wider, it was extended to commercial relationships.

25 "Chescun graunt et chescun demaunde par resound du graunt doit ester par especialté. Mès d'autre contracte com de baille, ou de apprest si puist homme demaunder par sute" ("Every grant and every demand by reason of a grant ought to be by specialty. But as

1.1 *Action of Covenant*

By the time of Bracton, agreements made on the basis of delivering objects[26] as security or personal sureties[27] faded in favour of other instruments. For important agreements, it was held best to formalise them in writing and as early as 1235, maybe also for reasons of widespread illiteracy, a seal was applied to written covenants by the parties as a sign of their acknowledgement of the written document.

In Bracton the action of covenant is described, apparently unknown to Glanvil. For a contract to be enforceable it must either be real, that is money or chattels have passed, or formal which, according to Bracton, requires a deed under seal with the *stipulatio*. The strict requirement of the seal means that beyond it becoming 'a promise well-proven', it had become a promise 'of a distinct nature of which a distinct form of action was provided'.[28] It transpires from Bracton that there was no room, at that stage, for the notion of a consensual contract.[29]

In the 13th century, and according to a statute of 1285,[30] the variety of writs of covenant was infinite and the action was applicable on the face of it to all consensual agreements. But this seemingly comprehensive action soon played only a minor role in the history of contract: a covenant was an agreement and the deed was evidence of an agreement by the early 14th century.[31] In other words, it was less a question of substantive law but rather one concerned with proof.[32] Sealed contracts were enforceable on the mere basis that they were formal and to contend, as was said from the mid-16th century, that a 'seal imports consideration' has little to do with the doctrine of consideration as we know it today. It is only with the action of assumpsit that the idea grew of informal agreements as actions in their own right.

---

regards other contracts, as, for instance, bailment or loan, one can demand by suit"), Frisk in *Loveday v Ormesby*, (1310) YB 3 Edw. II, 25, or 20 Selden Society at 191.

26 The Anglo-Saxon *wed*, called *gage* after the Norman Conquest consisted of a valuable object (though its value could be of symbolic nature).

27 The Anglo-Saxon *borgh*, called pledge after the Norman Conquest consisted of a person rather than a thing.

28 O.W. Holmes cited by Th. Plucknett (1956) *A Concise History of the Common Law*, London: Butterworth, at 634.

29 W.S. Holdsworth (1923) *A History of English Law*, vol. II, at p. 277; vol. III, at 416.

30 Statute of Wales 1284, c. 10, in: J. Baker, S. Milsom (1999) *Sources of English Legal History: Private Law to 1750*, London: Butterworth, at 281.

31 *Anon.* (1304) in: J. Baker, S. Milsom (1999) at 284.

32 S.F.C. Milsom (1981) *Historical Foundations of the Common Law*, London: Butterworth, at 247–248.

Agreements to do something could not be enforced in the King's Court without a sealed document. However, this rule did not apply to obligations to pay money or to deliver goods. Sealed documents were not always practicable in commercial undertakings. Therefore, actions of debt and detinue could be brought on the basis of a *quid pro quo*.

1.2 *Action of Debt*

The authors of *Glanvil* and *Bracton* wrote about *causa debendi*[33] (reason for owing) in the language of the *ius commune*. However, in the Year Books this was set out in terms of *quid pro quo*. The action of debt was applicable to formal contracts under seal specifying a sum (debt on an obligation) and to real contracts where a *res* had passed between the parties (debt on a contract). The latter was a way to protect creditors claiming on the basis of informal contracts, the premise being that the defendant had received something (a *res*) from the plaintiff and, hence, there had been a *quid pro quo*. Barton[34] argues that the expression was not exclusively associated with the action of debt. Milsom[35] has traced the development of the action of debt, also in its relation to *quid pro quo*. In an action from 1458, it was argued that debt will lie when there is a *quid pro quo*, and it was held, *per* Moyle and Davers, that something which was of no benefit to the defendant could constitute a *quid pro quo*, or be at least an equivalent.[36]

At the early stages when a common law action was used to enforce informal contracts on the basis of debt (specific sums lent or otherwise owed) or detinue (chattels sold or lent), there was nothing resembling a general idea of civil obligation based on promise or agreement or some sort of consensual contract.[37] The action of debt was based on a proprietary notion rather than promissory one. In other words, it evolved around the fiction that the lender was claiming what belonged to him, rather than what the object of the promise

33 The *causae debendi* listed in *Glanvil* are five examples of contracts in the *ius commune*: *mutuum*, *commodatum*, sale, lease and deposit (*Glanvil*, x. 3).

34 J.L. Barton (1969) The Early History of Consideration, in: 85 *Law Quarterly Review*, 382–383.

35 S.F.C Milsom (1961) Sale of Goods in the Fifteenth Century, in: 77 *Law Quarterly Review*, 257–284.

36 "...il n'est un mere contract, uncore il est tant en effet: car l'accord fuit q il prendra la file a feme; en ql cas le def. ad Quid p quo..." in Y.B. 37 Mich. Hen VI, 8, 18, or LBEx.

37 Mc Govern challenges that view: W. McGovern (1969) Contract in Medieval England: The Necessity for Quid Pro Quo And a Sum Certain, in: 13 *American Journal of Legal History*, 173–201, at 173–174.

was. While the actions of debt and detinue constitute the earliest recognition of the enforceability of oral agreements, these are not as such the origin of modern contract law in relation to informal agreements. The action of debt was riddled with technicalities and procedural complexities that excluded many meritorious claims for enforcing informal agreements. The common law only recognised parol agreements that were based upon a *quid pro quo*, but it took a rather broad view of this concept.

The common law courts, eager to expand their jurisdiction, began to develop tort[38] actions in trespass based on a very flexible form of writ, 'actions on the case', that provided a remedy in the form of damages for the invasion of personal or property interests and could be used in many different situations. It was tried by jury, hence moving away from wager of law.[39] Among the torts that were developed at that time, was an action in which the plaintiff alleged that the defendant had entered into an informal agreement with him and subsequently caused him some damage by a defective performance. That 'trespass on the case' became known as assumpsit.

2 Making Informal Agreements Actionable: Assumpsit and Its Forerunner Trespass on the Case

The medieval King's Courts, though aware of the ideas of contract, were not very pro active in the development of notions and principles relating specifically to contract law as we know it today.[40] As explained above, the instruments most used were covenant and debt, but their development was hampered by technical rules: the insistence on a sealed document for the former and the application of the doctrine of *quid pro quo* for the latter. Milsom pointed out that with the rise of assumpsit, the term 'covenant' was disabled from its original function and was gradually replaced by the term 'contract'. However,

38 The term 'tort' was first used in English in the legal context in the 1580s. The word is derived from Old French and Anglo-French *tort* (injury), which has its origin in the Medieval Latin *tortum*. The term was used in Law French well before then in phrases such as *tort e force* and *de son tort demene*.

39 A wager of law was a medieval form of trial in which the defendant was required to produce a set number of witnesses who could swear to his or her innocence.

40 A proper doctrinal system of contract law only materialised from the writings of the 19th century doctrinal writers, who borrowed extensively from the 17th and 18th century natural lawyers.

the latter came with its own medieval meanings, which added to the confusion among historians.[41]

The action of assumpsit became common at the beginning of the 16th century, and arose primarily from the action of trespass on the case, that is of a wrongful act directly causing harm or injury. It consisted in the recovery for the negligent performance of an undertaking. Actions in trespass providing a remedy in damages for the invasion of personal or property interests, developed long before there were actions on the case.[42] There was a time when trespass was a broad enough category to include felony, criminal misdemeanour and disseisin, as well as those remedied by the actions of trespass and trespass on the case. Later, trespass stood for a large category of original writs, though none of these writs actually employed the word 'trespass'.[43] But trespass are essentially actions of tort not contract, and liability only arose in a scenario where the plaintiff was passive and did not participate in any way. It is the element of an assumpsit, of having made an undertaking, that would render such cases actionable.

The term assumpsit has its origin in the Latin term *assumere* and, in the context of the law, was used within the phrase *assumpsit et fideliter promisit*. The defendant 'assumed and faithfully promised' to the plaintiff to do something. While the basis in a trespass action had been the occurrence of damage, in the case of assumpsit it became the breaking of a promise. The way the action of assumpsit crystallised and developed was a way of seeking a new form of action within the limits of what had already been established, such as in the action of covenant and debt, by gradually pushing the boundaries, but without making any major changes to the law. Ames qualifies it as:

> hard to find a better illustration of the flexibility and power of self-development of the Common Law. [...] In its origin an action of tort, [assumpsit] was soon transformed into an action of contract, becoming afterwards a remedy where there was neither tort nor contract. Based at first only upon an express promise, it was afterwards supported upon an implied promise, and even upon a fictitious promise. Introduced as a special manifestation of the action on the case, it soon acquired the dignity of a distinct form of action, which superseded debt, became concurrent

41 S.F.C. Milsom (1981) *Historical Foundations of the Common Law*, London: Butterworth, at 249.

42 S. Milsom (1985) *Studies in the History of the Common Law*, London: The Hambledon Press, at 1–90.

43 J. Baker (2007) *An Introduction to English Legal History*, Oxford: OUP, at 60–61.

> with account, with case upon a bailment, a warranty, and bills of exchange, and competed with equity in the case of the essentially equitable quasi-contracts growing out of the principle of unjust enrichment.[44]

The rise of assumpsit does not take a linear path of evolution: the need to create some action making parol undertakings enforceable came from different quarters. The account that follows is not to be taken as a linear description, but an attempt to describe the various strands of cases and legal thinking that led to the development of the concept of consideration.

2.1 *Malfeasance*

Among the reports in the early Year Books that cover the first quarter of the 14th century, two cases stand out as situations where money was exchanged for the making of a promise subsequently not honoured. In the Year Book of 14 Edward II (1321), we find an early example of a surgeon's negligence case: forty shillings were exchanged for the promise to cure a hand wound, but the hand was lost instead.[45] It was held that there was a lack of speciality required for a covenant. During the Eyre of Northamptonshire of 1329–30[46] a certain William Seymour took fees from two different gentlemen for the term of his life and promised to assist them rightfully or wrongfully.[47] It was claimed this was a customary thing to do. The case was held not to be one of conspiracy but of ambidexterity.[48] In neither case, can we find the sort of language that will become characteristic for later trespass on the case or assumpsit actions.

As we move into the second half of the 14th century, there are a number of cases where the resulting loss or damage or destruction of chattels were construed as quasi-trespasses – Milsom[49] calls them 'naturally trespassory' – while, with today's perspective, the nature of the situation was fundamentally more contractual, but could not be sustained as such back then for want of a covenant without deed. The common law had generally been more advanced

---

44 J.A. Ames (1913) *Lectures on Legal History and Miscellaneous Legal Essays*, Cambridge: Harvard University Press, at 166.

45 "*…ly promist de ly garrir de la play pur xl. S., et il resceut les xl. S. et il nad my garry, eynz par sa defaute il ad perdu sa mayn*" (1321) 14 Edward II, or 86 Selden Society at 353.

46 (1329–1330) 3 & 4 Edward III, or 97 Selden Society at 237.

47 "*…prist de lui argent e feez e lui promist de eyder a torte e a droit en mesme le plee*".

48 Ambidexterity here refers to jurors taking bribes from both sides for their verdict. Incidently, this is the earliest sense in English of the word, before it was used in the more general language sense.

49 S.F.C. Milsom (1981) *Historical Foundations of the Common Law*, London: Butterworth, at 316.

in developing the notion and principles of tort rather than those relating to contract and a series of cases had served to "introduce the idea of contract into actions of trespass".[50] In other words, notions of trespass were being used to overcome outmoded and excessively technical pleading procedures in matters of contract. Milsom[51] argues that, for example, in the *Humber Ferry case*[52] the ferryman was not liable in covenant because the complaint was of damage actually caused, rather than of failure to fulfil a 'contractual' obligations. These cases were actions of trespass for wrongfully inflicted physical harm on persons, goods and land. Referring to the medieval notion of legal liability in tort, Ames argues that such actions could only be brought when the plaintiff did not participate in any way. In the words of Newton C.J.:

> Perhaps he applied his medicines *de son bon gré*, and afterwards your horse died; now, since he did it *de son bon gré*, you shall not have an action.[53]

These trespass cases did not fit squarely into the original notion of tort that the injury was caused by the negligent conduct of a stranger without the participation of the plaintiff, because the latter voluntarily allowed for the defendant to come into contact with his person/property. This authorisation meant that the plaintiff took upon himself the risk of injury/damage, unless the defendant undertook (assumpsit) to do something in accordance with his skills and professional status. In the words of Newton, C.J.:

> If I have a sore on my hand, and he applies a medicine to my heel, by which negligence my hand is maimed, still I shall not have an action unless he undertook to cure me.[54]

Ames[55] insists that in these early cases of recovering damages for injuries to person or property caused by the active misconduct of the defendant, the

50 Th. Plucknett (1956) *A Concise History of the Common Law*, London: Butterworth at 637.

51 S.F.C. Milsom (1981) *Historical Foundations of the Common Law*, London: Butterworth, at 317.

52 see below (Lib. Ass. 22 Edw. III Folio 94a-94b, pl.41, or LBEx).

53 Case against a horse-doctor mentioned by J.A. Ames (1913) *Lectures on Legal History and Miscellaneous Legal Essays*, Cambridge: Harvard University Press, at 131, fn. 5.

54 J.B. Ames (1913) at 132.

55 J.B. Ames (1913) at 130.

action was regarded as actions in tort, not contract, because the notion of negligence was at issue, not that of assumpsit. It is the element of an assumpsit, of an express, unilateral undertaking, that rendered such cases against surgeons, carpenters and also bailees[56] actionable.

The first case usually associated with this development is the *Humber Ferry Case* or *Bukton v Tounesende* of 1348.[57] Ferryman Tounesende undertook to carry Bukton's mare over the river.[58] The horse was lost in the process as Tounesende had overloaded his vessel.[59] As the common law stood then, the plaintiff should have brought an action in contract/covenant. However, this required a sealed document and only applied to failure to perform agreements. Bukton would not have succeeded going down that road in his local court. A stroke of luck had it that the King's Court was sitting in York just at that time. They had developed the action of trespass for wrongfully inflicted physical harm on persons, goods and land. Yet, at that stage these actions still required proof of the use of *vi et armis,* or force and arms and a breach of the King's peace. Surprisingly, the King's Bench found in favour of the plaintiff's action of trespass to apply to the damage and loss caused by a badly-performed agreement.[60]

This case has sometimes been hailed as landmark in the history of contract law and one of the "earliest cases in which an assumpsit was laid in the declaration".[61] According to Holdsworth, it illustrated that "special variety of trespass or deceit on the case which came to be known as the action of assumpsit".[62] However, Plucknett[63] argues that although the report of the case includes the Law French words *empris a carier* (undertake to carry), there was no actual mention of an assumpsit. The action was not in case, which had not yet been developed, but in trespass. Plucknett contended that:

56 For a detailed discussion of actions on the case against bailees for negligence in the custody of the things intrusted to them, see J.A. Ames (1913) *Lectures on Legal History and Miscellaneous Legal Essays*, Cambridge: Harvard University Press, at 132–136.

57 Lib. Ass. 22 Edw. III Folio 94a-94b, pl.41, or LBEx.

58 "*...avoit empris a carier sa jument pris en son bateau oustr l'eau de Humbr safe & sain...*" Lib. Ass. 22 Edw. III Folio 94a-94b, pl.41, or LBEx.

59 "*...per quel surcharge le jument perist, a tort...*" Lib. Ass. 22 Edw. III Folio 94a-94b, pl.41, or LBEx.

60 "*...Il semble que vous luy fistes tresp' quant vous surcharge le bateau, p que sa jument perist...*" Lib. Ass. 22 Edw. III Folio 94a-94b, pl.41, or LBEx.

61 J.B. Ames (1913) at 130.

62 W.S. Holdsworth(1923) *History of English Law* vol. III, at 430.

63 Th. Plucknett (1956) *A Concise History of the Common Law*, London: Butterworth, at 441–442.

> the proceedings were initiated, not by writ, but by the less formal bill or querela which still lingered in the provinces and which explains the anomaly of trespass successfully applied without any direct and unauthorised act of interference. The case, in short, was not a precedent but a freak.[64]

Kiralfy argues[65] that since the action was for trespass without relying on *vi et armis*, the emphasis was not on the defendant's act but rather on his default. For Kiralfy, the fact that assumpsit was not mentioned was a main difference with later assumpsit actions but not an essential one in view of the fact that the formula mentioned on the original roll of this case resembles substantially the 'formulae' of subsequent assumpsit actions. Either way, once the action was admitted it "offered a fruitful soil for experiment".[66] In 1370, just over twenty years later, the decision in *Waldon v Marshall*[67] went the same way. The defendant, who undertook (*manucepit*) to cure the plaintiff's horse, had done so negligently (*ita negligenter*) and the animal died.[68] He argued unsuccessfully that the action rested upon an undertaking and thus a covenant requiring a deed. Plucknett[69] contends that all parties involved recognised a fundamentally contractual situation, but opted for "juggling with trespass because they felt unable to sustain an action in covenant without a deed". The court found against the defendant on the grounds that his negligence had caused the plaintiff damage.[70]

These cases where plaintiffs seek to recover damages for physical injuries to person or property caused by the active misconduct of the defendant,[71] cannot

64 Th. Plucknett (1956) at 441–442.

65 A.K.R. Kiralfy (1951)*The Action on the Case*, London: Sweet & Maxwell, at 53.

66 C.H.S. Fifoot (1949) *History and Sources of the Common Law: Tort and Contract*, London: Stevens, at 331.

67 Y.B Mich. 43 Edw. III, 33, 38, or LBEx.

68 "... *quod praedictus Johannes manucepit equum praedicti Will' de infirmitate, & postea praedictus John' ita negligent' curam suam fecit, quod equus suus interiit...*" Y.B Mich. 43 Edw. III, 33, 38, or LBEx.

69 Th. Plucknett (1956) at 632.

70 "... *pcq vo fists vostre cure ita negl', issint q le chival morust, p q il est reason de maint cest bre espec ...*" Y.B Mich. 43 Edw. III, 33, 38, or LBEx.

71 *Surgeons undertaking to cure the plaintiff or the plaintiff's animals*: Y.B. 43 Edw. III, 6, 11; 11 Rich. II, Fitz. Abr. Act. on the Case, 37; Y.B. 3 Hen. 36, 33; Y.B. 19 Hen. VI, 49, 5; Y.B. 11 Edw. IV, 6, 10; *Powtuary v Walton*, 1 Roll. Abr. 10, 5, *Slater v Baker*, 2 Wills. 359; *Sears v Rentice*, 8 East, 348; *Prior v Rillesford*, 17 Yorks. Arch. Soc, Rec. Ser., 78; *Blacksmith laming a horse while shoeing it*: Y.B. 46 Edw. III, 19, 19; Y.B. 12 Edw. IV, 13, 9; *Carpenter who built house unskilfully*: Y.B. 11 Hen. IV, 33, 60; Y.B. 3 Hen. VI, 36, 33; Y.B. 20 Hen. VI, 24, 4; Y.B. 21 Hen. VI, 55,

be regarded as actions of contract but are more akin to claims in tort. Stating assumpsit played an increasingly essential part in the count, but any notion of consideration, as an element of return or detriment incurred, was of no relevance at that stage. Stating assumpsit was one of the elements that led to the damage of person or property,[72] but it was not the basis on which an action of contract could be brought. During the 15th century, this view continued to be held. It is eloquently set out by Newton[73] in a trespass action on the case in 1436:

> ...if a carpenter makes a covenant to make a house good and strong and of a certain form, and he makes me a house which is weak and bad and of another form, I shall have an action of trespass on my case. So if a smith makes a covenant with me to shoe my horse well and properly, and he shoes him and lames him, I shall have a good action. So if a leech takes upon himself to cure me of my diseases,[74] and he gives me medicines, but does not cure me, I shall have an action on my case. So if a man makes a covenant with me to plough my land in seasonable time, and he ploughs in a time which is not seasonable, I shall have an action on my case. And the cause in all these cases that there is an undertaking and a matter in fact[75] besides that which sounds merely in covenant ... the plaintiff has suffered a wrong in all the aforementioned cases.

It is interesting to note that there is no use of the technical term 'assumpsit', the undertaking is still described in the vocabulary of general language. While it is an action of trespass on the case and, hence, a claim in tort, the repeated use of the term covenant, cannot deny a link to contractual thinking.

2.2 *Nonfeasance*

So much for the malfeasance of an express undertaking that results in damages for the plaintiff. An altogether different scenario was failing to act on an undertaking, which arose from situations of nonfeasance. Cases brought on

12; 18 Hen. VII, Keilw. 50, 4; 21 Hen. VII, Keilw. 77, 25; Y.B. 21 Hen. VII, 41, 66; *Coggs v Bernard*, 2 Ld. Ray. 909, 920; *Elsee v Gatward*, 5 T.R. 143; *Benden v Manning*, 2 N.H. 289.

72 The defendant undertook to do something and did it badly. Consequently, the plaintiff who relied upon the undertaking, suffered damages.

73 Y.B. 14 Hen. VI, 18, 58, or LBEx.

74 "*...enprend sur luy a me sainer de mes maladies...*" Y.B. 14 Hen. VI, 18, 58, or LBEx.

75 "*...un empris & un matier en fait...*" Y.B. 14 Hen. VI, 18, 58, or LBEx.

nonfeasance at the beginning of the 15th century were unsuccessful.[76] In *Watton v Brinth*,[77] one of the carpenter cases of a house, begun but not finished, the issue of negligence was mentioned[78] but not discussed, and the case was dismissed for want of a deed in an action of covenant. From the discussion of the 1436 case mentioned above, it appears no distinction was made between misfeasance and nonfeasance, it was all just a question of covenant.[79] The basic idea of trespass/quasi-trespass was not helpful to the nonfeasance scenario and this lay at the heart of the difficulty of bringing nonfeasance cases under the misfeasance type of assumpsit action. A new legal principle was needed, and it was found in the notion that breaching an undertaking amounts to a deceit.[80]

The original writ of deceit goes back to the beginning of the 13th century and, like the bill of deceit at that time, these were essentially penal in nature concerned with abuse of legal procedure.[81] In the late 14th century, the action of deceit was used to render express warranties of the quality of goods sold enforceable. From coupling express warranty with deceit, it was only a small step of imagination to use it in cases of a breach of an express assumpsit, which in turn offered a solution to the issue of nonfeasance. In 1428, a plaintiff brings an unsuccessful claim of nonfeasance on the basis of a writ of deceit.[82] In the *Somerton's Case*[83] (1433), the defendant, as legal counsel for the plaintiff, undertook the duties to purchase or lease a manor. But instead he became someone else's counsel and negotiated the lease for that person.[84] The legal

76 Entries for assumpsit for nonfeasance can be found in the plea rolls in 1370, though no reported cases in the Year Books before 1400. See S.F.C. Milsom (1981) *Historical Foundations of the Common Law*, London: Butterworth, at 323, fn. 1 and 2.

77 Case of 1400 in Y.B. 2 Hen. IV, 3, 9, or in LBEx.

78 "*...le chose ust ester commence, & puis p negligence nient fait...*" Y.B. 2 Hen. IV, 3, 9, or in LBEx.

79 "*...car la nul tort est sup q le fesance dun chose, eins le non fesance dun chose, le quell sonne seulemt en un covenant...*" Y.B. 14 Hen. VI, 18, 58, or in LBEx.

80 Th. Plucknett (1956) *A Concise History of the Common Law*, London: Butterworth, at 640; in his discussion on deceit Ames also deals with false warranty: J.A. Ames (1913) *Lectures on Legal History and Miscellaneous Legal Essays*, Cambridge: Harvard University Press, at 136.

81 Th. Plucknett (1956) at 640, in particular fn. 7, 8 and 9.

82 "*Un hom port un br sur son Case n natur de br de Deceit*". Y.B. 7 Hen. VI, 1, 3, or LBEx. The action failed for want of a *quid pro quo*, hence lacking a bargain.

83 Original writ: Y.B. 11 Pasch. Hen. VI, 1, 25, or LBEx.; arguments should be read in the following order: Y.B. 11 Hen. VI Trin., 55, 26; *ibid.*, Hil., 18, 10; *ibid.*, Pasch., 24, 1, or LBEx.

84 "*...le dit W. assumpsit ... il fauremt & en deceit de luy ad disco ve son consel; & fuit devenu Consel' ove u R. a luy fait achet l'dit man...*" Y.B. 11 Trin. Hen. VI, 55, 26, or LBEx.

argument evolved around issues of covenant, but there was a mention that issues of covenant may be transformed into deceits by subsequent events.[85] The facts in this case do not relate strictly speaking to nonfeasance because the defendant, by making the lease with someone else, acted in a way that made it impossible for his undertaking to be honoured. Similar arguments based on similar facts were voiced in the *Doige's Case*,[86] where the case was adjourned. But Brooke in his abridgement of that case makes a distinction between the action of deceit, in which the defendant disables himself, from that of an action on the case for nonfeasance.[87] Milsom[88] argues that *Doige's Case* was not an attempt to obtain a remedy in tort for the failure to perform a promise, nor was it a test case aimed at liberalising contract law. The decision was whether the claim of deceit was sufficiently separate from covenant, although the latter would not have succeeded for want of a sealed document. In 1476, an action of 'deceit on the case'[89] was successfully upheld against the defendant, who had been paid the purchase price for some land and enfeoffed another. Nonfeasance of undertakings made for money was finally recognised as actionable in 1504.[90] It is important to note that equity was ahead of the common law courts in providing relief to a purchaser who had paid but had not delivered, a particularly aggravated sort of deceit because the plaintiff's loss enriched the defendant.[91]

The next stage in the evolution of consideration came when, during the 16th century, this was extended to cases where the defendant enjoyed no benefit from the deceit that caused loss or damage to the plaintiff. In 1520, an action was successfully brought on a sale made by the plaintiff to a third person on

85 "*...il duit av' acc d Covenant, mes s'il discove s consel, & deviant del' Consail un aut a purchaser cest man a luy, or c'est un deceit de ql j'aurai acc sur mon cas...c'ê un deceit & changer tout cest q fuit devant forse covenant entr les parties, des ql deceit il aura...*" Hil. Hen. VI, 18, 10, or LBEx.

86 (1442) Y.B. 20 Trin. Hen.VI, 34, 4, or LBEx.

87 "*... ou home pmise per un consideration de fair act, et ne fait, que action sur le cas gyst, mes ou home fayte son promise faucement, que donque action de dyscept gyst...*" in: R. Brooke (1573) *La Graunde Abridgement*, Disceit, no. 4.

88 S.F.C. Milsom (1981) *Historical Foundations of the Common Law*, London: Butterworth, at 330.

89 "En un action de Disceit s son case..." in Y.B. 16 Pasch. Edw. IV, 9, 7, or LBEx.

90 "*...si jeo covenant p argent de fair un mese p tiel jour, & jeo ne fay, Acc sur le cas gist p le non fes...*"; "*...Et pofito que jeo covenant denfeoffer un home de un acre pcel' de mon man, & jeo vens tout le man a un autr; icy Action sur le cas gist p cest deceit...*" Y.B. 20 Mich. Hen. VII, 8, 18, or LBEx.

91 Th. Plucknett (1956) *A Concise History of the Common Law*, London: Butterworth, at 642.

the strength of the defendant's promise that the price should be paid.[92] No benefit to the defendant arose from the declaration nor from its breach, but the deceit meant a loss for the plaintiff. The point was taken up by St German:[93]

> if he to whom the promise is made have a charge by reason of the promise ...he shall have an action ... though he that made the promise had no worldly profit by it.

This was a definite signpost that points to the recognition of parol agreement and a stepping stone for the next stage in the development: that of the recognition of mutual promises. The basis of assumpsit had gradually moved from the 'end of the story' – deception of the plaintiff – to the 'beginning of the story' – the assumpsit and hence matters were discussed in terms of promises (contract) rather than deceits (tort).[94] Thus opening the door to the concept of mutual promises was the ultimate springboard allowing for the leap from tort (deceit) to contract (promise) to be completed. In *Norwood v Reed* (1558)[95] it was said that "every contract executory is an assumpsit in itself" and in *Strangborough v Warner* (1589)[96] it was acknowledged that "a promise against a promise will maintain an action upon the case".

2.3 Indebitatus assumpsit

In the middle of the 16th century the action of *indebitatus assumpsit* materialised, which was primarily a new form of procedure, rather than the creation of a substantive new right. Two elements, hitherto established, came together in this new action: debt and deceit. Since the 12th century, the action of debt was not based on any promissory element but on the presence of a *quid pro quo* (e.g. a *res* had passed). *Indebitatus assumpsit* arose from situations where the indebted (*indebitatus*) defendant (expressly) undertook (*assumpsit*) to pay a particular sum of the debt by a certain date. It is possible to argue that in such situations, the plaintiff has a classic action in debt, but also one in assumpsit on the subsequent promise to pay, if he was deceived by the defendant who was not fulfilling his undertaking. For a while, the distinction between the two actions was upheld, and thereby the boundary between debt/contract and

92 Y.B. 12 Mich. Hen. VIII, 11, 3, or LBEx: "*...le testat dit a luy, s'il ne paie a vous, jeo vous paier, s ql promes le pl' deliv les bns a le dit J.N. & le dit J.N. devint niet d paier le pl...*".

93 Ch. St. German (1518/1974), *Doctor and Student*, Second Dialogue, Chapter 24, edited by Th. Plucknett, J. Barton (1974) for the Selden Society, vol. 91.

94 Th. Plucknett (1956) *A Concise History of the Common Law*, London: Butterworth, at 643.

95 (1558) 1 Plowd. 180, or 75 Eng. Rep. 277.

96 (1589) 4 Leonard 3, or 74 Eng. Rep. 686.

trespass/deceit/tort. This was spelt out in a case of 1535: a plaintiff could only have an action in debt if there was *quid pro quo*. Alternatively, an agreement could be actionable under covenant if there was speciality. In the absence of either of these elements, an action on the case was possible by virtue of an assumpsit.[97] Brooke,[98] in his *Graunde Abridgement* mentions the same case by drawing, nevertheless, a sharper distinction between debt and promise:

> ...home est endetted a moy et il promise de payer devant Michelmas ieo puis aver accion de dett sur le contract ou accion del case sur le promise et issint ceo est in divers respectes, car sur le promise ne gist acc de dett...

It is interesting to note the absence of the word promise in the original reports, almost as though it needed these few more years between the Year Book report and Brooke's Abridgement for the promissory element to be named in more definite terms.

For these early *indebitatus assumpsit* cases to succeed, it was necessary to show an express promise which was subsequent to the debt – *quod postea assumpsit* – because if the undertaking was made at the time of the contract, debt would lie and not assumpsit.[99] Debt based on a simple contract required a *quid pro quo*, words of agreement were said in creating the debt. An action of assumpsit had to be distinguished from the initial debt and demanded, therefore, a new promise made subsequent to the debt. But as actions of assumpsit became more commonplace throughout the 16th century, it was getting increasingly more complex to distinguish between promises to pay money and promises to do other things.

The next stage in the development of the action of assumpsit may have less to do with fine minds wanting to advance legal thinking, but more with the rivalry and power struggle between the courts. Assumpsit, considered as a form of trespass, could be brought in both the King's Bench and in the Common Pleas. Actions of debt, however, were restricted to the Common Pleas. In an

---

97 "*...car jeo enten que on n'aura br de Det mes ou un contract est, car le defendant n'ad quid pro quo, mes l'action est solemt fonde s l'assumpsit, q sonne meremt in covenat: & s'il fuit p especialte, le pl' aura cc d Covenat, mes etat q il n'ad espec, ceo me see, il n'ad auc remedy si no Action sur son cas... car l'agréement le pl' apres fait ceo un assumpstion a luy in Ley...come me semble il n'aura acc de Det: car icy n'est asc contract, ni le def.,'ad quid pro quo; purq il n'ad auc remedy sino Acc sur son cas...*" Y.B. 27 Mich. Hen.VIII, 24, 3, or LBEx.

98 R. Brooke (1573) *La Graunde Abridgement, Action sur le cas*, pl. 5.

99 "*...il duist av dit quod postea Assumpsit, car sil Assumpsit al temps del contract donqs det gist sur ceo & nemy Assumpsit mes si apres le contract il assume, tunc action gist sur lassump autermt nemy...*" (1572) in Dalison 84, 35, or 123 Eng. Rep. 293.

attempt to gain the upper hand in the fierce competition for jurisdiction between the courts, the King's Bench began to allow for assumpsit to be used in actions to recover specific sums of money, instead of insisting on an action of debt, which was outside its jurisdiction. Consequently, the King's Bench was keen to make *indebitatus assumpsit* equivalent to debt: where a debt existed, a subsequent assumpsit was presumed in law.[100] This brought considerable business to the King's Bench, as the process was swifter and litigants could use barristers instead of the costly serjeants.

In its rivalry with the Common Pleas, which continued diligently to make the distinction outlined above, the King's Bench decisions tended to be reversed by the Exchequer Chambers[101] that consisted only of Common Pleas judges. This wrangling came to a head and was settled in the final instalment of the *Slade's Case* in 1602,[102] in which Coke appeared for the plaintiff and Bacon for the defendant. Slade had bargained and sold wheat and rye to the defendant who promised to pay a sum of money at a fixed date in the future. He failed to honour this undertaking and pleaded *non assumpsit modo et forma*. It was held that the case could lie upon simple contract as well as an action of debt. There must have been reluctance amongst the members of the Exchequer Chamber, but it was Coke's report of the case that came to matter.[103] *Indebitatus assumpsit* became an alternative to debt at the plaintiff's choice, and the plaintiff could recover damages as well as the original debt, but such a recovery would be a bar to an action of debt. If the debt was one of instalments,

100 *Edwards v Burre* (1573) Dalison 104, 45, or 123 Eng. Rep. 310.

101 The Exchequer was the oldest of the three common-law courts. It has a complex story of divisions into various different institutions. The Court of Exchequer Chamber at the time of *Slade's Case* referred to here is the appellate court for common law civil actions which heard references from the King's Bench, the Court of Exchequer and, from 1830, the Court of Common Pleas.

102 *Slade v Morley*, 4 Co Rep. 92 a or 76 Eng. Rep. 1074; literature on *Slade's Case*: J. Baker (1971) New Light on *Slade's Case*, Part I in: *Cambridge Law Journal* 29 (1), 51–67, Part II in: *Cambridge Law Journal* 29 (2), 213–236; D. Ibbetson (1984) Sixteenth Century Contract Law: *Slade's Case* in context, in: *Oxford Journal of Legal Studies* 4 (3), 295–317; H. Locke (1965/1966) *Slade's Case* and the Origin of the Common Counts, in: 81 *Law Quarterly Review*, Part I: 422–538, Part II: 539–561, Part III in: 82 *Law Quarterly Review* 81–96; S. Milsom (1981) *Historical Foundations of the Common Law*, London: Butterworth, at 346–356; Th. Plucknett (1956) *A Concise History of the Common Law*, London: Butterworth, at 637–656; B. Simpson (1958) The place of *Slade's Case* in the history of contract, in: 74 *Law Quarterly Review*, 381–396; B. Simpson (1975a) *A History of the Common Law of Contract: The Rise of the Action of Assumpsit*, Oxford: Clarendon Press, at pp. 281–299; S. Stoljar (1975) *A History of Contract at Common Law*, Canberra: Australian National University Press, at 76–82.

103 S.F.C. Milsom (1981) *Historical Foundations of the Common Law*, London: Butterworth, at 353.

assumpsit could be brought on the first default, while debt could only be brought when all payment deadlines had passed. Holding that the mutual executory agreement of both parties imports in itself action upon the case, as well as action of debt, and that every executory contract imported in itself an assumpsit, meant that the assumpsit need not be proved but would be assumed. Having thus made *indebitatus assumpsit* equivalent to debt meant that the distinctions between debt/contract and deceit/tort became blurred and the scheme of forms of actions was less clear and certain. In *Edgcomb v Dee*[104] the Slade decision was described as an:

> illegal resolution ... grounded upon reasons not fit for a declamation, much less for a decision of law... And that which is so commonly now received, that every contract executory implies a promise, is a false gloss, thereby to turn actions of debt into actions on the case: for contracts of debts are reciprocal grants.[105]

Having moved from assumpsit brought upon explicit undertakings, then allowing *indebitatus assumpsit* to lie upon a subsequent promise, to the possibility of bringing an action based on the original contract rather than on the subsequent assumpsit, the next step was to also imply a contract, because if assumpsit can be implied, it follows that contract can be implied. By extending the legal presumption of an assumpsit to that of contracts, the possibility was created for a large variety of implied contracts and eventually quasi-contracts to be remedied by the action of assumpsit. The decision of *Warbrook v Griffin*[106] in favour of allowing 'an implied promise of every part' confirmed this shift in legal thinking. It became rapidly clear that the potentially open-ended scope of the action of assumpsit would need a controlling element to ring-fence promises that show genuine undertakings because not every promise made can be deemed enforceable. A detriment or debt for which the promise was made, would be such an indicative element that distinguished enforceable promises from a bare promise.

•••

104 (1670) Vaughan, 101, or 124 Eng. Rep. 984.

105 The decision was also criticised because the new procedure meant that wager of law was no longer a part of it. For some (more conservative) it was a sort of constitutional right of the English, the loss of which compromised a valuable safeguard.

106 (1610) 2 Brownl. & Golds. 254, or 123 Eng. Rep. 927.

We have travelled a long way from the original trespass cases against surgeons and carpenters, where it was necessary to show the making of an undertaking. It is from these original uses of assumpsit to enforce an undertaking made by the defendant that the technical action of special assumpsit eventually emerged, which was more akin to a contractual action but retained elements of the tort action of deceit.

With the notion of (informal) promises, comes the question of their enforceability and, as we have seen so far, a corpus of doctrine had developed during the 16th century, to delimit the actionability of informal promises. It is in this context that we can find (some of) the roots of the idea of consideration such as the circumstances in which a promise was made and as the motivation for making a promise enforceable. The question that now required resolution related to the underlying reason for the promise. This may appear as akin to *quid pro quo*, but that particular concept was originally rooted in proprietary thinking, in the recovery of a *res*. Approaching the issue from the angle of why a promise was made, appeals to a promissory concept. It may also appear to relate to the civil law doctrine of *causa*, yet continental legal thinking tended to theorise entire legal constructs and contractual doctrines, which was rather foreign to the English common law lawyer, whose formulary system was not equipped to consider the field in its entirety. Contracts were not perceived as an overreaching construct but compartmentalised according to specific forms of actions.

2.4 Causa *as a Romano-Canonical Import*

Lorenzen[107] contends that the common law doctrine of consideration evolved and remained outside the influences of the *ius commune*, and all that was borrowed was the phrase *ex nudo pacto non oritur actio*, which incidentally described something very different in English law than it did in the *ius commune*. In *Rann v Hughes*[108] the court said:

> It is equally true that the law of this country supplied no means nor affords any remedy to compel the performance of an agreement made without sufficient considerations. Such agreement is *nudum pactum ex quo non oritur actio*; and whatsoever may be the sense of this maxim in

107 E. Lorenzen (1919) Causa and consideration in the law of contracts, in: 28 *Yale Law Journal*, 621–646, at 636.

108 C.H.S. Fifoot (1949) *History and Sources of the Common Law: Tort and Contract*, London: Steven & Sons, at p. 430; pleadings and arguments: 4 Brown, P.C. 27, or 2 Eng. Rep. 18; judgement of Skynner, L.C.B. in 7 T.R. 350, note.

> the civil law, it is in the last-mentioned sense only that it is to be understood in our law.

In the substantial bulk of assumpsit/consideration case law we find a relatively frequent occurrence of the word 'cause' often used interchangeably with 'consideration'. As late as 1574, consideration was defined as "cause or meritorious occasion".[109] But this usage can be attributable mainly to the fact that the word 'cause', imported from French, was much used in the language of legal actions and in a specific technical way. The use of the word 'cause' was wide spread in the legal jargon well before the rise of assumpsit. Adopting this word later in the context of consideration need not point to any Roman origin of either word or concept. The *ius commune* division of contracts/enforceable pacts and nude pacts found no corresponding distinction in the common law. Not all common law agreements based upon good consideration would be recognised as contracts or vested pacts in the *ius commune*. In addition, a common law agreement without consideration may be enforceable in the *ius commune* if it was a *mandatum, constitutum* or an agreement to make a gift (*donation*).

The influence the canon law doctrine of *causa*, used by the ecclesiastical Chancellors during the late 15th century, may have had on the development of the concept of consideration is unclear. In his very comprehensive account of contract in equity, Barbour concluded, though with "considerable hesitancy [...] to make any generalisations" and after having studied the chancery proceedings:

> The chancellor held that one might make a valid promise to do anything which was reasonable and possible, and that the obligation resulting from such a promise ought to be performed because the promisor had deliberately and intentionally assumed the obligation. By this I do not mean that the chancellor enforced any and all promises. But in his analysis of parol contract he did not require as an essential condition to a right of action that the promise should have been deceived or that the promisor should have been benefited. Rather did he enquire whether the enforcement of a particular promise would further some general interest. If the promisor has led the promise to alter his position on the strength of the promise, there lies upon him a moral duty to fulfil that promise. It is desirable, in the interests of the community at large, that

109 *Calthorpe's Case* (1574) 3 Dyer 334b, or 73 Eng. Rep. 756.

> such promises should be enforced. [...] I believe that such a promise [of money for a marriage] was enforced because of the purpose of which it was given.[110]

Barbour's explanation shows clearly that, at a time when the common law still considered primarily the promisee and whether he sustained damages due to a malfeasance or nonfeasance/deceit, chancery examined the position of the promisor and the circumstances and purposes for which the promise was made. Questions of detriment to the promisee and benefit to promisor were of secondary importance. Barbour continues:

> ...I do believe that all these cases [in equity] can be explained from the principles of canon law. Therein seems to me the only adequate and reasonable explanation. It is very probable that the chancellor as a judge in the chancery did not proceed to the same lengths as he would have done in the ecclesiastical court. But when confronted with a new situation in chancery he did apply so far as possible the principles of that system in which as a churchman he was trained. This indirect reception is not demonstrable with mathematical precision; it seems to me, however, that the whole line of decision in equity points unequivocally towards the canon law.[111]

In other words, it appears that the canon law principle of cause was applied in equity and that was a known fact. In 1414, the Commons complained that the Chancery was undermining the common law with romano-canonical imports.[112] But there is no hard evidence as to any reception into the common law, though some cross-fertilisation cannot be excluded.

A comparison between the concept of consideration and the civil doctrine of *causa* reveals a more narrow interpretation of what constitutes good consideration by the English courts. Most agreements supported by good consideration and actionable in the common law would also be valid according the

---

110 W.T. Barbour (1914) The History of Contract in Early English Equity, in: P. Vinogradoff (ed.) *Oxford Studies in Social and Legal History*, vol. IV, Oxford: Clarendon Press, at. 166–167.

111 W.T. Barbour (1914) at 167–168.

112 4 Rot. Parl. 84, no. 46.

broader doctrine of *causa*. However, the opposite is not true.[113] Lord Wright[114] contends that the *cause* as a precondition for the validity of a contract, written into the French Civil Code (Articles 1108 and 1131) is even wider "than what used to be described as moral consideration [...] it would, it seems, include the motive or impulse of charity or generosity"

The influence the civil law doctrine of *causa* had on Lord Mansfield and some of his colleagues, in particular in relation to the notion of a moral obligation inherent in the making of a promise, and the concept they developed of moral consideration to support a contract, will be discussed in Section 4 of this chapter.

It is from the context of the motivations for a promise that the use of the phrase *in consideratione* emerged, namely to describe precisely these underlying reasons for the existence of the promise. Once assumpsit was presumed, it was the matter fixed in the consideration clause that pointed to the defendant's obligation, independently of whether he had subsequently acknowledged the obligation. Here lies the immediate (though not only) origin of the consideration clause and terminology.

3 Concept of Consideration

3.1 *Terminology*

As we saw earlier, from the moment that an undertaking to carry out a bargain began to be separated from the principle bargain during the 16th century, it became necessary to find some word or phrase that would link the recital of the principal bargain to the subsequent assumpsit clause in order to explain the motivation of the undertaking. Otherwise, and as the Student told the Doctor,[115] the undertaking was held to be without a cause and hence unenforceable because it must be considered as *nudum pactum*. Here lies the origin of the 'in consideration of' clause, but at that early stage its semantic content

113 Lorenzen discusses such cases, e.g. a written guarantee without valuable consideration nor with any intention to make a donation, but made with a desire to act fairly and generously in the execution of a contract previously entered into, would fail under common law for want of good consideration but would be seen as sufficient *causa* for the guarantee in a civil law tradition; see E. Lorenzen (1919) Causa and consideration in the law of contracts, in: 28 *Yale Law Journal*, 621–646, at 639.

114 R. Wright (1936) Ought the doctrine of consideration to be abolished from the Common Law? in: 49 *Harvard Law Review*, 1225–1253, at 1237.

115 Ch. St. German (1518/1974), *Doctor and Student*, Second Dialogue, Chapter 24, edited by Th. Plucknett, J. Barton (1974) for the Selden Society, vol. 91.

did not go beyond expressing a technical requirement for an action on the case upon a promise – it was still a long way off being a principle in its own right.

Anyone reading the substantial bulk of assumpsit/consideration case law, is struck by the relatively frequent occurrence of the word 'cause' often used interchangeably with 'consideration'. But this was mainly attributable to the fact that the word 'cause', imported from French,[116] was much used in the language of legal actions and in a specific technical way. When reading, for example, the Edward I and Edward II Year Books in the original French language, the use of the word 'cause' is very prominent. Some were general language usages, and these were generally translated by non-contemporaneous translators with 'reason' or 'motive'. But the bulk of the occurrences were in a technical legal context, often embedded in a description of legal procedure, such as for example:

cause de forfeture (cause of forfeiture)[117]
cause accioun (cause of action)[118]
cause del doun (cause of the gift)[119]
qil est cause de la garde (he is the cause of the wardship)[120]
la cause de ceti bref fut accepte de la Chancerie (the cause of this writ was entertained by the Chancery)[121]

Or bound up with some legal procedure, such as for example:

responet a la cause (answer to the cause, which was the leasing of tenements on consideration of marriage)[122]
quidez vous par ceste cause aver seisine (do you think for this cause to have seisin)[123]
ceo est la cause del abatement de vostre bref (it is the cause of the abatement of your writ)[124]

---

116 The medieval Latin *causa, caussa* migrated into the living languages as Italian and Spanish and Provinçal *cosa*, Old Northern French *cose*, but also the French *chose*, in the sense of matter or thing, which is the sense of *causa* to be found in the Salic Law, in Gregory of Tours and the Capitularies. From the 13th century, the Latin *causa* could be found in the French of the law courts in the form of *causa* or cause, or *encheson*, meaning cause or by the reason of.

117 (1304) 4 YB Hil. 32 Edw. I, in: Year Books of the Reign of King Edward the First, Selden Society Publications and the History of Early English Law (www.heinonline.org), at 37.

118 (1304) 4 YB Hil. 32 Edw. I, *ibid* at 37.

119 (1303) 3 YB Mich. 31 Edw. I, *ibid* at 389.

120 (1305) 5 YB Mich. 33 Edw. I, *ibid* at 39.

121 (1304) 4 YB Mich. 32 Edw. I, *ibid* at 341.

122 (1294) 2 YB Mich. 22 Edw. I, *ibid* at 499.

123 (1307) 5 YB 35 Mich. Edw. I, *ibid* at 439.

124 (1294) 2 YB Mich. 22 Edw. I, *ibid* at 349.

> *le tenant par cause fit remuer la parole par un recordari* (the tenant, for a cause, removed the plea by a Recordari)[125]

The use of the word 'cause' was widespread in the legal jargon well before the rise of assumpsit. Adopting this word later in the context of consideration need not point to any *ius commune* origin of either word or concept. Nor does it exclude that there may have been a link.

In the late 15th and early 16th century, *quid pro quo* was frequently mentioned in the same breath as consideration, or at least as the element that makes a parol agreement enforceable. Holmes[126] famously said that:

> the requirement of consideration in all parol contracts is simply a modified generalization of *quid pro quo* to raise a debt by parol.

Quid pro quo was traditionally associated with debt, but as Barton[127] and Milsom[128] have shown, the concept of reciprocity expressed by *quid pro quo* has also appeared in actions other than debt and did not always apply to just proprietary exchanges. It included a situation where something that was of no direct benefit to the defendant could be considered as *quid pro quo* or at least equivalent to one.[129] While the action of debt was still in use, a sharp distinction between *quid pro quo* and consideration was not always made. For example, in *Bret v J.S.*[130] the term *quid pro quo* was used to distinguish a valuable consideration (a mother's love for her son) from one that consisted of an element given in return (the son's continued board).

Since the times of Glanvil, a sale was executed by delivery[131] – detinue for the goods could be brought by the buyer once the money was paid, while the seller could bring debt for the price once the goods had been delivered; it followed that if neither party performed there was no action. Writs were phrased in the simplest of terms to reflect such a notion of reciprocity: 'whereas, in return for a sum of [*pro*] money agreed or paid beforehand, A had undertaken to do X for B…' The action arose either through nonfeasance or misfeasance, *viz* A failed to carry out his undertaking. The resemblance to the 'in consideration

125 (1306) 5 YB Hil. 34 Edw. I, *ibid* at 153.

126 O.W. Holmes (1885) Early English Equity, in: *Law Quarterly Review*, 162–174.

127 J.L. Barton (1969) The Early History of Consideration, in: 85 *Law Quarterly Review*, 382–383.

128 S.F.C Milsom (1961) Sale of Goods in the Fifteenth Century, in: 77 *Law Quarterly Review*, 257–284.

129 "… *uncore il est tant en effet* …" in Y.B. 37 Mich. Hen. VI, 8, 18, or LBEx.

130 (1600) Cro. Eliz 755, or 78 Eng. Rep. 987.

131 *Glanvil* x. 14; *Bracton* f. 62, *Fleta*, ii. 58, §8.

of' clause does not escape today's reader, but during the 15th century, we are still firmly within a proprietary notion of exchange and reciprocity. During the 16th century, the undertaking to carry out a bargain began to be separated from the principle bargain. Baker[132] has called this a 'verbal divorce', designed to circumvent the technical problems of overlapping remedies. The *pro*-clause was re-phrased: 'whereas, for a sum of money agreed or paid, A had agreed to do X for B [= bargain], *and* A had agreed to do X within a certain time [= undertaking]'. Here, it is difficult to justify the undertaking in terms of a sum of money paid, the word 'and' being the only element that links it to the principle bargain. This has meant that the action either lies on the bargain or covenant, or on the mutual promise. In the case of the former it would fail on procedural and evidential grounds, in case of the latter, it was necessary to show that the promise is actionable independently. Baker[133] cites *Marler v Wilmer*,[134] an unreported King's Bench case of 1539, as an example for this type of dilemma. One of the points discussed was:

> that it does not appear in the declaration for what cause [*quam ob causam*] he made the aforesaid undertaking, either for money paid beforehand, or receipt of part of the aforesaid goods, and so *ex nudo pacto non oritur actio*.

This confirms what the Student had told the Doctor: that an undertaking without a *causa* is unenforceable because it is *nudum pactum*.[135] It became necessary to find some word or phrase that would link the recital of the principal bargain to the subsequent assumpsit clause in order to explain the motivation of the undertaking. Here lies the origin of the 'in consideration of' clause, but at that early stage its semantic content did not go beyond expressing a technical requirement for an action on the case upon a promise.

On examining the King's Bench Rolls, Baker[136] found that the *in consideratione* clause appeared for the first time in 1539, then again the next year and at least thirty-two times until 1550, but he found little uniformity in their form or

132 J Baker (2013) Origins of the doctrine of consideration 1535–1585, in: J. Baker, *Collected Papers on English Legal History*, vol III., Cambridge: CUP, at 1179.

133 J. Baker (2013) at 1180.

134 KB 27/1111, m. 64, see Baker (2013) at p. 1180, fn. 11.

135 Ch. St. German (1518/1974), *Doctor and Student*, Second Dialogue, Chapter 24, edited by Th. Plucknett, J. Barton (1974) for the Selden Society, vol. 91.

136 J. Baker (2013) at 1181–1182.

function. Sometimes the phrase was combined with the word *pro*, other times a mere alternative or when it was more apt and elegant to use it. The phrase could, however, also express something more akin to reason/motivation, as can be found in the general form *pro diversis aliis causis et considerationibus ipsum E adtunc et ibidem moventibus.*[137] This relates to the concept of *causa* and it can be argued[138] that the consideration clause combines the *quid pro quo* and *causa* notion, which may be an important element why that phrase finally triumphed over its terminological rivals and was widely adopted from the mid-16th century.

On the question of terminology, Holdsworth[139] contends that, at first, words such as 'cause' and 'occasion' were used in a general sense,[140] as it became "obvious that some word or expression was needed to differentiate the agreements which could be enforced [...], from the agreements which could not".[141] In Chapter 24 of St. German's Second Dialogue, where the student explains what a nude contract or naked promise is and whether any action may lie thereupon, we find in a text of 2589 word tokens only one occurrence of the term *quid pro quo*, 3 uses of 'consideration', 7 of 'cause' and 7 of 'recompense'. The word 'promise' occurs 74 times, but the discussion surrounding the issue is hardly matched by settled vocabulary. As late as 1579, Rastell[142] makes an entry for a bare or naked contract, which does not include the word consideration, but rather 'recompense'. He defines contract in terms of bargain and covenant (*contracte est vn bargeine ou couenaunt per enter ii. parties*) and equates consideration with *quid pro quo* or "one thing given for another" (*vn chose est done pur auter que est appelle quid pro quo* [...]*en consideration de* [...] *que vous dones*

137 *Newman v Gybbe* (1549) KB 27/1152, m. 135, see J. Baker (2013) Origins of the doctrine of consideration 1535–1585, in: J. Baker, *Collected Papers on English Legal History*, vol III., Cambridge: CUP, at p. 1182, fn. 21.

138 J. Baker (2013) at 1181.

139 W.S. Holdsworth(1925) *History of English Law* vol. VIII, London: Methuen, at 3–4.

140 *"par lescrit qil mest avant il suppose qe il nous fra certein services les queux sont la cause de sa demande..."* Y.B. 6, 7 Edw. II, or 36 Selden Society at 83 *per* Westcot *arg.*; "dont del hure qe ceste annuite fu grante issint pur les services issint les services sont loccasion..." in: (1312) Y.B. 5 Edw. II, or 33 Selden Society at 2, *per* Herle *arg.*

141 see definition of consideration as "cause or meritorious occasion" in *Calthorpe's Case* (1574) 3 Dyer 334b, or 73 Eng. Rep. 756. A keyword search of 'occasion' in the corpora constituted for this research does not confirm a frequent use of the word in assumpsit cases.

142 W. Rastell (1579) *Exposition of Certaine Difficult and Obscure Wordes and Termes of the Lawes of This Realme, Newly Set Fourth & Augmented, Both in French and English, for the Helpe of Such Younge Studentes as Are Desirous to Attaine the Knowledge for the Same. Whereunto Are Also Added the Olde Tenures*, 1 v., London: In adibus Richardi Totelli, www.heinonline.org – Selden Society Publications and the History of Early English Law.

a moy ceux font bone contractes, pur ceo que il ad vn chose pur auter). There is no separate entry for 'consideration'. But over fifty years later, a contract is defined as "a covenant or agreement with a lawful consideration or cause" in Cowell's *Interpreter*.[143] It is interesting to note that way into the 17th century 'consideration' and 'cause' are still used as synonyms, but this definition demonstrates a move away from the notion of bargain towards something more akin to a meeting of minds and the use of the word 'lawful' gives us to understand that there is a legal definition of 'consideration', which is given separately as the "material cause of a contract, without the which, no contract bindeth". In *Sharington v Strotton*[144] a familiar friend and acquaintance was considered as:

> no sufficient cause for the payment [...] as is requisite in contracts, and also in covenants upon consideration.

A more general description of 'consideration' can be found in *Calthorpe's Case*:[145]

> A consideration is a cause or meritorious occasion, requiring a mutual recompense, in fact or in law. Contracts and bargains have a *quid pro quo*.

From these examples it appears that the terminology used in discussing the concept of consideration was not settled. But there are also cases where the use of the consideration clause was more in line with the later terminology when the concept was well established:

> In an action upon the case, the plaintiff declared, that the defendant, assumed and promised to pay to him...[146]

By the end of the 16th century, the use of the consideration clause became more common place, signposting the facts which were relied upon to make the contentious promise enforceable by assumpsit. In *Whorwood v Gybbons*[147] it was the opinion of the whole court that (my emphasis):

143 J. Cowell (1637) *Interpreter: Or Booke, Containing the Signification of Words*, London: Printed for William Sheares, www.heinonline.org – *Selden Society Publications and the History of Early English Law*.

144 (1564) 1 Plowden 298, at 302, or 75 Eng. Rep. 460.

145 (1574) 3 Dyer, 334b at 337a, or 73 Eng. Rep. 756, at 759.

146 *Joscelin v. Shelton* (1557) 3 Leo. 4, or 74 Eng. Rep. 503.

147 (1587) Gouldsborough 48, or 75 Eng. Rep. 986.

> insomuch as the proviso was made by him by whom the debt was due, that it is a good consideration, and that it is a *common course* in actions upon the case against him by whom a debt is due, to declare without any words in consideratione.

Similarly, in the *Sidenham and Worlington's Case*[148] it was said (my emphasis):

> if there be a moving cause or consideration precedent; for which cause or consideration the promise was made; and such is the *common practice* at this day: for in an action upon the case, upon a promise, the defendant, for, and in consideration of 20l. to him paid, (postea scil.) that is to say, at a day after super se assumspit, and that is good...

But in many of these cases, including the last one just mentioned, the words 'cause' and 'consideration' still frequently appear side by side as synonyms.

3.2 *The Concept of Consideration*

As discussed previously, the concept of consideration emanated from a diversity of legal sources and this may in part be a reason why its terminology settled only hesitantly. The use of terms such as, for example, 'cause' and '*quid pro quo*' would inevitably have intertextual connotations that may have interfered, at times, with the new emerging legal thinking. In *Manwood v Burston*,[149] Chief Baron of the Exchequer Manwood mentions three "manners of considerations upon which an assumpsit may be grounded". Subsequently, this was often considered as a definition of consideration, but the plural form points to a list, rather than a doctrine. Yet, such a 'list' of conditions under which actions of assumpsit would lie is an important step for establishing that "compendious word"[150] which would differentiate the promises that could be enforced from those that could not.

In his lectures on legal history, Ames[151] identifies three theories advanced by different legal scholars on the origins of the concept of consideration. Holmes believes consideration to be a 'modified generalisation' of *quid pro quo*. Salmond sees consideration as originating from the *ius commune* principle of *causa*, introduced into the common law via equity. Finally, Hare traces

148 (1585) 2 Leonard, 224, at 225, or 74 Eng. Rep. 497, at 498 (my emphasis).

149 (1587) 2 Leonard 203, or 74 Eng. Rep. 479.

150 W.S. Holdsworth(1925) *History of English Law* vol. VIII, London: Sweet & Maxwell, at 7.

151 J.A. Ames (1913) *Lectures on Legal History and Miscellaneous Legal Essays*, Cambridge: Harvard University Press, at p. 129, see also fn. 2, 3 and 4.

a straight line back to the action on the case for deceit, making the plaintiff's detriment a forerunner of the consideration of all parol contracts. Whatever the merits of these theories, it reveals that it is impossible to link consideration to just one single source, which is also Ames' conclusion. This takes us back to the introductory paragraphs of this chapter, namely that the rise of assumpsit and the development of the concept of consideration did not take a linear path of evolution, because the need for an action that makes parol undertakings enforceable came from different quarters originating in a diversity of distinct legal issues and situations.

We have seen how the element of loss to the promisee due to a deceit of the promisor, was a part of the original nature of the action of assumpsit. This led to what was then generally known as special assumpsit and can be found in today's theory on consideration as detriment to the plaintiff. Another source was the action of debt, when some actions of debt began to be absorbed within the more general field of contract, though the development of *indebitatus assumpsit* and consideration became a way of demonstrating the motivation for making a promise. In addition, mutual promises in consensual contracts also developed the notion that a promise could be the consideration for a counter-promise. This constitutes what we would call today a bilateral contract and it enables either side to sue for breach unilaterally without averring performance. The extent of the influence the canon law doctrine of *causa* had on the development of the concept of consideration has not clearly been demonstrated.

During the late 16th and 17th centuries, the notion that a promise can only lie if the motivation of the undertaking can be demonstrated was gradually being kneaded into a doctrine, pushing the limitations of established actions and procedures by degrees. But the diversity of the legal ideas from which that concept sprang has led to contradictory rulings, sometimes based on rather similar facts. There appeared no general will to forge any general principles that may underlie the application of the concept and courts took their decisions, each following their own agenda of their particular locality raised by the facts of the specific cases at hand. It is, therefore, difficult to offer a strictly linear and chronological account of how the concept of consideration evolved during that period. We will, therefore, discuss the development of the concept of consideration by following how certain principles originally raised by the application of special assumpsit or *indebitatus assumpsit* evolved in the subsequent case law. Re-tracing the path consideration took from concept to doctrine goes hand in hand with comprehending the evolution of what constituted consideration. Originally, it arose from the need for an element to ring-fence the enforceability of parol undertakings. The extent and effect of the concept was decided gradually through case law.

Some have made attempts to define what consideration meant. In *Sidenham v Worlington*[152] Periam, J. called it:

> ...a moving cause or consideration precedent, for which cause or consideration the promise was made.

In an earlier case,[153] the type of consideration that would impose liability was described as:

> ...a cause or occasion meritorious, requiring a mutual recompense in fact or law.

Also relevant to this were notions such as the benefit/detriment analysis and *quid pro quo* was never very far away. These criteria will be discussed in greater detail below.

3.2.1 Adequate Consideration

One issue raised by different sets of facts was the question of what constituted adequate consideration. The English commercial mind has never been much preoccupied with the value of what was given in an exchange. If people are foolish enough to accept inadequate consideration in return for lavish promises, this will not be interfered with by the courts. In the words of Hobbes:

> The value of all things contracted for, is measured by the appetite of the contractors: and therefore the just value, is that which they be contended to give.[154]

This is also reflected in the common law decisions. In *Sturlyn v Albany*[155] the court adjudged for the plaintiff "for when a thing is to be done by the plaintiff, be it never so small, this is a sufficient consideration to ground an action". Admittedly, *Sturlyn v Albany* was less about bargaining power or value and more,

152 (1585) 2 Leonard 224, or 74 Eng. Rep. 497.

153 *Calthorpe's Case* (1574) 3 Dyer 334b, or 73 Eng. Rep. 756.

154 Th. Hobbes (1651/1996) *Leviathan*, Oxford: OUP ; Part I, Chapter 15, paragraph 14, at 100 (p. 75 in the original 1651 edition).

155 (1587) Cro. Eliza. 67, or 78 Eng. Rep. 327.

as Simpson pointed out, about whether trivial or nominal acts could impose liability in assumpsit in a case where the liability of the defendant was established anyway.[156]

But the question of adequacy is bound up with whether consideration is seen in the *causa* sense, in which case it touches on motivation that may extend its span to past and continuing events. If consideration is taken in the *quid pro quo* sense, the focus remains on the reciprocal exchange promised or done. Adequacy in a *quid pro quo* scenario can, in theory, only be properly evaluated in relation to some sort of reciprocal exchange and remuneration. But such inadequacy of consideration has never been recognised as a defence in the medieval common law.[157] This would suggest that the essence of the concept of consideration lies indeed in the notion of whether there is good reason for the promise, other than material/value reciprocity, which is treated as legally insignificant. An exception to this would be if the promise and consideration could be valued in precise monetary terms. The action in *Richards v Bartlett*[158] raised precisely that point, but it was decided, not on the absence, but rather on the inadequacy of the consideration. The disparity of monetary value was thought relevant because it showed the lack of consideration.

3.2.2 Consideration in Time

Simpson[159] has listed four elements of time as important for evaluating consideration:

- past or executed consideration
- continuous consideration
- present consideration
- future or executory consideration.

Consideration that is executed and past at the time of the promise is not good consideration. This was first implied by the Student in his dialogue with the Doctor when he argued that only contracts involving imminent or future

---

156 B. Simpson (1975a) *A History of the Common Law of Contract: The Rise of the Action of Assumpsit*, Oxford: Clarendon Press, at 447. Rent was due by the defendant who promised to pay if the plaintiff would show him a deed proving the rent was due.

157 B. Simpson (1975a) at 456.

158 (1584) 1 Leonard 19, or 74 Eng. Rep. 17.

159 B. Simpson (1975a) at 452–465.

mutual exchanges can be enforced.[160] In common law this principle was laid down in *Hunt v Bate*[161] when it was held that (my emphasis):

> there is no consideration wherefore the defendant should be charged for the debt of his servant, unless the master had *first* promised to discharge the plaintiff before the enlargement and mainprize made of his servant, for the master did never make request to the plaintiff to do so much, but he did it off his own head.

In the second case reported under that name a distinction was made for cases where marriage was the consideration, which was held as:

> good cause, although the marriage was executed and past before the undertaking and promise, because the marriage ensued the request of the defendant.

The rule established in *Hunt v Bate* was subsequently followed in many cases.[162]

The notion of 'continuous' consideration was raised in a case also involving marriage. In *Marsh v Rainsford*:[163]

> the father's natural affection doth continue, and her advancement is sufficient cause of the promise.

The continuity of the father's affection made the fact that there had been no request irrelevant. Thus a continuous consideration was seen as a present consideration. This also allowed for a debt precedent to be held as good consideration for a subsequent promise to pay a debt: "The debt here always continues, and no charge can be made of this, but by payment of it".[164]

---

160 Ch. St. German (1518/1974), *Doctor and Student*, Second Dialogue, Chapter 24, edited by Th. Plucknett, J. Barton (1974) for the Selden Society, vol. 91.

161 (1568) Dyer 272, or 73 Eng. Rep. 605.

162 *Sydenham v Worlington* (1584) Godbolt 31, 2 Leon. 224 or 74 Eng. Rep. 497; *Moore v Williams* (1574) Moore K.B. 200, 72 Eng. Rep. 542; *Pearl v Unger* (1587) Cro. Eliz. 94, 78 Eng. Rep. 353; *Jeremy v Goochman* (1594) Cro. Eliz. 442, 78 Eng. Rep. 683; *Rigges v Bullingham* (1598) Cro. Eliz. 715, 78 Eng. Rep. 949; *Bosden v Thinne* (1603) Yelverton 40, 80 Eng. Rep. 29; *Jones v Clarke* (1613) 2 Bulstrode 73, 80 Eng. Rep. 969; *Cotton v Westcott* (1616) 1 Rolle 381, 81 Eng. Rep. 549; *Townsend v Hunt* (1635) Cro. Car. 408, 79 Eng. Rep. 955.

163 reported as Marsh v Kavenford (1587) in Cro. Eliz. 59, or 78 Eng. Rep. 319; as Marsh and Rainsford's Case (1588) in 2 Leonard 111, or 74 Eng. Rep. 400.

164 *Hodge v Vavisour* (1616) 3 Bulstrode 222, or 81 Eng. Rep. 188.

Accepting future or executory consideration appears an obvious premise and it was frequently raised in relation to marriage agreements. But the assertion of future or executory consideration must be distinguished from cases where a promise was averred as consideration.[165] This distinction between present promise to perform an act and future act was made in *Fuller's Case*.[166] If the plaintiff is to rely on a future act rather than a promise to perform an act as consideration, he needs to show performance, because the defendant could not have sued if the act had not been performed. If, on the other hand, the plaintiff alleges a promise as consideration, an action by the defendant would be allowed without having to show performance. This was set out nicely in the subsequent case of *Lampleigh v Braithwaite*:[167]

> For wheresoever I build my promise upon a thing done at my request, the execution of the act must pursue the request, for it is like a case of commission for this purpose [...] But if it be executory, as in consideration, that you shall serve me a year, I will give you ten pounds; here you cannot bring your action 'till the service performed. But if it were a promise on either side executory, it needs not to aver performance, for it is the counter-promise, and not the performance, that makes the consideration...

The distinction between promise and future act as consideration was also made indirectly in cases dealing with mutual promises as consideration. It is clearly set out in the passage from *Lampleigh v Braithwaite* quoted above. But the issue was dealt with much earlier in *West v Stowell*[168] when a promise to pay £10 was made against the promise to win an archery match. The decision was not reported, but the argument in favour of holding that mutual promises is good consideration was argued by Mounson J.:

---

165 B. Simpson (1975a) *A History of the Common Law of Contract: The Rise of the Action of Assumpsit*, Oxford: Clarendon Press, at p. 458 ; see also *Joscelin v Shelton* (1557) 3 Leonard 4, or 74 Eng. Rep. 503; *Pecke v Redman* (1556) 2 Dyer 113a, or 73 Eng. Rep. 248 ; *Simmes v Westcott* (1588) 1 Leonard 299, or 74 Eng. Rep. 273; *Applethwait and Nertleys Case* (1590) 4 Leonard 56, or 74 Eng. Rep. 727.

166 (1586) Godbolt 95, or 78 Eng. Rep. 58.

167 (1616) Hob 105, or 80 Eng. Rep. 255.

168 (1577) 2 Leonard 154, or 74 Eng. Rep. 437;

> ...the consideration is sufficient, for here this counter promise is a reciprocal promise, and so a good consideration, for all the communication ought to be taken together.

Manwood J. objected on the grounds that the bettor was not a party to the archery match and such consideration could only hold if both promising parties were also both involved in the match. The principle to recognise mutual promises as good consideration can be found in many subsequent cases.[169]

3.3 *Types of Consideration – Some Examples*

From the early common law premise that a promise was actionable if it was given in return for a payment or some sort of recompense (i.e. the concept of bargain as a two-sided agreement)[170] emerged the idea that promises made for considerations other than money or recompense could also be enforceable. In the *Golding's Case*, Egerton said that:

> In every action upon the case upon a promise, there are three things considerable, consideration, promise and breach of promise.[171]

3.3.1 Recompense – Benefit/Detriment

Beyond the notion of recompense as consideration emanated the more general principle that a benefit to the promisor constitutes good consideration. Actions involving marriage as consideration (see below) are good examples for this line of thinking. Also relevant in this context are cases where the plaintiff

169 *Sackford v Phillips* (1593) Owen 109; Moore K.B. 690, 72 Eng. Rep. 842; *Gower v Capper* (1596) Cro. Eliz. 543 78 Eng. Rep. 790; *Metcalfe's Case* (1597) Moore K.B. 549, 72 Eng. Rep. 750; *Wichals v Johns* (1599) Cro. Eliz. 703, Moore K.B. 574, 78 Eng. Rep. 938; *Lea v Exelby* (1602) Cro. Eliz. 888, 78 Eng. Rep. 1112; *Bettisworth v Campion* (1609) Yelverton 133, 80 Eng. Rep. 90; *Nichols v Raynbred* (1615) Hob. 88, 80 Eng. Rep. 238; *Spanish Ambassador v Gifford* (1616) 1 Rolle Rep. 336, 81 Eng. Rep. 526; *Lampleigh v Braithwaite* (1616) Hob. 105, 80 Eng. Rep. 255; *Browne v Downing* (1620) 2 Rolle 194, 81 Eng. Rep. 745; *Bibble v Cunningham* (1628) Hetley 89, 124 Eng. Rep. 365; *Shann v Bilby* (1651) Style 280, 82 Eng. Rep. 710; *Ernly v Lord Falkland* (1655) Hard. 103, 145 Eng. Rep. 349; *Bennett v Astell* (1660) 1 Lev. 20, 83 Eng. Rep. 276; *Anon.* (1662) 1 Lev. 87, 82 Eng. Rep. 311; *Peters v Opie* (1671) 1 Vent. 177, 86 Eng. Rep. 120.

170 "...a bargain and sale is, when a recompense is given by both parties; as if a man bargains his land to another for money, here the land is a recompense to the one for the money, and the money is a recompense to the other for the land, and thus is properly a bargain and sale". *Sharington v Strotton* (1564) 1 Plowden 298 at 303, or 75 Eng. Rep. 454 at 461.

171 (1586) 2 Leonard 72, or 74 Eng. Rep. 367.

has performed some service of the promisor.[172] The rule that a benefit to the promisor or a detriment to the promisee can constitute good consideration was set out by Coke in *Stone v Wythipol*:[173]

> ...no consideration can be good, if not, that it touch either the charge of the plaintiff, or the benefit of the defendant, and none of them is in our case, for the plaintiff is not at any charge, for which the defendant can have any benefit, for it is but the forbearance of the debt, which she was not compellable to pay...

A series of cases brought in the Elizabethan courts have adopted this principle[174] and these are the best evidence to refute the premise that the concept of consideration emanates from the single source of *quid pro quo*.

While the facts in many cases can be seen in terms of both benefit to the promisor and detriment to the promise, there are situations when an actual benefit is non-existent, such as for example in cases of gratuitous contracts of bailment or loan which lacked an element of remuneration.[175] In St. German the student says:

> ...if I promise to another to keep him such certain goods safely to, such a time, and after I refuse to take them, there lies no action against me for it. But if I take them, and after they be lost or impaired through my negligent keeping, there an action lies.[176]

---

172 (1572) *Rogers v Snow*, Dalison 94, or 123 Eng. Rep. 301; also *Onely v Earl of Kent* (1577) Dyer 355b, or 73 Eng Rep. 797; *Webb's Case* (1577) 4 Leonard 110, or 74 Eng. Rep. 763; *West v Stowell* (1577) 2 Leonard 154, or 74 Eng. Rep. 437.

173 (1588) 1 Leonard 113, or 78 Eng. Rep. 106, or (1593) Cro. Eliz. 126, or 78 Eng. Rep. 383; see also *Richards v Bartlet* (1584) 1 Leonard 19, or 74 Eng. Rep. 17.

174 *Webb's Case* (1577) 4 Leonard 110, or 74 Eng. Rep. 763; *Gill v Harewood* (1586) 1 Leonard 61, or 74 Eng. Rep. 57; *Preston v Tooley* (1587) Cro. Eliz. 74, or 78 Eng. Rep. 334; *Foster v Scarlett* (1587) Cro Eliz. 70, or 78 Eng. Rep. 330 ; *Wichals v Johns* (1599) Cro. Eliz. 703, or 78 Eng. Rep. 938.

175 e.g. *Fooly v Preston* (1586) 1 Leonard 297, or 74 Eng. Rep. 270; *Byne v Playne* (1590) 1 Leonard 220, or 74 Eng. Rep. 202; *Riches v Briggs* (1602) Yelverton 4, or 80 Eng. Rep. 4, or Cro. Eliz 883, or 78 Eng. Rep. 1108: this decision was reversed in the Exchequer Chamber, the reversal was commented as erroneous in: *Game v Harvie* (1604) Yelverton 50, or 80 Eng. Rep. 36; *Pickas v Guile* (1608) Yelverton 128, or 80 Eng. Rep. 86; *Wheatley v Low* (1623) Cro Jac. 668, or 79 Eng. Rep. 578.

176 Ch. St. German (1518/1974), *Doctor and Student*, Second Dialogue, Chapter 24, edited by Th. Plucknett, J. Barton (1974) for the Selden Society, vol. 91.

This may also include situations when work that was requested was performed without the success hoped for and thus without benefit to the promisor, as was the case in *Lampleigh v Braithwaite*[177] where the plaintiff did not obtain the pardon from the King that the defendant had asked him to secure. Here the promisor enjoyed no benefit but the promisee, having relied on the promise for payment, had to bear the detriment of having journeyed at his own expenses to see the King.

3.3.2 Forbearance

Linked to the benefit/detriment debate is another scenario, namely that of an act of forbearance and whether it could constitute sufficient consideration to uphold an agreement. Holdsworth[178] identifies three types of cases where an act of forbearance is at issue:

i. when the promise was made in consideration of a forbearance to prosecute a groundless claim: in *Stone v Wythipol*[179] it was held that forbearance to prosecute an invalid claim was no consideration. While a case[180] three centuries later confirmed this rule, forbearance to prosecuting a *bona fide* claim did amount to good consideration.
ii. when a promise was made by a creditor to his debtor that, in consideration that the debtor would pay or promise to pay his debt wholly or in part, the creditor would release him: in *Pinnel's Case*[181] a rule which had already been voiced in previous cases, was confirmed that:

> ...the payment of a lesser sum on the day in satisfaction of a greater, cannot be any satisfaction for the whole, because it appears to the judges that by no possibility, a lesser sum can be satisfaction to the plaintiff for a greater sum...

This was about the discharge of an agreement and the rule laid down that the payment of the whole or a part cannot constitute a discharge nor can it be a consideration for an agreement to discharge a contract. However, in another line of cases, the court held that obtaining a speedy, though only partial payment but without a legal action was good consideration

---

177 (1616) Hob 105, or 80 Eng. Rep. 255;

178 W.S. Holdsworth(1925) *History of English Law* vol. VIII, London: Sweet & Maxwell at pp. 18–25; see also J.B. Ames (1899) Two theories of Consideration, in: 12 *Harvard Law Review*, 515–539 and 13 *Harvard Law Review*, 29–42.

179 (1588) 1 Leonard 113, or 78 Eng. Rep. 106, or (1593) Cro. Eliz. 126, or 78 Eng. Rep. 383.

180 *Callisher v Bischoffsheim* (1870) L.R. 5 Q.B. 449.

181 (1602) 5 Co. Rep. 117a, or 77 Eng. Rep. 237.

for a promise to release a debt because of the benefit derived from such part-payment by the promisor. In *Reynolds v Pinhowe*:[182]

> all the court held that it to be well enough; for it is a benefit unto him to have it without suit or charge.

This was confirmed in subsequent cases[183] until the matter was finally settled in the 19th century: a part payment by a debtor to his creditor cannot be good consideration for a promise by the creditor to release his debtor.[184]

iii. when a promise was made by a third party that he would do something for one of the parties to a subsisting valid contract, if that party would perform or promise to perform his duty under the contract: this situation arose rarely[185] and is reminiscent of a promise-in-consideration-of-a-promise scenario where consideration has been recognised as valid. But the courts went further in these cases by stressing that the receipt of payment was a benefit to the creditor and this was the main reason for them to hold the consideration as valid.

3.3.3 Charitable Promises

The rule that promises failing to provide a benefit to the promisor should also be actionable is reiterated by the Student in his dialogue with the Doctor:

> all promises shall be taken in this manner: that is to say, if he to whom the promise is made have a charge by reason of the promise, which he has also performed, then in that case he shall have an action for that thing that was promised, though he that made the promise have no worldly profit by it.[186]

If this applies to 'all' promises that should also include charitable promises and those made for the benefit of third parties. This may involve promises to pay school/tuition fees for a youngster or to pay a medical doctor to cure a poor

182 (1595) Cro. Eliz. 429, or 78 Eng. Rep. 669.

183 e.g. *Bagge v Slade* (1613) 3 Bulstrode 162, or 81 Eng. Rep. 137; *Flight v Crasden* (1625) Cro. Car. 8, or 79 Eng. Rep. 612; *Johnson v Astell* (1667) 1 Lev. 198, or 83 Eng. Rep. 367.

184 *Foakes v Beer* (1884) 9 A.C. 605.

185 *Sherwood v Woodward* (1600) Cro. Eliz. 700, or 78 Eng Rep. 935; *Bagge v Slade* (1613) 3 Bulstrode 162, or 81 Eng. Rep. 137.

186 Ch. St. German (1518/1974), *Doctor and Student*, Second Dialogue, Chapter 24, edited by Th. Plucknett, J. Barton (1974) for the Selden Society, vol. 91.

man etc. The common element in these scenarios is the lack of direct benefit for the promisor. This is reminiscent of the many cases involving promises of payment in consideration of a marriage, but as described below, the account of marriage was distinguished from other charitable promises on the grounds that the father enjoyed the pleasure of the advancement of his daughter. Injurious reliance without benefit to the promisor was at issue in *Lord Grey's Case*[187] which explicitly approved an earlier decision.[188] Simpson[189] recounts the discussions from a number of further cases, some of which were inconclusive but, as he points out, in none of them was there explicit reference to the charitable nature of the promises in question. But he believes it was likely that the demands of Christian charity may have swayed the courts to allow gratuitous promises to be actionable in assumpsit. However, it would be erroneous to conclude that the element of detriment was seen as consideration for the promise. Simpson[190] argues that:

> the natural requirement derived from a theory of injurious reliance is that the detriment must be induced by the promisor, not that it should be the motive for the promise, and the difference, though nice, is not always unimportant.

3.3.4 Friendship, Love and Natural Affection

The area most associated with the *causa*/motivation outlook was that of natural love and affection. The consideration clause has been used prominently in the context of marriage. Anyone systematically reading assumpsit/consideration cases will be struck by the relatively high proportion of actions where marriage is at issue. This is also borne out by examining the corpus of the Year Books and Law Reports that was constituted for this research. In the texts dating from the 16th and 17th century (annex 2 under VI.i, ii, iii & iv), we find the word 'marriage' 76 times in a proximity span of 20 words to the left and to the right of 'consideration'. 'Promise' yields the same figure, while there are 60 instances of 'covenant', 59 instances of 'debt', 37 instances of 'assumpsit but only 12 proximity hits for 'contract'.

---

187 (1567) reported in: J. Baker & S.F.C. Milsom (1986) *Sources of English Legal History. Private Law to 1750*, London: Butterworth, at 492.

188 *Jordan's* or *Tatam's Case* (1535) Y.B. 27 Mich. Hen. VIII, 24, 3 or LBEx.

189 B. Simpson (1975a) *A History of the Common Law of Contract : The Rise of the Action of Assumpsit*, Oxford: Clarendon Press, at 430–431.

190 B. Simpson (1975a) at 432.

Friendship and affection (outside the family/marriage) was held to be insufficient consideration.[191] Though temporarily questioned in *Lord Grey's Case*[192] by linking friendship to benefit consideration, the principle established in *Hunt v Bate* prevailed. The case law provides a more complex answer to the question of whether love and affection within the family constitutes consideration. In *Sharington v Strotton*[193] several aspects of love and natural affection as consideration were discussed and Plowden argued that the continuance of male heirs constituted good consideration because:

> men are for the greatest part more reasonable than women, and have more discretion to guide and manage things than women have, for to govern and direct is more suitable to the capacity of the male than of the female.

Also, excluding female heirs in favour of men ensured a continuance of the name. It must be stressed that the central issue in this case was whether a use would lie. The argument against allowing this consideration was clearly grounded in a *quid pro quo* approach, arguing that brotherly love and long acquaintance constituted no monetary value:

> ...the consideration ought to be to him that is seized of the land, for if he has no recompence, there is not cause why the use of his land should pass; And none of the considerations contain a recompence here, for the continuance of the land in his blood and name of B. is no recompence to him, nor cause worthy to raise a use; no more is the brotherly love and favour which he bore to E.B., or to his other brothers, for although these causes induce affection, yet every affection is not sufficient cause to alter the use. For if a man grants to J.S. that in consideration of their long acquaintance, or of their great familiarity, or of their being scholars together in their youth, or upon such like considerations, he will stand seized of his land to his use, this will not change the use, for such considerations are not looked upon in the law as worthy to raise a use, because they don't import any value or recompense [...]

191 *Hunt v Bate* (1568) Dyer 272, or 73 Eng. Rep. 605: "...promises for this friendship to save him...".

192 (1567) reported in J.H. Baker & S.F.C. Milsom (1986) *Sources of English Legal History. Private Law to 1750*, London: Butterworth, at 492.

193 (1564) 1 Plowden 298, or 75 Eng. Rep. 454.

The counter-argument favoured looking beyond purely monetary value at the wider motivation for an undertaking:

> If I make a contract with another, that if he will take my daughter to wife, I will give him £20, in this case if he takes her to wife, he shall have an action of debt for the £20 [...] and yet I have nothing for it, and if it was not out of regard to nature, this should be called a nude contract, *et ex nudo pacto non oritur actio*. But, Sir, my daughter is advanced by the marriage, which is a sufficient consideration to me for the £20. So that a consideration proceeding from nature is a sufficient consideration in our law. And from these reasons and cases it is manifest that things proceeding from nature are respected not only in philosophy, but also in our law, and are of great force and operation in our law, and therefore are esteemed to be good and sufficient considerations. From whence it follows that the consideration of A.B., here expressed for the provision of his heirs males is a sufficient consideration to raise a use in the land [...]
>
> [...] the continuance of the land in the name of B. [...] seems to be a good consideration to raise a use [...] here A.B. deserves to be praised and commended for his gratuity by all those of the name of B. And therefore for these reasons there is a sufficient consideration in the limitation of the name to raise a use. [...] the continuance of the land in his brothers and others of his blood, it is also founded upon nature. [...] From whence we see that by the law of nature, and by the law of the realm, and by the law of God (which in intent approves them both) brotherly love and advancement of one's blood is taken to be of great effect, and seems to be a sufficient consideration to raise a use in land [...]

In 1588,[194] the decision went the other way (this was partly also because the consideration was past):

> Love is not a consideration, upon which an action can be grounded; the like of friendship...

But maybe more important for the debate was that in cases where love/affection was declared as consideration to pass a use, it was held as constituting good consideration. It appears that when passing a use the wider underlying motivation, namely to strengthen family settlements in particular in relation to landed property, was given more prominence. This can also be traced back

194 *Harford and Gardiner's Case* (1588) 2 Leonard 30, or 74 Eng. Rep. 332.

to actions where marriage was considered good consideration to support a covenant to pass a use[195] and to the recognition of consideration in equity.[196]

Cases involving marriage as consideration offer yet another scenario. In the second case reported under *Hunt v Bate,*[197] a definite distinction was made between cases involving friendship as consideration and those where marriage was the consideration. In cases of the latter sort, the promise and consideration were frequently not contemporaneous, but love and natural affection was seen as constituting continuous consideration, even in cases that did not involve a use. In *Sidenham v Worlington*[198] Anderson said that "marriage is always a present consideration". This was confirmed in *Marsh v Rainsford*[199] where Wrey, J. held that:

> here the natural affection of the father to his daughter, is sufficient matter of consideration.

In other words, love and natural affection in the context of family and marriage is continuous, precisely because of the family/marriage bond and, as part of a wider principle, it should be upheld as good consideration. In *Browne v Garborough,*[200] Shuttleworth appears to confirm the family restriction by arguing that the woman at the centre of a marriage deal:

> was a mere stranger to the defendant; and there was no reason for him to give her one hundred pounds in marriage.

In the event, the court found that a family link between the woman and the defendant did exist and the issue was therefore not discussed further.

Barker v Halifax[201] was also about past consideration, but assumpsit in consideration of a marriage was held as good "for the affection and consideration

---

195 *Assaby v Lady Manners* (1516) Dyer 335a, or 73 Eng Rep. 520.

196 Discussing the equitable doctrine of consideration is beyond the scope of this paper; for this and contract in equity in general see, for example, W.T. Barbour (1914) The History of Contract in Early English Equity, in: P. Vinogradoff *Oxford Studies in Social and Legal History*, Oxford: Clarendon, at pp. 66–169; H. Barlow (1793) *Treatise on Equity*, vol. 1, Dublin: Byrne, Moore, Jones, Lynch and Watts, at pp. 326–379; B. Simpson (1975a) *A History of the Common Law of Contract: The Rise of the Action of Assumpsit*, Oxford: Clarendon Press, at. 455.

197 *Hunt v Bate* (1568) Dyer 272, or 73 Eng. Rep. 605.

198 (1585) 2 Leonard 224, or 74 Eng. Rep. 497.

199 (1586) 2 Leonard 111, or 74 Eng. Rep. 400.

200 (1587) Cro. Eliz. 64, or 78 Eng. Rep. 324.

201 (1599) Cro. Eliz 741, or 78 Eng. Rep. 974.

always continues". The element of continuity was also accepted in *Brett v. J.S. and his Wife*[202] where natural affection of a mother for her son was not accepted as a sufficient consideration to ground an action without an express *quid pro quo*, which was the son's continued board in this case:

> ... But it is here good, because it is not only in consideration of affection, but that her son should afterwards continue at his table, which is good as well for the money due before, as for what should afterwards become due...

Similarly, in *Townsend v Hunt*[203] *per* Berkley J.:

> it had been a consideration continuing, as in consideration of marrying his daughter or cousin, which is a gift in frank-marriage, it had been good...

From this line of cases, it can be concluded that love and natural affection in the context of family/marriage constitute an exception to the general principle that past consideration is not enforceable, because the family/marriage link renders the consideration continuous. In other words, while love and natural affection do not, as such, constitute consideration in assumpsit, a promise made in consideration of love and natural affection and in consideration of a past act could be actionable.

•••

From the discussion so far it is striking to observe that the (mainly) 16th century case law concerned itself with exploring the issue of when a breached promise was actionable rather than laying down what constitutes a binding promise. This can be explained in part by the evolution from the refusal (13th/14th c.) to enforce any agreement wanting a seal or *quid pro quo*, stretching actions of trespass to include misfeasance and later non-feasance during the late 14th and 15th centuries, to allowing certain undertakings and informal promises to become legally enforceable in the late 15th and 16th centuries. With this last step came the inevitable necessity to ring-fence the possibility of bringing an action for a breached promise. In the words of Plowden reporting *Sharington v Strotton:*

---

202 (1600) Cro. Eliz. 756, or 78 Eng. Rep. 987.

203 (1635) Cro. Car. 408, or 79 Eng. Rep. 955.

> And, Sir, by the law of this land there are two ways of making contracts or agreements for lands or chattels. The one is, by words, which is the inferior method; the other is, by writing, which is the superior. And because words are oftentimes spoken by men unadvisedly and without deliberation, the law has provided that a contract by words shall not bind without consideration.[204]

In other words, consideration was used to check the floodgates from opening too wide, and to limit assumpsit action to those where the promise was supported by consideration. It was not devised as part of an overall doctrine of contract law. Indeed, there was no general common law theory of contract law at the time – that would be initiated only in the 18th century by Blackstone and his treatise-writing contemporaries. Today's contract law doctrine of offer and acceptance as the moment when a promise becomes binding, was unknown then and there was no requirement, as there is in modern contract law, for the plaintiff to show that a contract had been made. Instead, it had to be demonstrated that a promise had been made for good consideration but had not been honoured. In the words of Houghton, J.:

> A contract by parole on good consideration is as strong (binding) as a covenant by deed…[205]

The rules about what type of consideration could be legally enforced evolved rather haphazardly, as we have seen from the description of the case law above. But as Simpson[206] points out, it would be inappropriate to view these rules as revealing some underlying reality in terms of social conditions or ideas.

4 Consideration as a Moral Obligation – The Concept in the 18th Century

Towards the end of the 17th century, the language and terminology used in cases involving consideration had settled and evolved into technical jargon. But the underlying concept, though much more ascertainable by then, had developed in a piecemeal fashion. It was only from the mid-18th century that

204 (1564) 1 Plowden 298 at 308, or 75 Eng. Rep. 460 at 470.

205 *Winter v Foweracres* (1618) 2 Rolle 39, or 81 Eng. Rep. 645.

206 B. Simpson (1975a) *A History of the Common Law of Contract: The Rise of the Action of Assumpsit*, Oxford: Clarendon Press, at 487–488.

treatise writers began to voice the need to search for a more general theory of contract, no doubt encouraged by the very comprehensive writings of Pothier on the subject.[207] An 1806 English translation of the *Traité des obligations* was widely known in both England and America, though some may have already read it in its French original, and it had a major influence on a great many Anglo-American writers on contract.

On a more general level, the late 17th and 18th centuries saw considerable shifts in socio-political thinking shaping Western societies and England was no exception to these influences of the Enlightenment, although as Fifoot interjects:

> England [...] had not yet abandoned the defects or privileges of insularity. Her contact with the Continent was precarious, and it was not surprising that an intellectual movement, European in essence, should be translated into terms at once less magical and less drastic...[208]

But the basic premise was similar, namely the rejection of extrinsic authority in favour of the voice of reason and natural law. A figure at the centre of these changes and a leader in wanting to move the law away from the land-centred outlook and rigid professional traditions and procedures was William Murray, 1st Earl of Mansfield. Of Scottish descent, he acquired, as a student at Oxford and in Lincoln's Inn, a broad legal knowledge that went well beyond the confines of the English legal system. He was well-read in French, Dutch and Scottish law and legal writings, and was particularly interested in a comparative approach, which served him well when he set about correcting the insularity of English law. He was a child of the century that followed the Glorious Revolution of 1688, when the political system was no longer grounded in authority but based on reason.[209] He is generally known for his contributions to the area of commercial and maritime law, aiming to make international commercial law an integral part of both the common law and equity. Relying on his knowledge of other systems of law, he went beyond the traditional thinking of

207 *Traité des obligations, selon les règles tant du for la conscience, que du for extérieur*, was first published in France in 1761–1764; a first American translation was published by F.X. Martin in 1802: *A Treatise on Obligations considered in a Moral and Legal View*, Newburn, NC: Martin & Ogden; an English translation followed in 1806 by Sir William Evans: *A Treatise on the Law of Obligations, Or Contracts* (republished in Philadelphia in 1826, 1839 and 1853).

208 C.H.S. Fifoot (1977/reprint of 1936 edition) *Lord Mansfield*, Aalen: Scientia Verlag, at 1.

209 N. Poser (2013) *Lord Mansfield. Justice in the Age of Reason*, Montreal & Kingston: McGill-Queen's University Press, at 3–10.

established categories and models and his comparative outlook allowed him to find solutions by breaking away from rigid professional traditions and procedures. His understanding of the learning of continental lawyers allowed him, on the one hand, to view critically the law and procedures he was confronted with, and on the other hand, he was able to adapt continental rules to the English legal system to modernise its workings. However, he was not advocating large legislative changes to the law; rather he worked towards an adaptation of old rules and principles to the new circumstances and needs of modern times. And by delving into his knowledge of continental systems of law and writings, he was able to ground his decisions on underlying principles that were acceptable to both the English and continental lawyers. His basic premise was that cases should always be interpreted in view of underlying principles. While he acknowledged that the workings of precedents cannot allow rules of law to be overturned, "the cases must if possible be so interpreted as to bring them into conformity with those principles".[210] This is reminiscent of Scottish law where:

> the search was not for the appropriate form of writ, but for the legal principle involved [...] The formulary system and the fictions of the English common law, the outcome of pure empiricism, find no counterpart in the history of the law of Scotland.[211]

It is also from Scottish law that Mansfield imported a theory of consideration he thought more appropriate than the concept that had been worked out in the English courts hitherto. His basic premise was to prevent unjust enrichment[212] and he developed this idea in *Moses v Macferlan* when he said that:

> If the defendant be under an obligation, from the ties of natural justice to refund; the law implies a debt, and gives this action, founded in the equity of the plaintiff's case, as it were upon a contract ("quasi ex contractu", as the Roman law expresses it).[213]

---

210 W. Holdsworth (1938/1966 reprint) *Some Makers of English Law*, Cambridge: CUP, at 166–167.

211 H.P. Macmillan (1932) Scots Law as a subject of comparative study, in: 48 *Law Quarterly Review*, 477–487, at 482.

212 M. Lobban (2010) Contract, in: W. Cornish, S. Anderson, R. Cocks, M. Lobban, P. Polden, K. Smith (eds.) *The Oxford History of the Laws of England*, vol. XII (1820–1914), Oxford: OUP, at 361–366.

213 (1760) 2 Burr. 1005, or 97 Eng. Rep. 676, at 678.

The first attempt to actively reform consideration can be found in his ruling of *Pillans and Rose v Van Mierop and Hopkins*,[214] a merchant law case in which the defendant's promise lacked consideration in any technical sense. It is a case well known for a number of innovative propositions, one of which was his equation of consideration with mere evidence of an agreement:

> I take it, that the ancient notion about the want of consideration was for the sake of evidence only: for when it is reduced into writing, as in covenants, specialties, bonds &c. there was no objection to the want of consideration.

He also affirmed that the law of merchants and the law of the land were the same and that the concept of *nudum pactum* did not exist in the usage and law of merchants. He concluded that:

> in commercial cases amongst merchants, the want of consideration is not an objection.

Mansfield's point was historically justifiable to the extent that consideration had been seen as part of the toolbox that ring-fenced agreements to distinguish enforceable and non-enforceable promises. Hence, consideration was part of a 'list' of technical conditions under which actions of assumpsit would lie. The question of evidence had been addressed by the 1677 Statute of Frauds[215] imposing the written form for certain types of agreements. Mansfield concluded that the statute replaced the older requirement of considerations.[216] This decision brought English law momentarily closer to continental laws by sketching deliberate intention as the test of a binding contract.

However, this attempt at reforming consideration was reversed in 1778 by the House of Lords' ruling in *Rann v Hughes:*

> …the present case did not afford a pretext of any benefit or indulgence stipulated for by the defendant, or anything to be done or omitted by the

214 (1765) 3 Burr. 1663, or 97 Eng. Rep. 1035.

215 *An Act for prevention of Frauds and Perjuryes*, Statute of the Realm: vol. 5: 1628–90, at 839–842; originally published by Great Britain Record Commission, s.l, 1819; www.british-history.ac.uk.

216 "And the Statute of Frauds proceeded upon the same principle" (1765) 3 Burr. 1663 at 1669, or 97 Eng. Rep. 1035 at 1038.

> plaintiffs, as a consideration for the promise stated to have been made by the defendant...[217]

This reversal did not prevent Mansfield from pursuing his reforms of the law relating to consideration. It led to his attempt to introduce the concept of moral consideration to support a contract. This was based on the notion that a moral obligation is inherent in the making of a contract and it was an attempt to import into the doctrine of consideration his own view that the basic function of a contract was to implement the intentions of the parties. If the basis of moral obligation could be accepted, it would allow for the distinction between written and oral agreements to become obsolete. Mansfield's efforts to reform the English law was a less glorious chapter, because although supported and propagated by several of his colleagues, the reforms did not last.

But to view moral obligations as the primary factor that makes a promise actionable, was not just an inspiration from across the Scottish border. The equitable conception of consideration had allowed for an exception to the rule that consideration must move from the promise. Furthermore, traces of the notion of moral consideration could already be found to a certain extent in the action of *indebitatus assumpsit*. The decision in the *Slade's Case*[218] had established that the existence of a preceding debt imports a promise and assumpsit will lie despite the fact that there had been no express promise to pay. In 1697, a defendant was held bound to a debt incurred during his minority[219] and a couple of years later a promise to pay a debt bared by the Statute of Limitation was enforceable.[220] In both cases, *indebitatus assumpsit* was brought on a preceding debt that had incurred but was not enforceable. The last two cases were used by Mansfield as precedent to support his view in *Hawkes v Saunders*.[221] But in contrast to the earlier cases, the Mansfield's reasoning relied entirely on equitable considerations, which weakens considerably the link to the earlier cases as precedents. In *Hawkes* Mansfield started by discussing:

> ...whether the defendant having assets sufficient to pay all the debts and legacies, is, or is not sufficient consideration for her to make a promise to pay the legacy in question? As to that point, the rules laid down at the

217 (1778) 4 Bro. P.C. 27, or 2 Eng. Rep. 18, or 7 T.R. 350.
218 (1602) 4 Co. Rep. 92a.
219 *Ball v Hesketh* (1697), Comb. 381, or 90 Eng. Rep. 541.
220 *Hyleing v Hastings* (1699) 1 Ld. Raym. 389.
221 (1782) 1 Cowp. 289, or 98 Eng. Rep. 1091.

> Bar, as to what is or is not a good consideration in law, goes upon a very narrow ground indeed; namely, that to make a consideration to support an assumpsit, there must be either an immediate benefit to the party promising, or a loss to the person to whom the promise was made. I cannot agree to that being the only ground of consideration sufficient to raise an assumpsit. Where a man is under a legal or equitable obligation to pay, the law implies a promise, though none was ever actually made. A fortiori, a legal or equitable duty is a sufficient consideration for an actual promise. Where a man is under a moral obligation, which no Court of Law or Equity can inforce, and promise, the honesty and rectitude of the thing is a consideration.

Referring to *Hyleing v Hastings* and *Ball v Hesketh*, he continues:

> As if a man promise to pay a just debt, the recovery of which is barred by the Statute of Limitations: or if a man, after he comes of age, promises to pay a meritorious debt contracted during his minority, but not for necessaries [...] In such and many other instances, though the promise gives a compulsory remedy, where there was none before either in law or equity; yet as the promise is only to do what an honest man ought to do, the ties of conscience upon an upright mind are a sufficient consideration.

In *Atkins v Hill*,[222] Mansfield talks about "obligations which would otherwise only bind a man's conscience". Similarly, in *Trueman v Fenton*[223] Mansfield relied on arguments akin to equitable principles, rather than the more restrictive common law view that the existence of a precedent debt is good consideration:

> The debts of a bankrupt are due in conscience, notwithstanding he has obtained his certificate; and there is no honest man who does not discharge them...

The concept of moral consideration survived Mansfield for a few decades and was adopted by a number of his colleagues. As Holdsworth point out, Mansfield's appeals to moral and natural law were:

---

222 (1775) 1 Cowp. 284, or 98 Eng. Rep. 1088.

223 (1777) 2 Cowp. 544, or 98 Eng. Rep. 1232.

> attractive to the minds of the lawyers of his day; and so the idea that a conscientious obligation could be consideration for a promise was speedily taken up.[224]

It had almost become an accepted doctrine. Twenty years after Mansfield's death, references to his idea of moral consideration were made in *Lee v Muggeridge*:

> Lord Mansfield C.J. thought the rule of *nudum pactum* was too strict, and that it was competent for parties to make their own agreements on deliberation, and if they did so think fit to make them, that they must be subject to them. It is now fully recognized in the law, that if there be, even in the strictest morality, the foundation for a promise, and the promise be accordingly made, it is binding. It is a new ligamen, though not a new consideration; for if there were a new consideration, it would be clearly good.[225]

In *Atkins v Banwell*[226] Lord Ellenborough C.J. said that "a moral obligation is a good consideration for an express promise". He confirmed this in *Wing v Mill*[227] with the words: "In this case both the legal and moral obligation obtain". As late as 1863, we can find Pollock C.B. referring to the concept of moral consideration, although this was perhaps more a linguistic expression lingering from the past than a discussion of the underlying concept. One of the questions under consideration was:

> ...whether an advance of money under such circumstances as to create no legal obligation at the time to repay it can constitute a good consideration for an express promise to do so. Such consideration has been sometimes called a moral consideration...[228]

But the concept had its critics well before then. In a note appended to their report of *Wendall v Adney*[229] Bosanquet and Puller attempted to limit the idea of allowing an express promise founded simply on an antecedent moral obligation to be sufficient to support an assumpsit. They argued that the expression

224 W.S. Holdsworth(1925) *History of English Law* vol. VIII, London: Sweet & Maxwell, at 27.
225 (1813) 5 Taunt. 36, or 128 Eng. Rep. 599, at 602.
226 (1802) 2 East 505, or 102 Eng. Rep. 462.
227 (1817) 1 B. & Ald. 104, or 106 Eng. Rep. 39.
228 *Flight v Reed* (1863) 1 H. & C. 703, or 158 Eng. Rep. 1067 at 1072.
229 (1803) 3 Bos. & P., 247 at 250, or 127 Eng. Rep. 137 at 138–141.

of this concept as used by Mansfield may appear of a general nature at first, but:

> ...yet the instances adduced by him as illustrative of the rule of law, do not carry that rule beyond what the older authorities seem to recognise as its proper limits; for in each instance the party bound by the promise had received a benefit previous to the promise [...] Lord Mansfield appears to have used the term moral obligation not as expressive of any vague and undefined claim arising from nearness of relationship, but of those imperative duties which would be enforceable by law, were it not for some positive rule, which, with a view to general benefit, exempt the party in that particular instance from legal liability [...] An express promise, therefore, as it should seem, can only revive a precedent good consideration, which might have been enforced at law through the medium of an implied promise, had it not been suspended by some positive rule of law, but can give no original right of action if the obligation on which it is founded never could have been enforced at law, though not barred by any legal maxim or statute provision.

This was an attempt to argue for a more restricted reading of the case law and that 'moral consideration' could not be reconciled with old cases. It was, however, not adopted in subsequent actions such as *Lee v Muggeridge*.

Eventually, in *Eastwood v Kenyon*[230] the court (*per* Lord Denman C.J.) returned to a more technically strict reading of consideration by putting aside the concept of moral consideration, saying that:

> the doctrine would annihilate the necessity for any consideration at all, inasmuch as the mere fact of giving a promise creates a moral obligation to perform it.

The Mansfield episode in the history of consideration is not only interesting from the point of view of legal theory, doctrinal developments and legal history, but also from the linguistics and terminological angle. The era of the Enlightenment comes not only with new ideas but also innovations in terminology and shifts in semantic contents. This will be explored in further detail in the following chapter.

---

230 (1840) 11 Ad. & E. 438, or 113 Eng. Rep. 482.

CHAPTER 6

Corpus Linguistic Analysis

Habent sua fata verba

In the previous chapters, we became acquainted with the cultural and linguistic landscape of multilingual England and its specific situation of medieval legal text production, as well as with the origins and historical evolution of the concept of consideration. From our 21st century perspective, this doctrine may appear carved in stone: as far back as the legal mind can remember, we see the concept and the language used to describe it as long-standing and well-established companions. Yet, from the discussion so far, we can observe that the path taken has been a tortuous mountain climb rather than a straight run on a stretch of motorway. The concept originated in a variety of legal issues and one needs to untangle the different strands to understand the process. It is, of course, in the nature of the common law, especially in its early stages, to evolve in a more organic fashion, pushing boundaries without making major changes to the law. Ames[1] believed that the action of assumpsit and later the concept of consideration were a picture book example of this.

In the context of the customary set-up of the common law, the twists and turns the concept of consideration went through can be examined by studying the case law, which can be found in the Year Books and Law Reports. These are neither systematic, nor official, nor standardised, but scant and personal at times, but still offer us plenty of insight into this development. In a second step, reported in this chapter, these same sources were exploited for examining the language describing the concept of consideration. The terminology was analysed diachronically to reveal the evolution of the conceptual perception, on the one hand, and the corresponding semantic shifts, on the other. The aim was to evaluate the concordance between the historical and conceptual development of 'consideration' and the way the relevant terms and vocabulary were used, changed and shifted throughout this evolution, most notably the increased abstraction and technicality of both the concept and the language.

The underlying premise for this approach is the deep-level and intrinsic link between language and law, as law cannot be imagined without the use of

1 J.A. Ames (1913) *Lectures on Legal History and Miscellaneous Legal Essays*, Cambridge: Harvard University Press, at 166.

 | DOI:10.1163/9789004436169_007

language and, in particular, without the use of written language. The account of language that is most appropriate to adopt is one which emphasises usage, communicative function and social contexts. A study of language as it is used in actual social situations and is concerned with meaning, communicative functionality and rhetorical purposes.[2] The function that is of particular interest to this research is the representational aspect, which encodes our experience of the world and thus conveys a picture of reality. Considering the vocabulary used in relation to the concept of making informal agreements enforceable, by looking beyond the traditional grammar classification of the words in question and examining the function they play, we can get a more complete and in-depth picture of the evolution of that vocabulary. This is best done by undertaking a diachronic linguistic and semantic analysis using corpus linguistics methodologies. It is important to stress that corpus linguistic work not only provides an empirical basis for examining the language, but it has also a heuristic function to the extent that the analysis of the material systematized in a corpus generates new knowledge. The researcher may be confronted with results that were unexpected. The theoretical framework and methodological choices were set out in Chapter 3 above.

1 Methodology

This section describes the process used to constitute the corpora that formed the basis for the study. Furthermore, it deals with the linguistic analysis and will describe the (statistical) results in detail.

1.1 *Sources*

The sources from which the texts were drawn for analysis are electronically accessible and searchable through the following databases:

i. www.anglo-norman.net – The Anglo-Norman On-Line Hub:
   - Anglo-Norman text base
ii. www.heinonline.org – Selden Society Publications and the History of Early English Law:
   - Ames Foundation Publications
   - Selden Society (Annual) Series

2 On systemic functional linguistics see Chapter 3 above; also C. Laske (2013) Translators and Legal Comparatists as Objective Mediators between Cultures?, in: J. Husa, M. Van Hoecke (eds.) *Objectivity in Law and Legal Reasoning*, Oxford: Hart Publishing, 213–227.

   – English Legal History Classics

iii. www.heinonline.org – English Reports:

   – English Reports – Full Reprint (1220–1867)

The full bibliographical information is listed in annex 1 and 2.

The texts in the databases were considered in their entirety. For the study of the general language register, the material in the Anglo-Norman On-Line Hub (i) was used as it is presented in the database. Since the Hub offers a series of linguistics and concordance tools, there was no need to download any texts to constitute a tailor-made subcorpus. As far as the specifically legal material (ii & iii) is concerned, the criteria for selection was that texts must report on cases judged in a common law court and that the original language version of the report was electronically accessible and searchable.

The sources are presented in both their original language (Latin, Anglo-French, Middle/Early Modern English) and an English translation undertaken by the editor at the time of the publication of the material. Most texts were written in two, sometimes three languages (Anglo-French, Middle/Early Modern English, Latin) though one language usually dominated. The earlier texts had many Latin passages or were entirely in Latin; these were not included in the study. The majority of the original language sources are in Law French and passages in Middle/Early Modern English tend to be transcripts of declarations made by one of the parties to the action. Only the main original language body of texts from the Anglo-French and Middle/Early Modern English sources were considered; all (English) translations, editors' footnotes and introduction, or other editorial explanations etc. were disregarded. No discrimination was made on the basis of legal content or importance of the legal decision in question: landmarks were included as much as unimportant ones.

Although the year books and reports listed were all studied, not all were used to constitute the corpus. This is the reason why the description of the diachronic terminological study below falls into two parts for every term: a more general section on the entirety of the texts studied and a more specific and detailed description of the corpus work.

1.2 *Corpora*

A corpus is usually defined as a systematic collection of naturally occurring texts of both written and spoken language[3] that has been computerised. It offers the empirical basis for carrying out linguistic investigations. The collection of texts is 'systematic' because the content and structure of the corpus is built

3 Naturally occurring language is language that has evolved naturally, is hereditary and in extended use.

according to extra-linguistic principles that relate to the way texts are chosen and sampled. The theoretical question underlying corpus design and its representativeness was discussed in Chapter 3 above. The corpus for this research was purpose-built, adapting traditional corpus linguistics methodologies to the specific situation of multilingual, medieval legal texts from the HeinOnline databases, which was constituted for the purpose of legal rather than linguistic study. The use of these texts for linguistic purposes in this research meant that it was necessary to construct a tailor-made corpus. This process was the result of trial and error, very much in the vein of what Biber[4] described as the cyclical movement of continuously revising the design following empirical research carried out on the initial pilot corpus in order to adjust the design parameters.

The sources as described above, were used to compile a series of diachronic subcorpora, except for the Anglo-Norman On-Line Hub, which is already constituted as a corpus for linguistics purposes:

- Anglo-Norman corpus (ANC): Anglo-Norman source texts include 76 texts in electronic form, containing more than 5 million tokens and covering all registers of Anglo-Norman usage. The majority of the sources are from the second half of the 14th century, though a few date from the mid-13th century. The majority of these documents can be dated and localised, which offers greater certainty that they come from the said periods and have not been subsequently rewritten. The corpus material consists, among others, of correspondence, chronicles in both prose and verse, government statutes and treatises, ordinances, romance and epic texts, religious and devotional prose, texts on hagiography, language pedagogy and philosophy etc. It is not a specifically legal corpus, though it includes legal texts.
- The 15th century corpus: this is based on the early legal sources (almost exclusively 15th c. except for one – Bellewe – from the late 14th c.), before informal contracts were enforceable, but trespass on the case actions began to materialise, the quasi-trespass nature of which being of a fundamentally contractual nature. The 15th century was also the time when the action of assumpsit appeared and with it the shift from primarily proprietary thinking to that of promissory exchange.
- The 16th century corpus: constituted mainly of texts from the Elizabethan reign that can be found in volumes 71, 73 and 123 of the English Reports Full Reprint (reports by Keilwey, Benloe, Dalison, Anderson, Savile). This was an era that saw the establishment of the concept of consideration as an element vital for the enforceability of promises and informal contracts.

4 D. Biber (1993) Representativeness in Corpus Design, in: *Literary and Linguistic Computing*, Vol. 8, No. 4, 243–257.

- The 17th century corpus: the texts in this corpus report decisions from either side of the Interregnum, mainly during the Stuart reign of James I and Charles II (reports by Rolle and Palmer). By that time, the concept of consideration was well established.
- The Mansfield corpus: constituted from a variety of reports. It is a collection of cases decided by Lord Mansfield and his colleagues, in which the idea of consideration as moral obligation was defended. These date from the mid-18th to the early 19th century.

The full bibliographical information is listed in annex 1 and 2.

All downloaded documents had to be reformatted in .txt form, so as to make them compatible with the linguistic software. These were subsequently put together in a series of subcorpora according to the following specific criteria.

The guiding principle of constituting the corpus was to structure the diachronic subcorpora in such a way that it follows the conceptual evolution of how an informal promise became legally enforceable. The 15th c. corpus represents roughly the period before the concept of consideration was established, while the cases in the 17th c. corpus show that the consideration had already become an abstract legal concept. The 16th c. corpus covers the period in between, when the concept was in full evolution. As mentioned previously the criteria for selection of text was that these must report common law court decisions in original language. There was no discrimination as to content. All decisions reported in a particular source were included. In other words, the selection was not content-driven. However, the Mansfield corpus was compiled in a different way: here case reports were selected if these were a part of the corpus of cases stipulating Mansfield's doctrine of consideration as moral obligation. Hence, this selection was content-driven.

In corpus linguistics, the size of the corpora involved in a study are frequently of similar sizes, so that comparisons can be made on similar basis. This was not possible in this research, due to the relative scarcity of the electronically accessible original language sources, in particular in relation to the earlier periods. For the Anglo-Norman texts, the word count was provided by the Anglo-Norman On-Line Hub. As far as the legal sources are concerned, HeinOnline has no tool that ascertains the word count for specific texts in its database. However, the linguistic software used for the study provides such information.

The word count for the corpora used for this research is as given in Chart 1. As the various subcorpora differ in size it is therefore essential that all comparisons should be made on the basis of relative frequency, which is the number of occurrences of a term in relation to the total number of words contained in a particular corpus. It is calculated by dividing the number of occurrences by the total number of words, multiplying the results by a figure in order to

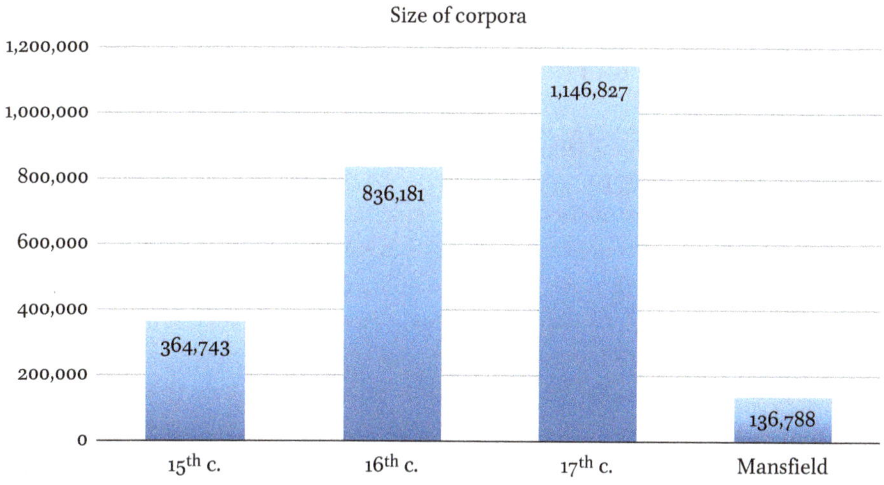

CHART 1 Word count in specially constituted subcorpora

move the decimal into a position that renders the result appropriate. In this study the relative frequency was calculated for every 100,000 words.

1.3 *Linguistic Analysis*

The linguistics software used for this study is the AntConc[5] concordance program, which is fully Unicode compliant, meaning that it can handle data in any language, including all European and Asian languages. Therefore, the multilingual nature of the corpus used for this research did not cause a problem. However, the diversity in medieval spelling could not be smoothed over by the software.

AntConc allows us to create word lists and search the text files for words, phrases and patterns, though not all the tools it offers are relevant to this study. Once a corpus is uploaded into the software, we can obtain the figures for the number of words the corpus contains (word tokens) and the number of unique word forms (word types) – as opposed to total numbers – that can be found in that corpus. It is important to stress that the statistics for the word types/tokens may be skewed by the medieval spelling variations as the software does

5 AntConc is a concordance program developed by Laurence Anthony, Director of the Centre of English Language Education at the Waseda University in Japan. There are versions available for Windows, Mac & Linux. The particular version used for this research is: AntConc 3.5.8m (2019). The program can be downloaded at the following pages, which also includes links to online guides and video tutorials: http://www.antlab.sci.waseda.ac.jp/antconc_index.html.

not recognise two different spellings of the same word as one word token. The study, therefore, did not include any discussion on type-token ratios for the texts in the corpus.

By far the greatest challenge of the linguistic analysis was the varying spellings or grammatical forms typical of medieval text production. While the HeinOnline database has a fuzzy search function that searches for terms similar in spelling, the linguistic software does not have this facility, though both allow for the possibility of wildcard searches, which are especially helpful in locating variations of a particular word. It has meant that certain search functions had to be done several times, once for each spelling variation, which could be as many as a dozen times for each search term. It is also likely that some freak spellings were not picked up. Proximity searches became exponential because every spelling of every term had to be tried in combination. At times this issue can be overcome by wildcard searches, which allow for a special character, usually an asterisk, to replace one or more characters at the beginning or end of a search term. This is, however, not always appropriate nor did it always deliver satisfactory results.

The different subcorpora were usually first searched for a series of terms and their various spelling variants relating to the concept of consideration and its forerunners. The search window size for this study will always be set at 100. The results were displayed in the so-called pre-set 'Key-Word-In-Context' format, which is the most common way to show concordance lines. KWIC places the search term in its context as found in the original text. These can then be sorted according to the words to the left and right of the search term and, hence, provide an excellent overview of the type of contexts in which the search terms occur. In Table 1 below we have an example of ten KWIC lines from the corpus extracted from volume 72 of the English Report on the basis of the search term 'consideration' and its various spelling variants (wildcard search of 'considera*'). The lines are cited here merely to illustrate the methodology. They were sorted according to alphabetical order of the word that precedes the search term.[6] This was adopted for all the KWIC tables used for this research. It facilitates looking for a particular terminological construction. By grouping these together it also gives us a precise idea of their numbers of

6 Level 1: 1L; Level 2: 1R; Level 3: 0.

TABLE 1 KWIC lines (extract) for 'considera*', vol. 72 of the English Report

upon full hearing whereof, and due and advised	consideration had of the said Conveyance, and of a
le case hors del court fuit referre al	consideration des 2 Chiefe Justices Popham & amp;
tiel proviso no sont pties queux ont asci5	considerae~n pur raiser lour estates. Et del auter
eclare sur estate execute, que ne besoigne ascun	consideraen: mes si fuisset use declare sur coven
sont mise en 1' endenture ils ne sont available	considera- csns, car les pols sont q ils ove
cestuy que vie; lc reason est default de	consideracin en cestuy que vie de jinder, si come
pur 24. ans est void estate pur fault de	consideracon en les covenantees, & donq le pchein
, quia n'est expss que el covenant en	consideration dadvanceibt ou pferiilt des issues
le fait que le covenant est fait en	consideration dadvancer les issues de son corps,
devant marriage Pson single nosme sans expsser en	consideracin de marriage ; en quel case ne fuit a

occurrence. These few lines are also a good illustration of the spelling variations, some of which can be quite unpredictable.

Besides the keyword search and KWIC display function, AntConc also offers the possibility of an 'advanced search' with more complex possibilities. It enables the search of KWIC lines with a second search term or set of search terms, either by typing them in one per line, or by uploading a list of search terms from another file. It is further possible to define the parameters for the context words and a word span which within the second (set of) search term(s) must appear. For example, a corpus is searched for the main search term 'consideration', which produces a number of KWIC lines. These lines can then be advance searched with a number of other terms, for example 'promise' or 'contract'. The word span adopted for this research is the widest possible context window that AntConc offers, namely 20 words to the left and 20 words to the right of the main search term – 'consideration' in this example. If, in our example, we find the word 'promise' to appear significantly more often than the word 'contract', we may conclude that the concept of consideration is more frequently discussed in a context of promise-making than in a context of contract.

The choice of secondary search term(s) to be used in specific advanced searches was guided by the doctrinal development of the concept of consideration. In view of the diversity of medieval spellings, these searches could be very time-consuming, hence it was a matter of producing the most effective results by searching the various time periods with the most relevant terminology.

Another possibility, searching for words or patterns that cluster together with the words immediately to the right or the left of the search term, is offered by the software's so-called clusters tool. The results can be ranked by frequency, range and probability. The cluster minimum and maximum size can be defined. For this study it was always set at minimum 2 and maximum 3. Table 2 presents a few examples selected from volume 72 English Reports. The column 'range' refers to the number of documents in which a particular cluster could be found.

Furthermore, the collocate tool was used in this study. It offers information on the sequence of words or terms that co-occur with the search term more often than would be expected by chance. The window span can be determined to the left and right of the search term. For this study it was always set at 5 words to the right and left of the search term. The results can be sorted by total frequency, frequency on the left or right of the search terms, or the start or end of the word, or by the value of a statistical measure between the search term and the collocate. In Table 3 are a few selected lines from the same reports by way of illustration (window: 5L, 5R).

The instability of spelling and grammatical forms in medieval texts meant that the results of these various linguistic search tools, could only be seen as indications rather than exact statistical information. Moreover, it is important to stress that the information obtained by using these various linguistics tools,

TABLE 2 Examples of clusters for 'consideration' in vol. 72 of the English Report

Rank	Freq.	Range	Cluster (search term on left)
1	17	13	consideration de
4	10	8	consideration que le
8	4	2	consideracon de marriage
11	4	3	consideracon que e pl
22	3	3	consideration ne fuit sufficient
			Cluster (search term on right)
1	27	16	en consideration
2	12	10	le consideration
6	5	5	bone consideration
9	4	2	available considerac
15	3	1	auters bone considerations

TABLE 3 Examples of collocates for 'consideration' in vol. 72 of the English Report

Rank	Freq.	Freq (L)	Freq (R)	Collocate
1	223	124	99	le
2	132	96	36	en
7	82	41	41	fuit
8	72	42	30	est
16	45	14	31	marriage
27	29	21	8	covenant

is *linguistic/lexico-grammatical* information, rather than *legal* information. We are, at this stage, less concerned with content and more with lexical and grammatical choices, with linguistic form and function that were used to realise meaning and convey a picture of reality as it was then in the legal minds.

Besides applying these automated linguistic tools, the analysis will also consider the language that provides the context in the concordance lines for the search terms. For this purpose, the language in the KWIC lines resulting from the various concordance searches has been grouped into three main types of language uses for the purpose of this study:

i. general language meaning/use:
   This is language comprehensible to the ordinary person.
   e.g.: "The court's decision was made in consideration of all the facts".
ii. general language meaning but use in a legal context:
   This is also comprehensible to all, but the legal context in which this language occurs adds legal meanings that may only be picked up by those with some legal training.
   e.g.: "The payment was promised in consideration of the marriage to his daughter".
iii. specialist/technical/abstract meaning and use:
   This language is abstract to a point that its meaning can no longer be understood by a non-specialist.
   e.g.: "The instrument imported a prima facie consideration".

To this categorisation the Latin uses have to be added. This does not refer to the Latin texts or passages, which have usually been disregarded altogether, but to the occurrences where the search term was embedded in a legal Latin phrase in an otherwise Anglo-French or Middle/Early Modern English text. There is, no doubt, some overlap between the different groups and the categorisation may appear somewhat artificial at times, but for the purpose of this study, it is essential to group concordance lines together for evaluation.

The main pointers to the use of a particular language register can be observed in the interaction between the lexical and grammatical patterning, because every meaning of a specific word will tend to have different patterns. Firth[7] famously said: "You shall know a word by the company it keeps". Grammar and lexis do not operate independently and as separate systems, but together as a single system.[8] Words with technical meanings 'behave' differently from the same words in general language contexts. In our example iii. above we find 'consideration' as a full noun, rather than in the causal link phrase of 'in consideration of' that is typical for general language usages.

The rest of this chapter discussing the results of the various linguistic studies, is structured chronologically, starting with the earliest actions of trespass on the case that predated the concept of consideration and ending on Mansfield's idea of consideration as a moral obligation. The description of the diachronic terminological study of specific terms falls into two parts for every term: a more general section on the entirety of the texts studied and a more specific and detailed description of the corpus work.

2 General Language Register

Before turning to the sources that are at the centre of this research, namely the Year Books and Law Reports, it may be of interest to take a brief look at texts in registers other than the legal one. This is to observe how the main lexical item in this study – consideration – is used in mainly non-legal texts.

A look at the definition in today's online Oxford English Dictionary shows 'consideration' to have manifold meanings. These can be divided into three groups:

7 J.R. Firth (1957) A synopsis of linguistics theory 1930–1955, in: *Studies in Linguistic Analysis*, Oxford: Philological Society, 1–32, at 11.

8 J. Sinclair (1991) *Corpus Concordance Collocation.* Oxford: OUP at 103; see also A. Goldberg (1995) *Constructions: A Construction Grammar Approach to Argument Structure,* Chicago: University of Chicago Press; S.T. Gries, D. Divjak (2009) Behavioral profiles: A corpus-based approach towards cognitive semantic analysis, in: V. Evand, S. Pourcel (eds.) *New Directions in Cognitive Linguistics,* Amsterdam and Philadelphia: John Benjamins.

- four of the eight definitions describe consideration in terms of careful thought/contemplation, viewing, observing typically over a period of time, taking into account, motives/reasons, deliberation/opinion/conclusion;
- two definitions deal with the notion of kindness/thoughtfulness for another and esteem, importance, consequences among men and for things;
- two definitions present consideration as payment or reward and as the promise/object of a contract.

In the English language, the beginning of the use of 'consideration' dates back to the Middle English of the 14th century (*consideracoun, consideracioun, consideracion*), with its etymological root in the Latin word *considerationem* (nom.: *consideratio* and the noun of the action from the past participle stem of *considerare* meaning to examine) and the Old French 12th century term of *consideracion*.

The definition in Anglo-Norman French of the word 'consideration'[9] that can be found in the Anglo-Norman Dictionary[10] is divided into four usages:

i. examination, reflection, study, contemplation;
ii. opinion, conclusion;
iii. idea, motive;
iv. legal decision, purchase.

The Anglo-Norman On-Line Hub also includes an electronically available corpus of 76 original language source texts, as described above in Section 1.1. Searching that corpus for the term 'consideration' in its various Anglo-Norman spellings, we obtained 62 hits, as follows:

- 32 hits for *"consideracion"*
- 1 hit for *"consideratione"*
- 17 hits for *"consideracioun"*
- 2 hits for *"consideraciun"*
- 10 hits for *"consideration"*

The majority of the sources are from the second half of the 14th century and a few date from the mid-13th century.

None of the results showed the use of the term in the legal sense, such as for the purposes of purchase/debt or in the context of a promise, agreement or exchange. The sense was always pertained to the general language register. In the majority of the cases, the meanings were: taking into account, having regard for, with regard to, in view of, etc. In two occurrences, the search term

9 The word can be found in following spelling variations: *consideracion, consideracione, consideracioun, consideraciun, consideration.*

10 Anglo-Norman Dictionary on the Anglo-Norman On-Line Hub www.anglo-norman.net.

appeared in the sense of contemplation/meditation and in both cases the source text was of a religious nature.

A collocates analysis revealed the following:

- 15 hits for *"priere"*, all of which occurred in the Anglo-Norman Letters and Petitions documents and not in specifically religious sources. The word was always a part of the same structure: *"considera* de ma/noz/nostre/susdites priere"*. It leads to the reasonable conclusion that it is probably a standard form in the register of petitions.
- 10 hits for *"regard"*, all except 2 following the pattern of: "considera*et regard". These all occurred in the same source, the Foedera, conventiones, litterae; et cujuscunque generis acta publica, inter regis Angliae, ab ingressu Gulielmi I. in Angliam, A.D. 1066. It may be reasonable to conclude that this is a part of the register of this sort of text.
- 10 hits for *"bon/bone"*, in 3 cases *bon** was found before *considera**, in 7 cases it was placed after the search term, in 3 of which it occurred in the same phrase: "consideration a ce qui/q'a/que, a l'effect que bone accorde".

An advanced proximity search of the Anglo-Norman Hub sources texts with a span of 20 words to the right and 20 to the left of the search term, confirmed that 'consideration' was not associated with typical contract words such as 'promise', 'covenant', 'contract' or 'agreement'. There were no proximity hits for any of the four terms, despite the fact that these terms occurred in the corpus:

- 443 hits for the various spellings of the word 'promise' (*promess, promès, promese, promis, promisse, pramesse, pramez, premés, premesse, premis*);
- 89 hits for the various spellings of the word 'contract' (*contract, contracte, contrait, contraite, contrat, contret*);
- 256 hits for the various spellings of the word 'covenant' (*covenant, covenand, covenaunt, covenaunte*);
- 3 hits with the various spellings of the word 'agreement' (*agreement, agrément, engrément*).

The proximity search with words that are particularly associated with medieval informal agreements, such as 'debt' and 'trespass', showed no proximity hits between the word 'consideration' and words like 'debt' and 'trespass', although these terms occurred in the corpus:

- 462 hits with the various spellings of the word 'debt' (*dette, det, dete, debt, debte, depte, deite, deitte, debit, decte, doite, duite, duyte, decies, dectes, dettus*)
- 743 hits with the various spellings of the word 'trespass' (*trespas, trespaas, trespace, trespase, trespass, trespasse, trespaz, trepas, trepaas, trepace, trepase, trespass, trepaz, treppas, tresspas*)

TABLE 4 'Contract' and 'covenant' as terms/proximity to other terms in the Anglo-Norman On-line Hub corpus

Search term	Hits	Proximity (20L, 20R)					
		Contract	Covenant	Debt	Promise	Trespass	Agreement
contract	89	–	19	15	1	11	0
covenant	256	19	–	17	6	14	0

TABLE 5 Search terms/proximity to 'consideration', 'contract', 'covenant' in the Anglo-Norman On-line Hub corpus

Search term	Hits	Prox. of consideration	Prox. of contract	Prox. of covenant
consideration	62	–	0	0
promise	443	0	1	6
contract	89	0	–	19
covenant	256	0	19	–
agreement	3	0	0	0
debt	462	0	15	17
trespass	743	0	11	14

However, a proximity search between 'contract' and 'covenant' and other terms typically associated with informal agreements, showed the results in Table 4.[11]

All quantitative information has been summarised in Table 5 (proximity search of 20 words to left and right).

The Anglo-Norman Hub is not a specifically legal source and it is relatively limited corpus material to the extent that given the wide-spread illiteracy, written texts were not very common and reflected the learned man's mind and

11 All the various spelling variations listed above have been respected in the search, which was carried out for every combination for spelling between both the search term and the proximity term.

vocabulary rather than those of the masses. The register of the collected texts is therefore also limited. Yet, it is reasonable to conclude that in the second half of the 14th century, the term 'consideration' tended to occur in general language meanings, such as examination, reflection, study, contemplation, opinion, conclusion, motive. It could not be found, as yet, in a general context of making promises or concluding agreements, contracts or covenants, nor in situations of debt or trespass, though admittedly the Anglo-Norman Hub includes very few specific legal texts.

3 Law Reporting

The Year Books and Law Reports were at the centre of this study, though for comparison's sake, abridgements and lexicons were also considered (see Sections 4 and 5). As explained, the common law sources were used to constitute the corpus with various diachronic subcorpora starting from the 15th century. Earlier sources were also studied and evaluated in relation to the research question. But these were not included in any corpus because they yielded too little data.

This section on law reporting is divided into three main parts, one for each of the following search terms: 'assumpsit', 'promise' and 'consideration'. Each of these subsections will be introduced with a chronological overview for every term. This includes a discussion of the earlier sources not considered for the corpus work. Then follows a detailed linguistic analysis using the AntConc software of every selected term in the corpus.

3.1 *Assumpsit and Its Forerunner Trespass on the Case*

As explained in the previous chapter, the concept of consideration was born from the action of assumpsit, the essence of which lies in the notion of making an undertaking to do something. Assumpsit materialised in the 15th century and arose primarily from the action of trespass on the case (13th century), that is of a wrongful act directly causing harm or injury and consisting in the recovery for the negligent performance of an undertaking. It is, therefore, also interesting to examine the language used in the formulation of this new action as the forerunner to the later evolving concept of consideration.

When studying the 14th century law reporting material from the reign of Edward II, Edward III and Richard II[12] we find no references to any conceptual thinking that informal promises may be enforceable. Any cases that could be

12 Detailed references for these Year Books can be found in annex 2.

considered as forerunners for the actions of assumpsit are all classified as trespass on the case actions. They are about making an undertaking, but were construed as quasi-trespasses because, although fundamentally of a contractual nature, procedurally speaking an action of covenant would not have succeeded for lack of deed under seal. While in the first half of the 14th century, we find very little evidence of such actions, these became more prominent in the latter part of that century.

The lack of references to the enforceability of informal promises is reflected in the lack of vocabulary that may express any such discussions. In the Edward II and Edward III Year Books, half a dozen uses of 'consideration' are all in the general sense of 'taking into consideration/having considered'. One mention of 'assumpsit' can be found in a Latin language context[13] and another, similar one, in the Anglo-French text.[14] Furthermore, we have 7 references to 'promise' in the original Law French text, four of which were part of declarative statements promising to undertake duties graciously, and that gifts and promises would not distract men from carrying out their duty to the best of their abilities.[15] Among the case reports of these early Year Books that cover the first third of the 14th century, two cases stand out as situations where money was exchanged for the making of a promise subsequently not honoured.[16] However, in neither case can we find the sort of language that will become characteristic of later trespass on the case or assumpsit actions.

Once we move into the second half of the 14th century, we come across actions like the *Humber Ferry case*,[17] which many considered the first action of taking the law into a new direction.[18] This was later disputed, among others by Plucknett, who considered that the case 'was not a precedent but a freak'.[19] Yet,

13 "...*illam conclusionem assumpsit*"; in: (1310) 3 & 4 Edward II, or 22 Selden Society at 118.

14 "...*de pus qe le baron ad assume la tenaunce en sa persone par son plee*"; in: (1329–1330) 3 & 4 Edward III, or 98 Selden Society at 598.

15 For example : "*En le comencement del eyre nous vous promismes de faire grace de ceo qe a nous appendoit*"; in: (1329–1330) 3 & 4 Edward III at 97, or 98 Selden Society at 195; "...*et ceo ne levrai pur doun ne pur promesse ne pur amur ne pur haungre ne pur nul ren qe issi ne servirai a moun power*"; in: (1321) 14 Edward II, or 85 Selden Society at 12.

16 (1321) 14 Edward II, or 86 Selden Society at 353; (1329–1330) 3 & 4 Edward III, or 97 Selden Society at 237. These cases are discussed in greater detail in Chapter 5.

17 *Bukton v Tounesende* (1348) Lib. Ass. 22 Edw III Folio 94a-94b, pl. 41, or LBEx.

18 J.B. Ames (1913) *Lectures on Legal History and Miscellaneous Legal Essays*, Cambridge: Harvard University Press, at 130: "earliest cases in which an assumpsit was laid in the declaration"; W.S. Holdsworth(1923) *History of English Law* vol. III, at 430: "special variety of trespass or deceit on the case which came to be known as the action of assumpsit". For more detailed discussion of this point, see Chapter 5 above.

19 Th. Plucknett (1956) *A Concise History of the Common Law*, 5th ed., Boston: Little, Brown and Co., at 441–442.

once the action was admitted it 'offered a fruitful soil for experiment'.[20] And with the decision in *Waldon v Marshall*,[21] just over twenty years later, we can safely say that the new action and its novel thinking were gaining definite ground. Admittedly, both reports are very short, but the language in both bears little resemblance to the linguistics expressions of the later assumpsit cases:

In the 7 lines of the *Humber Ferry Case* (1348), the main key words are:

avoit emprist a
a tort
nul tort
covenant
trespass

In the 17 lines of *Waldon v Marshall* (1369), we have the main key words:

manucepit
emprist
contra pacem
peace
covenant
negligence

Following those cases and in the YB 40–50 Edward III (1366–1377), we find an extensive use of the term 'trespass', frequently collocating with *vi & armis*,[22] which was a precondition in these early cases: proof was required of the use of force and arms and a breach of the King's peace for such trespass action to succeed. This was a remnant of criminal law from which these actions originated. Beside the typical trespass vocabulary, such as *maliciose fixit*, 'damages', 'tort', 'diligence' and 'guarantee', we increasingly come across terms that describe the making of undertakings, mainly in the form of *il emprist/imprist* ('he undertakes'). In *Waldon v Marshall*[23] the action is worded in Latin with *manucepit* as the term to signal the undertaking made. In a surgeon's negligence case of

20 C.H.S. Fifoot (1949) *History and Sources of the Common Law: Tort and Contract*, London: Stevens, at 331.

21 Y.B Mich. 43 Ed. III, 33, 38, or LBEx.

22 e.g. YB 46 Edw. III, 19b, or LBEx ("*Trespass port devers un Ferrer, de ceo q il enclowe son chival*").

23 YB 43 Edw. III, 33, 38, or LBEx.

1374[24] we find, in the 43 lines, 12 uses of *emprist* (or variants) to describe the action. We find 5 uses of *emprist* (and variants) in the 36 line report. In the 7 volumes of the Richard II Year Books[25] we have no match for the key word search of 'assumpsit'.

As we come to the 15th century sources, we find a continued use of the trespass vocabulary, as well as *emprist* often in a context of covenant. For example: *Emprise de faire at pl' un novel meason deins un certain temps ... my fait le meason a tort.*[26] During Henry VI's reign (1422–1461), actions on the case dealt increasingly with the notion of deceit. These arose from facts, not of mal feasance, but of non feasance. Hence, the notion of trespass or quasi-trespass was no longer appropriate and a new principle was needed: the breach of an undertaking became considered as deceit. In cases where the plaintiff's loss enriched the defendant, it was seen as aggravated deceit. The use of the word *emprist* gave way to a frequent use of assumpsit in Latin phrases[27] together with an increased occurrence of terms such as 'deceit', 'bargain', 'covenant' a *quid pro quo*. In the discussion of some of these cases, the judges allude to past cases or hypothetical scenarios, but again the terms used are usually dominated by bargain and covenant, rather than *emprist* : for example: "*...le covenant le def. fuit; jeo face covenant ove un carpend pur me fair un meason; face covenant ove moy a fair* etc..."[28]

In the 16th century reports we find a timid use of the term 'assumpsit' or similar. Assumpsit cases were still not labelled as such in the early 16th century. Many were categorised in the Index of Subjects by the (modern) editor as such, but the word 'assumpsit' did not often appear in the reports. It was the nature of the case that attracted the label. In other words, while the new action was increasingly becoming a legal reality, the textual evidence did not shown the term 'assumpsit' as an established legal technical term or category. The key words in the actual case reports tended to be: 'undertaking', 'condition', 'obligation' and the legal vocabulary is 'covenant', 'debt', 'contract', 'trespass'. These

24 YB 48 Edw. III, 6, 11, or LBEx (*"Action sur le case vers Surgeon, que emprist de curer home del plague, & luy mahim"*).

25 Detailed references in annex 2/II, electronically accessible on HeinOnline.

26 YB 11 Hen. IV, 33, 60, or LBEx (*"Action sur le case vers carpenter pur non feasant de meason"*).

27 Action on the case examples: 7 Hen.VI,1, 3, or LBEx: deceit, bargain, quid pro quo; 9 Hen. VI, 53, 37, or LBEx: deceit sur le cas, bargain; 11 Hen. VI, 18, 24, or LBEx: extensive Latin use of *assumpsit* and Anglo-French use of *assumpc, assumer, assumption*; 14 Hen. VI, 18, 58, or LBEx: extensive use of covenant; 20 Hen. VI, 34, 4, or LBEx: deceit, bargain, covenant.

28 14 Hen. VI,18, 58 ; see also : 26 Hen. VI, 55, 12, or LBEx.

assumpsit cases were often reported by paraphrasing, in conditional clauses, what one of the parties is alleged to have said or promised:

> ...Si jeo baile biens a un home a garder savement, et il *emprent* a ceo faire...[29]
>
> (If I bail goods to someone to keep safely, and he undertakes to do this)
>
> ...le testatour dit a luy, si il ne paya vous jeo voile payer, sur quel promesse le pleintife delyver lez bienz...[30]
>
> (the testator said to him, 'If he does not pay you, I will pay'; upon which promise the plaintiff delivered the goods)
>
> Si home *assume* sur luy a moy a arrer et seminer ma terre...[31]
>
> (If a man undertakes for me to plough and sow my land...)
>
> ...home *assume* sur luy de paier...[32]
>
> (a man took upon himself to pay)

In the Caryll Reports, the editor lists five reports as dealing with assumpsit, three of which actually contain the word 'assumpsit', as well as *emprist/emprent* ('undertook/undertakes'). In these cases, 'assumpsit' tends to be a part of a Latin phrase, rather than integrated into the Anglo-French text as it was later. The key words in the other two are trespass, debt and covenant.

In *Johnson v Baker*[33] (1493)

> ...le deffendant de ceo [fair] accordant *super se assumpsit* [...] A que le deffendant dit que *non assumpsit modo et forma* [...] le pleintiffe ad alledge que *emprist* le charge sur luy [...]ceo fuit le chose que covient estre traverse et nemy *quod non assumpsit*...
>
> (...the defendant took upon himself (*super se assumpsit*) to do this accordingly [...] To this the defendant said *Non assumpsit modo et forma* [...] the plaintiff has alleged that the defendant undertook the charge [...] and that was the thing which ought to have been traversed (not *Non assumpsit*)...)

29 *Hayden v Raggeldon*, CP 40/992, m. 451, in Caryll Reports, or 116 Selden Society at 608.

30 *Cleymond v Vyncent*, YB Trin. 27 Hen. VIII, 23, 21, or 119 Selden Society at 46–47.

31 From BL MS. Hargrave 322, 13v, in Dyer Lost Notebooks, or 110 Selden Society at 466.

32 *Lord Zouche v Digby*, in Dyer Lost Notebooks, or 110 Selden Society at 416.

33 C.P., Hil. 1493. Record CP 40/914, m. 104, in: 115 Selden Society at 135.

In *Orwell v Mortoft*[34] (1505)

> …, quel chose a faire le defendant *super se assumpsit* […]
> et luy chargera per cest parol '*super se assumpsit*'…;
> (…the defendant took upon himself to do this […] and charge him by the words 'took upon himself (*super se assumpsit*)').

In *Hayden v Raggeldond*[35] (1510)

> …Si jeo baile biens a un home a garder savement, et il *emprent* a ceo faire…;
> (…If I bail goods to someone to keep safely, and he undertakes to do this…)

In the Selden Society edition of the Year Books 12–14 Henry VIII (1520–1523), the Index of Subjects lists the action of assumpsit as relevant in two cases. Yet the word does not appear in the reports. The key words that describe the actions are 'promise' and 'damage',[36] 'covenant', 'contract', 'grant', 'condition' and 'favour'.[37] Similarly, in the English translation of the Dalison reports (1552–1558), we find 'assumpsit' twice to describe the type of action at hand,[38] but the action is not described as such in the French original text.

In the second volume of the Dyer Lost Notebooks (second half of 16th c.), six cases come under the category of 'assumpsit', the reports of which show more extensive use of the word 'assumpsit' (7 hits in the six reports), as well as other synonyms, such as *assume/assuma* (4 hits) and *assumption* (5 hits). All were translated by Baker with 'undertake/undertaking', which underlines that we are well within the ambit of meaning that is fundamental to an action of assumpsit – someone undertaking to do something. Staying with this Dyer Lost Notebook for the moment, we can observe that the act of making an undertaking can be expressed using the verb form, such as:

> …home assume sur luy de paier…[39]
> (a man took upon himself to pay)

34 CP, Mich. 1505, in: 116 Selden Society at 494.
35 CP 40/992, m. 451, in: 116 Selden Society at 608.
36 *Cleymond v Vyncent* (King's Bench 1520), in: 119 Selden Society, at 46.
37 *Southwall v Huddelston and Reynolds* (Common Pleas 1523), in: 119 Selden Society, at 139.
38 *Benger v Pert* (1552 King's Bench) KB 27/1162, mm. 89, 134; *Rolf v Aucher* (1557 King's Bench) KB 27/1182, mm. 40,156, 169, 186;
39 *Lord Zouche v Digby*, in Dyer Lost Notebooks, or 110 Selden Society at 416.

> Si home assume sur luy a moy a arrer et seminer ma terre...[40]
> (If a man undertakes for me to plough and sow my land...)

We also find uses of the noun form in specifically legal phrases:

> ...In evidence sur lissue Non assumpsit modo et forma, fuit agree per curiam...[41]
> (In evidence upon the issue non assumpsit modo et forma, it was agreed by the court...)

> Action sur le case sur assumption/assumpsit[42]
> (action on the case of an undertaking/assumpsit)

The remaining noun form uses, accompanied by an article or adjective, are more akin to abstract concepts or discussions thereof. For example, in a case[43] from the Northampton assizes on the autumn circuit of 1571, we can read:

> ...Lassumpsit covient estre all plaintife mesme, ou al ascun auter a que le plaintife agree, autrement nest bon. Et sil count dun simple assumpsit, et levidence prove un conditionell assumpsit, levidence nest bon...
> (An *assumpsit* must be to the plaintiff himself, or to some other person to whom the plaintiff agrees, or else it is not good. And if he counts of a simple *assumpsit*, the evidence proves a conditional *assumpsit*, the evidence is not good.)

Other examples:

> Et per luy si lassumpsit soitt conditionell, destre performe del parte le defendant, et il dit Ne assuma point modo et forma, cest conditionell promis del parte le defendant ne garrante lissue le defendant, car conditionell assumption est assumption.[44]
> (And, according to him, if the undertaking is conditional [on something] to be performed on the defendant's side, and he says 'He did not undertake in the manner and form [alleged]', this conditional promise on

40 BL MS. Hargrave 322, fo.13v, in Dyer Lost Notebooks, or 110 Selden Society at 466.
41 Northampton assizes, autumn circuits 1559, in Dyer Lost Notebooks, or 110 Selden Society at 420.
42 in Dyer Lost Notebooks, or 110 Selden Society at 453 (dated 1573) and 466 (undated).
43 Northampton assizes, autumn circuits 1571, in 110 Selden Society at 452.
44 From Chr. Yelverton Rep., BL MS. Hargrave 322, fo. 13r, in 110 Selden Society at 457.

the defendant's side does not warrant the defendant's issue, for a conditional undertaking is an undertaking.)

...fuit agree per curiam [...] que un express promise et assumpsit a paier le monie pur le baraine...[45]

(...it was agreed by the court [...] that there should be given and put in evidence an express promise and undertaking to pay the money for the bargain...)

The word 'assumption' can also be found interchangeably with 'assumpsit' in a non-Latin context. For example, compare *levidence prove un conditionell assumpsit*[46] with *car conditionell assumption est assumption.*[47] This case of metalinguistic[48] use appears to suggest that by virtue of the definitional description, the term is established. Similarly, *un expres promise et assumpsit a paier"*[49] and *le defendant trauerz le promis et lassumcion.*[50] We even have assumption in the legal phrase *El port sur le cas sur assumption.*[51] The verb form describes the process of making an undertaking. This descriptive form renders the action less abstract.

3.1.1 The 15th c. Corpus

This corpus contains 364,743 words. To search for the term assumpsit, the wildcard option 'assump*' was taken, as that covers the necessary possibilities of spellings. 'Assumpsit' is discussed in only two cases and the term appears 5 times in the whole 15th c. subcorpus, this represents a relative frequency of 1.37 per 100,000 words. This does not mean that making informal promises legally enforceable was not discussed or dealt with in the courts, it just means that the term 'assumpsit' was less in use than other phrases such as 'trespass on the case'. Indeed, when searching this corpus for 'trespass' ('trespa*') we can find 410 hits. Not all of these occurrences deal with trespass on the case in the sense of informal promises, but it shows that in this particular corpus informal undertakings were still discussed using the "older" terminology of trespass on the case.

45 Dyer Lost Notebooks, or 110 Selden Society at 420.
46 Dyer Lost Notebooks Reports, or 110 Selden Society at 452.
47 Dyer Lost Notebooks Reports, or 110 Selden Society at 457.
48 'Metalinguistic' here relates to the function of language in which the language itself is discussed.
49 Dyer Lost Notebooks Reports, or 110 Selden Society at 420.
50 Spelman Reports, or 93 Selden Society at 3–4.
51 Dyer Lost Notebooks Reports, or 110 Selden Society at 466.

The advanced proximity search function, that looks for other terms in the vicinity of 20 words to the left and to the right of the primary search term, has shown no terms typically associated with formal or informal contractual undertakings, such as 'consideration', 'contract', 'covenant', 'debt', 'promise' and *quid pro quo*. As the primary term search only yielded 5 lines, it would not have been reasonable to make any fundamental deductions from examining the KWIC lines in details. Similarly, the clusters and collocates tools did not reveal meaningful results.

3.1.2 The 16th c. Corpus

The subcorpus for the following century was considerably larger, it contained 836,181 words. The terms 'assumpsit' ('assump*') occurs 77 times, with a relative frequency of 9.21 per 100,000 words.

From the textual evidence, we can observe that the use of the term 'assumpsit' was more extensive in the 16th century than in earlier sources as described above. Also, there was no longer the previous great variety of forms and spellings. Other terms that tended to appear in actions on the case and actions of assumpsit in the earlier sources continued to be prominent in this mainly Elizabethan corpus. The use of the terms such as 'debt' and 'covenant' are still more frequent than 'contract' or 'promise', though it is striking that in the proximity search, both 'promise' and 'contract' score highest among the secondary search terms, despite the fact that their relative frequencies are among the lowest.

The template for Table 6 has been used throughout the statistical analysis for this study. The second and third columns give the absolute (N) and relative frequencies with which each term occurs in the specific (sub) corpus. The subsequent three columns provide information on the proximity of some secondary terms to the primary term, which is 'assumpsit' in the table below. The fourth column (P) shows the number of times the secondary terms occurs in a proximity of 20 words to the right and to the left of the primary search term. The fifth column (P/N_0) expresses that frequency of proximity (P) in relation to the number of occurrences of the primary term (N_0). For the last column the frequency of proximity of the secondary term (P) is calculated in relation to its own absolute frequency (N). For example, in the table below 'assumpsit' occurs 77 times and 'consideration' 240 times. On three occasions, 'consideration' is within twenty words of 'assumpsit', which represents 3.9% of the 77 occurrences of 'assumpsit' (P/N_0) and 1.3% of the 240 occurrences of 'consideration' (P/N).

The collocate tool has shown the words 'plead', 'verdict' and 'promise' to be among the first in the frequency list. The clusters search yielded the results in Table 7.

TABLE 6 Search terms/proximity to 'assumpsit' in the 16th c. corpus

Search term (incl. various spellings)	Hits (= N)	Rel. freq. (100,000 words)	Proximity occurrences (= P)	Prox. to 'assump*' (= P/N_o)	Relative proximity (= P/N)
assump*	77 (= N_o)	9.21	N/A	N/A	N/A
consideration	240	28.70	3	3.9%	1.3%
contract	111	13.27	5	6.5%	4.5%
covenant	476	56.93	0	0	0
debt	707	84.55	5	6.5%	0.7%
promise	94	11.24	10	13%	10.6%

TABLE 7 Clusters for 'assumpsit' in the 16th c. corpus (cluster size min. 2, max. 3)

Rank	Freq.	Range	Cluster (search term on left) 142 cluster types; 154 cluster tokens
1	3	2	assumpsit modo
4	3	1	assumpsit plead verdict
6	2	1	assumpsit secum quator
14	1	1	assump-tionis & promissionis
Rank	**Freq.**	**Range**	**Cluster (search term on right)** 123 cluster types; 154 cluster tokens
1	13	5	non assumpsit
4	3	3	plead non assumpsit
5	3	2	plede non assumpsit
6	3	1	sur non assumpsit
7	2	1	in assumpsit

It shows that legal phrases tend to cluster with the term 'assumpsit'. This is confirmed by the examination of the concordance lines where we can observe that the term appears firmly embedded into the Law French language as a word in its own right, no longer needing an accompanying explanation, nor necessarily placed within a Latin context or phrase. It occurs as a term expressing an established concept. It never occurs in a Middle English context.

TABLE 8 Language register for 'assumpsit' in the 16th c. corpus (836,181 words)

Language	Matches	% of total
general language	1	1%
general legal language	4	5%
technical language	54	70%
Latin	18	24%
Total	77	–

The distribution of the language register in the 'assumpsit' concordance lines also confirms the use of technical language in the textual context of the word. In almost three quarter of the term's occurrences are we dealing with a specifically legal technical language register (see Table 8).

The immediate surrounding language is also littered with technical legal terms, almost exclusively in noun forms. Of the 54 KWIC lines, where 'assumpsit' has a technical meaning, only three show no technical language in the immediate vicinity of 'assumpsit'. In 13 KWIC lines, we can observe general legal language as well as technical terms. We frequently find the legal phrase *action sur le case sur assumpsit* or similar variants and it acts as the signpost for the nature of the action. While in earlier sources, it tended to be the modern editors who labelled actions as assumpsit, in this corpus we find the categorisation clearly highlighted in the original sources. The term is used in a specifically technical way. Not only can it be found between two full stops as a simple statement of fact or signposting the type of action, but it is frequently combined with a definite article (*l'*/*le*) or with prepositions such as *en*, *in*, *sur*, and *pur*. We can also see 'assumpsit' repeatedly occurring in combination with *non*, such as *sur non assumpsit* or *plead non assumpsit*, and a few times in Latin phrases, such as *indebitat*(*us*) *assumpsit*, *non assumpsit modo & forma* or *super se assumpsit*.

3.1.3 The 17th c. Corpus

In the 1,146,827 words of the 17th c. corpus, 'assumpsit' can be found on 303 occasions, which represents a relative frequency of 26.42 per every 100,000 words. Whilst the relative frequency for all selected terms have risen, the proximity search does not necessarily show the same trend. Comparing the percentages in the last two column of Table 9 below with the figures for the 16th c. (see Table 6 above), we can observe that, in the 17th c., the term 'consideration' can be found more frequently in the close context of 'assumpsit', whereas there is a drop for 'contract' and 'promise', which is particularly steep for the latter. In the case of 'contract', it is interesting to note that the drop is more marked

TABLE 9 Search terms/proximity to 'assumpsit' in the 17th c. corpus

Search term (incl. various spellings)	Hits (= N)	Rel. freq. (100,000 words)	Proximity occurrences (= P)	Prox. to 'assump*' (= P/N_0)	Relative proximity (= P/N)
assump*	303 (= N_0)	26.42	N/A	N/A	N/A
consideration	744	64.87	34	11.2%	4.6%
contract	280	24.42	5	1.7%	1.8%
covenant	1099	95.83	4	1.3%	0.4%
debt	1388	121.03	14	4.6%	1%
promise	324	28.25	10	3.3%	3.1%

TABLE 10 Language register for 'assumpsit' in the 17th c. corpus (1,146,827 words)

Language	Matches	% of total
general language	0	0%
general legal language	0	0%
technical language	303	100%
Latin	0	0%
Total	**303**	–

in relation to the occurrence to 'assumpsit'. In the 17th c. corpus 1.8% of the occurrence of 'contract' can be found in the proximity of 'assumpsit' (4.5% in the 16th c.) while in only 1.7% of the occurrence of 'assumpsit' can we find 'contract' in its proximity, as opposed to 6.5% in the 16th c. 'Covenant' and 'debt' remain both low, despite their high relative frequency.

A more detailed study of the concordance lines reveals that these all lie within the technical language register (Table 10).

A closer contextual examination shows that in a third of the KWIC lines we can find, beside the technical legal language, also general legal language. In 22% of the KWIC lines there are references to financial matters, which is in marked contrast to the contextual language in the 16th c. corpus, where in a mere 8% of the KWIC lines do we find references to financial matters. This is also reflected in the search for clusters, where payment figures in the highest ranking clusters with the search terms to the left (Table 11).

The application of the collocation and the clusters tools confirms 'assumpsit' collocates and clusters with specifically legal technical terms (Tables 11 and 12).

TABLE 11 Clusters for 'assumpsit' in the 17th c. corpus (cluster size min. 2, max. 3)

Rank	Freq.	Range	Cluster (search term on left) 433 cluster types; 606 cluster tokens
1	15	5	assumpsit fuit
3	10	4	assumpsit de
14	5	3	assumpsit de payer
24	3	2	assumpsit modo & forma
31	2	2	assumpsit en consideration
Rank	**Freq.**	**Range**	**Cluster (search term on right)** 276 cluster types; 606 cluster tokens
1	50	9	non assumpsit
3	36	8	case sur assumpsit
8	15	5	plead non assumpsit
9	9	5	indebitatus assumpsit

TABLE 12 Collocates for 'assumpsit' in the 17th c. corpus (collocate types: 675; collocate tokens: 3,030; sorted by frequency)

Rank	Freq.	Freq (L)	Freq (R)	Collocate
1	273	139	134	le
4	78	71	7	case
7	64	53	11	action
19	26	9	17	consideration
25	22	15	7	defendant
28	21	2	19	plaintiff

3.2 *Promise*

Before studying the term 'consideration' in depth, it may be of interest to pause and examine the use of the word 'promise', the notion of which is an important signpost on the road to the concept of consideration.

In the early Year Books and Selden Society sources we can observe an increase with time of the use of 'promise' (Table 13). As it is not possible to ascertain the word count for these sources and hence to calculate a relative frequency, the

TABLE 13 Frequencies of 'promise' in a selection of the Selden Society (Annual) Series and Ames Foundation Publications[a]

Date	Source	'promise'
end 13th c.	Earliest Engl. Reports (111, 112, 122, 123 SS) – 947 pages	2
14th c.	Y.B. Edward II & III – 6449 pages	7
end 14th c.	Y.B. Richard II – approx. 759 pages	3
1422	1 Henry VI (50 SS) – 131 pages	none
1409/1470	10 Edw. IV & 49 Hen. VI (47 SS) – 172 pages	none
1477–1509	Select Cases Before The King's Council in The Star Chamber, vol. I (16 SS) – 278 pages (Middle English)	4
1485–1509	Select Cases in the Council of Henry VII (75 SS) – 169 pages (Middle English)	6
1489–1522	Caryll Reports part 2 (116 SS) – 349 pages	3
1502–1540	The Reports of Sir John Spelman, vol. I (93 SS) – 238 pages	12
1509–1544	Select Cases Before The King's Council in The Star Chamber, vol. II (25 SS) – 331 pages (Middle English)	11
1520–1523	Y.B. 12–14 Henry VIII (119 SS) – 192 pages	12
1541–1581	Lost Notebooks Dyer vol. I & II (109 & 110 SS) – 468 pages	21

a Detailed references can be found in annex 2 (iii) and (iv).

number of pages are provided for each document to give an rough indication of the length of each reports.

As the concept of consideration originated from the growing need to allow informal agreements to become enforceable under certain circumstances, the earliest actions were (quasi-)trespass on the case, from which the action of assumpsit developed. Viewed from our 21st century perspective, we clearly consider these to be situations at the heart of which a promise was made and relied upon.

We can observe from the Anglo-Norman sources, which date from roughly the same period, that the word 'promise' occurred 443 times, which is a similar frequency to 'debt' (462 instances). We also find 256 instances of 'covenant' and 743 instances of 'trespass', but only 62 instances of 'consideration'. In the early legal sources the use of the word promise appears rather reluctant and, hence, the corresponding notion somewhat tentative. Instead, the meanings are expressed in terms of undertakings to be assumed. The step from the hitherto proprietary thinking of a contractual exchange in actions of debt, was still too deeply rooted, to give way to the new promissory thinking of assumpsit and later the concept of consideration.

Only seven matches for promise could be found in the late 13th/14th c. Year Books of Edward II and his successor Edward III.[52] It must be stressed that these specific sources represent a substantial corpus by themselves, covering three quarters of a century, while most other sources only cover about half of that time span. Four references were part of declarative statements promising to undertake duties graciously, and that gifts and promises would not distract men from carrying out their duty to the best of their abilities.[53] Of the seven matches for 'promise', only one – promising to cure a wounded hand – described a situation that was characteristic for trespass on the case or assumpsit actions.[54] In the Year Books of the reign of Richard II, which covered the last quarter of the 14th century, we find three references to 'promise', all in the report of the same case, namely a 1383 action in debt for the payment of a hundred shillings or a pipe of wine for developing businesses on behalf of the defendant.[55] This 13th and 14th century textual evidence, confirms that the use of the term 'promise' in the context of making an informal agreement enforceable was not widespread.

Moving to the 15th century sources, we do not find a vastly increased use of the word 'promise' either. In the *Select Cases Before The King's Council in The Star Chamber*, vol. I[56] and the *Select Cases in the Council of Henry VII*,[57] the term occurs ten times, but in only three cases does it relate to a contractual situation. It is also interesting to note that these two reports are in Middle English rather than Law French and there is a more frequent use of 'promise' in the non-contractual/legal sense.

52 Listed in annex 2.

53 For example : *"En le comencement del eyre nous vous promismes de faire grace de ceo qe a nous appendoit"* ; in: (1329–1330) 3 & 4 Edward III, or 97 Selden Society at 195; *"...et ceo ne levrai pur doun ne pur promesse ne pur amur ne pur haungre ne pur nul ren qe issi ne servirai a moun power"*; in: (1321) 14 Edward II, Part I, or 86 Selden Society at 12.

54 *"...ly promist de ly garrir de la play pur xl. S., et il resceut les xl. S. et il nad my garry, eynz par sa defaute il ad perdu sa mayn"* ; in: Eyre of London, (1321) 14 Edward II, Part II, or 86 Selden Society, at 353.

55 (1383) 6 Richard II, or Ames Foundation Publications, at 217.

56 *Select Cases Before the King's Council in the Star Chamber commonly called The Court of Star Chamber*, vol. I (A.D. 1477–1509) 16 Selden Society.

57 *Select Cases Before the King's Council in the Star Chamber commonly called The Court of Star Chamber*, vol. II (A.D. 1509–1544) 25 Selden Society.

By the end of the 15th and beginning of the 16th century, informal agreements could no longer be disregarded for lack of deed. Relief was granted to damages due to malfeasance, nonfeasance and deceit, but also in cases where the defendant had no benefit from the deceit, yet the plaintiff suffered loss and damage. In 1523 St. German wrote in his Dialogue[58] which was not a law report but more akin to a treatise:

> "if he to whom the promise is made have a charge by reason of the promise [...] he shall have an action [...] though he that made the promise had no wordly profit by it".

This clearly indicates that the focus of the newly evolving action, was less the plaintiff's deception/defendant's deceit (tort) but rather the promise/undertaking (contract) made at the start of the interaction between the two parties. Yet, despite the fact that St. German uses the term 'promise' in his writings, it took a while to trickle through and feature prominently in the law reports to describe and discuss the enforceability of informal agreements.

During the Elizabethan reign in the 16th century and into the early 17th century, the use of the word 'promise' not only increased, but also adopted a more specifically legal meaning, as it appeared in restricted contexts of contract formation.

3.2.1 The 15th c. Corpus

A wildcard search for 'promis*' to cover spelling variations showed the term occurred 8 times in the 15th c. corpus that contains 364,743 words. This represents a relative frequency of 2.19 per 100,000 words.

The word 'promise' is never a technical term. It always describes the act of making a declaration or assurance to another person, stating a commitment to giving/doing/refraining from doing something or guaranteeing that a specific thing will or will not happen.[59] In view of the low number of concordance lines, no general conclusions could reasonably be made from their examination. More specifically none of the 8 KWIC lines show the term to be used in a contractual context (i.e. the exchange of a promise in consideration of something). The advanced proximity search function looking for other terms in the vicinity of the primary search term, has shown no terms typically associated with formal or informal contractual undertakings, such as 'consideration',

58 Ch. St. German (1518/1974), *Doctor and Student*, Second Dialogue, Chapter 24, edited by Th. Plucknett, J. Barton (1974) for the Selden Society, vol. 91.

59 See definitions in the Oxford English Dictionary.

'contract', 'covenant', 'debt', 'promise' and *quid pro quo*. Similarly, the clusters and collocates tools did not reveal meaningful results.

3.2.2 The 16th c. Corpus

In the much larger subcorpus for the following century, containing 836,181 words, the term 'promise' ('promis*') occurs 94 times, with a relative frequency of 11.24 per 100,000 words.

From the advanced proximity search, we can learn that 'consideration' figures most prominently among the terms in the proximity of promise, although the percentage for the relative proximity is much lower (Table 14). While the term 'assumpsit' shows the lowest relative frequency, the proximity figures are both high in relation to the other secondary search terms.

Whilst 'promise' is strictly speaking not a technical term, it appears to associate in this corpus with more technical terms. From the highest ranking clusters and collocates, presented in Tables 15 and 16, we find that 'pay', 'defendant' and 'case' are amongst such terms.

Considering the KWIC lines in more details, we can observe that, although the term is used in a general legal language register, including legal technical vocabulary. In contrast to the corpus of the previous century, the context is always contractual or quasi-contractual (Table 17) and in a third of the concordance lines, the surrounding language relates to financial matters.

TABLE 14 Search terms/proximity to 'promise' in the 16th c. corpus

Search term (incl. various spellings)	**Hits (= N)**	**Rel. freq. (100,000 words)**	**Proximity occurrences (= P)**	**Prox. to 'promis*' (= P/N$_0$)**	**Relative proximity (= P/N)**
promis*	94 (= N$_0$)	11.24	N/A	N/A	N/A
consideration	240	28.70	16	17%	6.7%
contract	111	13.27	4	4.3%	3.6%
covenant	476	56.93	0	0	0
debt	707	84.55	2	2.1%	0.3%
assumpsit	77	9.21	10	10.6%	13%

TABLE 15 Clusters for 'promise' in the 16th c. corpus (cluster size min. 2, max. 3)

Rank	Freq.	Range	Cluster (search term on left) 155 cluster types; 188 cluster tokens
1	7	2	promise a
2	6	2	promise fuit
5	4	1	promise pur pay
9	2	1	promise et declare
Rank	**Freq.**	**Range**	**Cluster (search term on right)** 143 cluster types; 188 cluster tokens
1	14	2	sur promise
3	4	2	le promise
4	3	1	ceo promise
8	3	1	le deft promise

TABLE 16 Collocates for 'promise' in the 16th c. corpus (collocate types: 440; collocate tokens: 940)

Rank	Freq.	Freq (L)	Freq (R)	Collocate
1	51	36	15	le
8	15	15	0	case
9	12	12	0	deft
15	9	0	9	pay
25	6	2	4	consideration

TABLE 17 Language register for 'promise' in the 16th c. corpus (836,181 words)

Language	Matches	% of total
general language	0	0%
general legal language	78	83%
technical language	0	0%
Latin	16	17%
Total	**94**	–

3.2.3 The 17th c. Corpus

In the over 1.1 million word 17th c. corpus, 'promise' occurs 324 times, which represents a relative frequency of 28.25 for every 100,000 words. The relative frequency of all search terms rise with a proportion between one and a half and three times between the 16th and 17th centuries. Yet the figures for the proximity searches tell a different story. There is a rise in the occurrence of the term 'consideration' in the proximity of promise. 'Covenant' and 'debt' also increase, whilst those for 'contract' fall and there is also a substantial drop for 'assumpsit' (see Table 18).

The register of the contextual language is, similar to the corpus of the previous century, general language used in a specifically legal context, including legal technical terms. We are dealing exclusively with contractual or quasi-contractual uses (Table 19).

TABLE 18 Search terms/proximity to 'promise' in the 17th c. corpus

Search term (incl. various spellings)	Hits (= N)	Rel. freq. (100,000 words)	Proximity occurrences (= P)	Prox. to 'promis*' (= P/N_0)	Relative proximity (= P/N)
promis*	324 (= N_0)	28.25	N/A	N/A	N/A
consideration	744	64.87	76	23.5%	10.2%
contract	280	24.42	4	1.2%	1.4%
covenant	1099	95.83	5	1.5%	0.5%
debt	1388	121.03	22	6.8%	1.6%
assumpsit	303	26.42	10	3.1%	3.3%

TABLE 19 Language register for 'promise' in the 17th c. corpus (1,146,827 words)

Language	Matches	% of total
general language	0	0%
general legal language	318	98%
technical language	0	0%
Latin	6	2%
Total	**324**	–

TABLE 20 Clusters for 'promise' in the 17th c. corpus (cluster size min. 2, max. 3)

Rank	Freq.	Range	Cluster (search term on left) 431 cluster types; 656 cluster tokens
1	42	7	promise a
3	14	2	promise a paier
5	11	3	promise fuit
17	4	3	promise en consideration
Rank	**Freq.**	**Range**	**Cluster (search term on right)** 390 cluster types; 656 cluster tokens
1	67	7	le promise
6	11	4	home promise
13	5	5	case sur promise
20	4	3	le defendant promise

TABLE 21 Collocates for 'promise' in the 17th c. corpus (collocate types: 773; collocate tokens: 3,280)

Rank	Freq.	Freq (L)	Freq (R)	Collocate
1	206	143	63	le
16	40	15	25	consideration
22	26	24	2	case
25	24	14	10	action
26	23	0	23	paier

Amongst the 318 vernacular KWIC lines, 76% include highly technical language in the immediate vicinity of the main search term, while 17% include financial related terminology. This is confirmed by both the clusters and collocates tools which show that technical terms and financial related terms tend to cluster and collocate with 'promise' (Table 20).

3.3 *Consideration*

Turning to the main focus of this analysis, namely the word 'consideration', we can observe a steady increase in its use in law reporting. But beside this quantitative rise in the occurrence of the term, we can also observe a semantic shift, in particular in the later corpora. By examining in greater detail the language that constitutes the context of the use of 'consideration', we are able to draw conclusions on the semantic evolution of that term.

In the 13th, 14th and 15th century law reporting sources,[60] the word 'consideration' is very rarely used and any occurrence has a general language meaning such as: considering a question, having regard to, in recognition of, etc. The original Latin texts frequently include the phrase *ideo consideratum est* which is also a general language use, though embedded in a specific legal context.

In the four volumes of the Earliest English Law Reports[61] all dated from the end of the 13th century, we can find no hits in any original Law French source texts for 'consideration' in its various spellings. The word is used neither in a general sense nor with a specifically legal meaning. In the eight Year Books of Richard II's reign, dating from 1378–79 and 1382–1390,[62] there are no hits in any original source texts for 'consideration' in its various spellings.

The 15th century sources edited for the Selden Society show similar trends. For example, the Year Book of Henry VI from (1422)[63] provides no hits for 'consideration'. The same is true for the Year Books of 10 Edward IV and 49 Henry VI (1470),[64] while in the Caryll Reports (1485–1499),[65] we find two matches for 'consideration', both used in general language contexts.

60 Earliest English Reports vol. I, II, III, IV (to 1284, 1285–1289, 1279–89) 111, 112, 122, 123 Selden Society; Year Books of Richard II (1378–79, 1382–1390) Ames Foundation Publications; (1422) Year Book 1 Henry VI, 50 Selden Society; (1470) Year Books of 10 Edward IV and 49 Henry VI, 47 Selden Society.

61 Edited for the Selden Society by Paul Brand: vol. I & II, 111 & 112 Selden Society, Oxford: Alden Press 1996; vol. III & IV, 122 & 123 Selden Society, Cambridge: CUP, 2006 & 2007.

62 (1378–79) 2 Richard II (edited for the Ames Foundation by Morris S. Arnold; London: William Clowes & Sons, 1975); (1382–83) 6 Richard II (edited for the Ames Foundation by Samuel E. Thorne; Michigan: Edwards Brothers, Ann Arbour, 1996); (1383–84) 7 Richard II (edited for the Ames Foundation by Maurice J. Holland; Michigan: Edwards Brothers, Ann Arbour, 1989); (1385–87) 8–10 Richard II (edited for the Ames Foundation by L.C. Hector and Michael J Hager; London: Spottiswoode, Ballantyne & Co., 1987); (1387–88) 11 Richard II (edited for the Ames Foundation by Isobel D. Thornley; London: Spottiswoode, Ballantyne & Co., 1937); (1388–89) 12 Richard II (edited for the Ames Foundation by George F. Deiser; Cambridge: Harvard University Press, 1914); (1389–90) 13 Richard II (edited for the Ames Foundation by Theodor F.T. Plucknett; London: Spottiswoode, Ballantyne & Co., 1929).

63 (1422) 1 Henry VI, 50 Selden Society, edited by C.H. Williams; London: Bernard Quaritch, 1933.

64 (1470) Year Book of 10 Edward IV and 49 Henry VI, edited by N. Neilson, 47 Selden Society, London: Bernard Quaritch 1931.

65 Reports of Cases by John Caryll, Part I (1485–1499), 383 pages & Part II, (1501–1522) 349 pages, edited by J.H. Baker, 115 & 116 Selden Society; Oxford: Alden Press 1999 & 2000.

It is only in the 16th century sources[66] that we find the term 'consideration' used more frequently in a legal context and in an increasingly technical legal sense. An example for each:

> Nota que si home a cest jour ou devant grant al auter per son fait que en consideration de son bon service que il ad fait ou a faire a luy ou en consideration que son file marier ove moye ou mon fittes que il avera tout le terre en un ville et cest graunt est per fait et nient enrolle que ore nul use est alterate sur cest graunt entant que il va per voy de graunt et done soit execute per liverey de seisin...[67]

> Et cest plee per Portman Justice et Gawdy Serjeant fuit tenus bon plee en barr et le bargaine bon et cest consideration alter le use en le terre coment que la est un rent reserve devant lestatute...[68]

In the Year Books of 12–14 Henry VIII's reign,[69] covering the years 1520–1523, we have 21 matches for 'consideration', exclusively used in the legal sense as payment or reward or as the promise/object of an agreement. A proximity search between 'consideration' and other contract vocabulary reveals that although there are similar numbers of hits for both 'consideration' and 'contract', these two search terms cannot be found in proximity of 20 words from each other. The same holds for 'promise', 'covenant' and 'debt'. There are, however, 14 proximity matches with 'grant/graunt' (out of a total of 215 hits for 'grant/graunt').

Similarly, in the Dalison reports[70] the 6 matches for 'consideration' are all in the legal sense. In the reports from the lost notebooks of Dyer,[71] the 36 matches

66 (1520–1523) Year Books 12–14 Henry VIII, 119 Selden Society; (1522–1558) The Reports of William Dalison, 124 Selden Society; Reports from the Lost Notebooks of Sir James Dyer 109 & 110 Selden Society.

67 "Note that if someone at the present day (or before) grants to someone else by his deed that, in consideration of his good service that he has done or is to do for him, or in consideration that his daughter should marry me or my son, he should have all the land in a vill, and this grant is by deed and not enrolled, no use is altered upon this grant inasmuch as it goes by way of grant and gift and takes no effect until the gift is executed by livery of seisin." in: Reports of William Dalison, or 124 Selden Society 50.

68 "And this plea was held a good plea in bar by Portman J. and Gawdy, serjeant, and the bargain good; and this consideration alters the use in the land even though there is a rent reserved before the statute..." in: Reports of William Dalison, or 124 Selden Society 60.

69 (1520–1523) Year Books 12–14 Henry VIII 192 pages, edited by J.H. Baker, 119 Selden Society; Oxford: Alden Press 2002.

70 The Reports of William Dalison (1552–1558) 148 pages, edited by J.H. Baker, 124 Selden Society, Cambridge, CUP, 2007.

71 Reports from the Lost Notebooks of Sir James Dyer, vol. 1 & 2 (1541–1581) 219 & 246 pages, edited by J.H. Baker, 109 & 110 Selden Society; Oxford: Alden Press 1994.

for 'consideration', only 9 are in the general sense, while the remaining 27 hits are all in the legal sense. The proximity searches in the Dyer Notebooks show the same trend as for the Henry VIII Year Books: 8 proximity matches between 'consideration' and 'grant/graunt' (out of a total of 162 hits for 'grant/graunt'), 2 for 'covenant' and 1 hit for 'promise' and none for 'debt' and 'contract'.

Interestingly, when the term consideration appears in a Middle English text, it is always in a general language context. For example:

> In tender consideration whereof, and for asmuch as the saied Lorde Dier did greatelie mislike our service and manner and dealing in the publique administration of justice....[72]

Its occurrence in a general language Anglo-French context becomes increasingly rare. For example:

> Sir, le deffendant gist languishant en son lict, par que nous priomus que il poit estre par attornay. Mes jeo say bien que sans tiel consideration il ne respondra par attorney, mes convient apere en proper person...[73]

It appears that the technical legal sense of 'consideration' was developed in Law French and not exported at this stage into Middle English.

As the 16th century progressed, and even more during the first half of the 17th century, we find 'consideration' used increasingly in specifically technical legal meanings. The lexical and grammatical patterning surrounding 'consideration' signposts an abstract and autonomous concept, rather than a descriptive general language context, which has been prominent hitherto. This will be discussed in detail below in relation to the later corpora under the heading for the specialist and abstract uses.

3.3.1 The 15th c. Corpus

The early 364,743 word corpus yielded 18 hits for the term consideration in its various spelling variations, which represents a relative frequency of 4.93 for every 100,000 words. The proximity search shows none of the secondary terms in the vicinity of consideration. In view of the small number of concordance

---

72 In: Reports from the Lost Notebooks of Sir James Dyer Part 2 or 110 Selden Society 314.

73 "Sir, the defendant is lying sick in bed, and so we pray that he may appear by attorney. I am quite aware that in other circumstances he would not be able to answer by attorney, but must appear in his own person." in: Reports of Cases by John Caryll Part 1, or 115 Selden Society 113.

TABLE 22 Language register for 'consideration' in the 15th c. corpus (364,743 words)

Language	Matches	% of total
general language	12	67%
general legal language	0	0%
technical language	0	0%
Latin	6	33%
Total	**18**	–

lines, neither the clusters nor the collocate tools provided any significant data. On closer examination the lines show that the term 'consideration' is mainly used in a general language register as well as embedded in Latin phrases (Table 22). The words that most frequently appear in the vernacular lines are 'diverse' and 'reasonable'.

3.3.2 The 16th c. Corpus

In the corpus for the following century, we can observe a significant increase in the use of the word 'consideration'. It occurs 240 times[74] with a relative frequency of 28.70 for every 100,000 words. The term 'promise' can be found most often in the proximity of 'consideration'. Interestingly, it also has a low relative frequencies in this subcorpus, in 17% of its occurrences it can be found in the proximity of 'consideration', while in 6.7% of the occurrence of 'consideration' we can find 'promise' in its proximity. These figures are far ahead from those for the other secondary search terms. The term with the highest relative frequency – debt (84.55) – can only be found in 0.7% of its occurrences in the proximity of 'consideration', followed by covenant (R.F: 56.93) with only 2.9% (Table 23).

The language register of the textual context tells a very different story from the previous century. In three quarters of the concordance lines, the term is now used in a general legal or specifically legal technical sense (Table 24).

This is also borne out by the results from the collocate and clusters tools. We find specifically legal terms such as 'use' and 'covenant' fairly high up the frequency ranking list for collocates (Table 25). 'Marriage' in the sense of a legal bargain tends to cluster around the term consideration, as we can observe in Table 26.

74 There were 254 KWIC but 14 KWIC lines were discarded (editor's notes).

TABLE 23 Search terms/proximity to 'consideration' in the 16th c. corpus

Search term (incl. various spellings)	Hits (= N)	Rel. freq. (100,000 words)	Proximity occurrences (= P)	Prox. to 'considera*' (=P/N_0)	Relative proximity (= P/N)
considera*	240 (= N_0)	28.70	N/A	N/A	N/A
assumpsit	77	9.21	3	1.3%	3.9%
promise	94	11.24	16	6.7%	17.0%
contract	111	13.27	2	0.8%	1.8%
covenant	476	56.93	14	5.8%	2.9%
debt	707	84.55	5	2.1%	0.7%

TABLE 24 Language register for 'consideration' in the 16th c. corpus (836,181 words)

Language	Matches	% of total
general language	32	13%
general legal language	46	19%
technical language	138	58%
Latin	24	10%
Total	**240**	–

TABLE 25 Collocates for 'consideration' in the 16th c. corpus (collocate types: 902; collocate tokens: 2,540)

Rank	Freq.	Freq (L)	Freq (R)	Collocate
1	122	61	61	le
2	86	25	61	de
3	79	70	9	in
5	45	20	25	est
14	21	6	15	use
19	18	9	9	covenant
20	18	16	2	bone
21	18	17	1	ascun
37	13	0	13	marriage
47	10	0	10	mariage
44	11	5	6	promise
50	8	5	3	terre

TABLE 26 Clusters for 'consideration' in the 16th c. corpus (cluster size min. 2, max. 3)

Rank	Freq.	Range	Cluster (search term on left) 408 cluster types; 508 cluster tokens
1	20	5	consideration de
3	7	4	consideration del dit
8	4	2	consideration de marriage
25	2	1	consideration de fesance

Rank	Freq.	Range	Cluster (search term on right) 388 cluster types; 508 cluster tokens
1	32	6	in consideration
2	10	4	le consideration
3	8	3	ascun consideration
4	8	3	bone consideration
19	2	1	cause ou consideration
28	2	1	feoffment sur consideration

Latin Uses

The word 'consideration' occurs 24 times in a Latin text context (Table 24). These were not included in this study, as it would contribute less to the understanding of how the language used in the development of the concept of consideration shifted from a general language use to a specialised one.

The Latin uses of 'consideration' can usually be found in a (or several) Latin phrase(s) within an Anglo-French text, rather than in an entirely Latin text. For example:

> ...in considertatione maritagii[75]
> ...quod quidem judicium quo ad consideration[76]
> ...ideo consideratum est.

Its use tends to be in the general language meaning of 'taking into consideration', rather than in the contractual sense of the element that makes an informal agreement enforceable.

75 1 Anderson 19, or 123 Eng. Rep. at 331–334, 1 Anderson 138, or 123 Eng. Rep. at 395–398.
76 2 Anderson 127, or 123 Eng. Rep. 581; 2 Anderson 131, or 123 Eng. Rep. 583.

General Language Uses

In the sub-section of general language use, consideration is to be understood in terms of careful thought/contemplation, viewing, observing typically over a period of time, taking into account, motives/reasons, deliberation, opinion or conclusion; also included is the notion of kindness and thoughtfulness for another and esteem, importance, consequences among men and for things. In 32 concordance hits of this 16th c. corpus, 'consideration' appears within the context of a general language meaning. For example:

> ...et apres argument & consideration del Case lea Justices...[77]
>
> ...monstra divers considerations & reasons al Roy en maintenance de son opinion[78]
>
> ...soit bone ou male, convenient ou inconvenient, ne besoign ascun grand consideration; car certenment a coo tener pur opinion est absurd...[79]

In the 184 concordance hits of the general legal language and technical language, we find the term 'consideration' appearing in a continuum of uses ranging from general language use in a legal context to a technical use in a specialised context. The general legal use can be defined in terms of consideration as payment or reward and as the promise/object of a contract. It describes a concrete situation of a causal link between two elements necessary to making an agreement: something is said/given/paid/done in consideration of something said/given/paid/done. These were the basic elements required for the formation of a legally binding informal agreement. When the term is used in an abstract way – e.g. "the instrument imported a prima facie consideration" – it no longer refers to a concrete causal link between two events, as is the case with the expression 'in consideration of'. Instead, it has become a cover term expressing an abstract concept or range of ideas.

While the collocation 'in consideration of' is a general language construct adopted in the legal context of contract, it can be used in a wide range of semantic meanings, both legal and non-legal. When consideration is used as part of a specialised language, it is restricted semantically to the specialised contexts in question. It tends to be combined with a relatively restricted set of technical words, which in itself points to technical language: the more limited the vocabulary in proximity, the more specialised the language. Grammatical features are further important pointers to the use of specialised language. In

77 1 Anderson 12, or 123 Eng. Rep. at 327.

78 Keilwey 183, or 72 Eng. Rep. at 360.

79 1 Anderson 335, or 123 Eng. Rep. at 503.

concordance lines that show a more abstract use of the word consideration, it tends to be used as full noun, sometimes even in a one-word sentence. To that extent it is a cover term that stands for abstracts concepts and thus becomes a part of specialised and technical language.

General Language in Legal Use and Context

In 19% or 46 of the 240 concordance lines (Table 24) we find the word 'consideration' in the causal collocation 'in consideration of' or different variations. The Anglo-French equivalents are *en/in consideration d'/de/del/do/dun* and include similar causal phrases such *en/in consideration que* and *pur consideration del*. In other words, while the term 'consideration' appears as a noun, it does not behave as a full noun, but rather depends on the phraseological pattern without which it would not have the same meaning. The function of this phrase is to provide a causal link between two events or elements at the centre of the concept of striking an informal agreement.

With reference to the functional linguistic conception of language, as discussed in Chapter 3/1,[80] the phrase 'in consideration of' was studied in relation to the experiential function and the meanings encoded from the experience of reality. In the case of this particular phrase, we are on the outer layer of the experience:

- something is (done) = PROCESS
- in relation to something or someone = PARTICIPANTS
- in consideration of = CIRCUMSTANCES

For example:

> ...le dit. def. pur ***consideration*** del marriage fait perenter le fitz...[81]
>
> ...il coo releas grantis sans prender riens in **considerae** de son releas.[82]
>
> ...si home a cest jour ou adevant grant a un aut p s fait q en **consideration** de Marriage ou de bon service fait a luy...[83]

'Consideration' in these general legal language uses is a part of what is represented by the outer blue layer of experience in Figure 3 (Chapter 3) above and thus twice removed from the inner core of the experience. We will see later

80 See in particular Figure 3 in Chapter 3/1.

81 Benloe 58, or 123 Eng. Rep. 45.

82 Dalison 89, or 123 Eng. Rep. 297.

83 Dalison 19, or 123 Eng. Rep. 239.

how this changes in the KWIC lines where 'consideration' can be found in a legal technical meaning.

When considering the KWIC concordance lines in greater detail, we can observe that the language *to the right* of the search term tends to describe common events, 'things' done or affections, duties and services undertaken by people. By far the most common word is 'marriage'. Similar matters such as natural affection, the bringing up of children, fatherly care or brotherly love, loyal service can also be found as elements in the consideration of which agreements are made. Furthermore, words relating to financial matters such as payments or debts or the mention of specific sums of money, as well as the words plaintiff or defendant are more frequently to the right of the phrase 'in consideration of'. The language *to the left* of the search term is of a more specialised nature. We can count considerably more technical terms describing legal instruments or legal persons or titles. 'Covenant' is the most prominent among the technical terms before the search term. The financial vocabulary is also more technical: we can find words such as 'fine', 'purchase', 'fee', which were far less prominent before the search terms. Furthermore, words relating to property and related legal instruments or legal titles occur more frequently before the search term, such as 'intestate', 'legacy', 'estate', 'grant', 'possession', 'heirs', 'testator', 'enfeoffor', 'executor', etc. In other words, the collocation 'in consideration of' in the context of law reporting appears to link specifically legal instruments or concepts with more common events, 'things' done or affections, duties and services undertaken by people, frequently in a private or family context.

From this textual evidence, we can observe that the word 'consideration' occurs in general language uses expressing the causal link between two elements or events that are necessary for striking an agreement. However, the textual context clearly shows that we are dealing with specialist technical matters of the law. While the collocation 'in consideration of' could be used in any situation of exchange, in this corpus we have a relatively restricted set of vocabulary concerned with legal instruments and persons, payments, indenture, estate, etc. in exchange of mainly marriage and other family matters. In other words, both the meaning and function of the collocation is in a general language sense but it is the lexical and semantic context that is highly technical.

Specialist and Technical Uses

In 58% or 138 of the 240 concordance lines (Table 24), the word 'consideration' can be found in a specialised context more akin to an abstract concept. It is frequently a one-word sentence, where the word is between two full-stops and

TABLE 27 Words associated with 'consideration' in the specialist/technical category of the 16th c. corpus

Words accompanying 'consideration'	Occurrence	Left of search term	Right of search term
verbs, e.g. *ester, aver, faire, raiser, enfeoff*	95	54%	46%
prepositions, e.g. *pur, sans, sur, de*	80	78%	22%
adjectives, e.g. *bon, effectual, sufficient*	58	95%	5%
determiners, e.g. *le, les*	29	79%	21%

thus signposting a conceptual meaning. As discussed above, the main pointers to the use of technical language can be observed in the interaction between the lexical and grammatical patterning. The word 'consideration' in the technical context is no longer embedded and dependent on a causal prepositional phrase but appears and behaves as a full noun and in combination with adjectives, articles, pronouns and prepositions.

The most common accompanying grammatical unit in the immediate vicinity of the search term are verbs. Only those directly associated with the noun 'consideration' were taken into account. Any verb relating to other nouns, even if in the immediate vicinity of 'consideration' was not taken into account. The verb mostly associated with the noun 'consideration' is *ester* ('to be'), in 29 of these concordance lines it can be found before and in 9 lines after the noun. No other verbs stand out as occurring particularly frequently, though it is interesting to note that most other verbs can be found to the right of 'consideration'.

All the verbs relating to the search term consideration represent material processes and associate the noun consideration in a function of participants within the clause.Of the 95 verb occurrences identified as relating to consideration, in 62% these associate with consideration in the traditional class of subject, while in 38% we find the noun can be categorised as object, usually directly linked to a verb.

Other frequent accompanying elements in the immediate vicinity of the search term are prepositions. These can be found 80 times in the KWIC lines, usually preceding the term consideration, such as *pur, sans, sur, de* etc. The combination with adjectives (58) is also frequent, such as good, effectual, false, sufficient etc. These are almost exclusively placed to the left of the search term. On 29 occasions we can find consideration combined with determiners, such as definite articles, mainly in the singular form: *le(s) consideration(s)* or quantifying determiners such as *nul*.

Moving beyond traditional grammar classification of words and considering the function they play, we refer to the functional linguistic conception of language, as discussed in Chapter 3/1. As the word 'consideration' appears in its specialised, technical and abstract uses, we can observe that the way experience and reality are encoded in those cases represents a major shift in the function of the use of 'consideration'. With reference to functional linguistics, as represented in Figure 3, the experiential function of 'consideration' moves from the outer blue layer to the middle green layer, namely to that of the participants in the process, most commonly realised by nominal groups. In this way, it becomes a signpost to signal an autonomous concept, rather than a causal connector, as discussed in the previous section on general language in legal use and context. Considering the unit of meaning rather than the unit of analysis according to traditional grammar, we find that the role in which the word consideration appears is that of participant (notion of 'thingness'), sometimes as actor, sometimes as goal. The examples given below show that the term tends to appear in a context of material processes (what-happened? or what-did-X-do?) rather than behavioural processes (encoding physiological or psychological behaviour) or mental processes (reflecting the inner world of cognition, perception, (dis)liking, inclination).

Examples for specialist language uses:

> ...lour reason fuit pur ceo que nul **consideration** est expresse en le fait pur raiser...[84]
>
> ...les Feffees sais **consideration** ou cause pur que ils aver use...[85]
>
> ...car la le **consideration** move de cestuy que est de aver le terre...[86]
>
> ...icy cest assumpcon est encounter le ley, ergo le Ley ne regarda le Consideracon...[87]

We find the function of 'consideration' at the heart of the experiential meaning of the language used. In the role of participant, it relates to a material process and the strength of the experiential meaning can be such that its use as a single word is sufficient to signify the concept. In 10 out of the 138 KWIC lines for this

84 1 Anderson 141, or 123 Eng. Rep. 397.

85 2 Anderson 201, or 123 Eng. Rep. 620.

86 1 Anderson 233, or 123 Eng. Rep. 447.

87 Benloe 90, or 73 Eng. Rep. 963.

specialist/technical category of the 16th c. corpus, we find consideration as a stand-alone term between two full stops. In other words, in the specialised and technical uses of the term, the strength of its experiential meaning has been underlined in comparison to its use in the phrase 'in consideration of', as described above.

In addition, the information generated by the linguistic software further underlines the technical nature of the texts and language. It shows that a dozen specifically legal terms can frequently be found both in the vicinity of the search term, and in the rest of the corpus: e.g. use, covenant, plaintiff, estate, assumpsit, indenture etc. Similarly, there are words that are not particularly technical in the sense that they come from everyday language use, but take on a specific legal significance in a legal context, such as 'marriage', '*terre*', 'promise', etc. In general, the term 'consideration' tends to be combined with a limited set of words, which is further indicative for the use of specialised language.

3.3.3 The 17th c. Corpus

In the over 1.1 million word 17th c. corpus, there were 744 relevant hits for the wildcard search 'considera*', which represents a relative frequency of 64.87 for every 100,000 words. The terms with the highest relative frequency – 'debt' (121.03) and 'covenant' (95.83) – are also among the lowest in their relative proximity to 'consideration' (Table 28). Only 4.2 of all occurrences of 'covenant' can be found in the vicinity of 'consideration', which is just ahead of the 3.9% for 'debt' and 3.6% for 'contract'. The proximity factor P/N_0 tells a similar story.

TABLE 28 Search terms/proximity to 'consideration' in the 17th c. corpus

Search term (incl. various spellings)	Hits (= N)	Rel. freq. (100,000 words)	Proximity occurrences (= P)	Prox. to 'considera*' (= P/N_0)	Relative proximity (= P/N)
considera*	744 (= N_0)	64.87	N/A	N/A	N/A
assumpsit	303	26.42	34	4.6%	11.2%
promise	324	28.25	76	10.2%	23.5%
contract	280	24.42	10	1.3%	3.6%
covenant	1099	95.83	46	6.2%	4.2%
debt	1388	121.03	54	7.3%	3.9%

TABLE 29 Collocates for 'consideration' in the 17th c. corpus (collocate types: 1, 464; collocate tokens: 7, 470)

Rank	Freq.	Freq (L)	Freq (R)	Collocate
1	406	223	183	le
2	265	122	143	que
3	259	58	201	de
5	204	115	89	est
16	71	54	17	bon
21	53	7	46	marriage
30	41	24	17	promise
33	36	25	11	assumpsit

TABLE 30 Clusters for 'consideration' in the 17th c. corpus (cluster size min. 2, max. 3)

Rank	Freq.	Range	Cluster (search term on left) 929 cluster types; 1494 cluster tokens
1	92	10	consideration de
4	28	8	consideration que le
7	15	6	consideration fuit
12	12	6	consideration est
16	8	5	consideration de marriage
28	5	3	consideration de service
30	5	4	consideration execute
Rank	**Freq.**	**Range**	**Cluster (search term on right)** 892 cluster types; 1494 cluster tokens
1	94	8	en consideration
3	60	9	le consideration
5	13	5	est bon consideration
12	10	5	valuable consideration
13	9	2	ascun consideration
26	6	5	nul consideration
32	5	4	sans consideration

TABLE 31 Language register for 'consideration' in the 17th c. corpus (1,146,827 words)

Language	Matches	% of total
general language	19	3%
general legal language	227	30%
technical language	481	65%
Latin	17	2%
TOTAL	744	–

Among the 744 hits for 'consideration', we find the term 'debt' in proximity in 7.3%, 'covenant' in 6.2% and 'contract' in 1.3% of the occurrences. The term promise continues to be ahead of all other terms, including in its relative proximity, followed by 'assumpsit'.

'Assumpsit' can also be found in the results of the collocation and cluster tools. But, as is the case for the 16th c. subcorpus, the term 'marriage' features most prominently in these results (Tables 29 and 30).

The story told by the language register of the textual context (Table 31) is very different from the 16th c. subcorpus. In 95% of the concordance lines, the term is now used in a general legal or specifically legal technical sense. The general language uses have fallen to 3% and the Latin uses to 2%. The semantic shift toward encoding more specialised meanings is undeniably revealed in this subcorpus.

General Language and Latin

The most obvious change in relation to the earlier corpora is the drastic fall in the general language use: from 67% of the concordance hits in the 15th c. subcorpus, and 13% in the 16th c. subcorpus to a mere 3% during the 17th c. subcorpus. The general language meanings relate to the court taking specific factors into consideration during the process of their decision. The Latin uses have dropped from 33% and 10% to a mere 2% and there is less variety in the Latin phrases in the present corpus. In 8/17 occurrences the word is part of the phrase *ideo consideratum est*, in 6/17 within the phrase *per considerationem*.

In 95% of the general language and technical language concordance lines, we find the word 'consideration' in a continuum of uses ranging from legal connotations to specialised legal language.

General Language in Legal Use and Context

In over 30% or 227 of the concordance hits (Table 31), the word 'consideration' is a part of the causal phrase 'in consideration of' and other variations, such as *en consideration d'un/de/del/que, in consideration d'un/de/del/inde/que* etc. As observed in the corpora discussed previously, the term appears as a noun, yet it does not behave as a full noun, but is embedded in a phraseological pattern without which it would not have the same meaning. The phrase provides a causal link between two events or elements at the centre of the concept making an informal agreement. However, the language surrounding the phrase is not specifically technical, as had been the case in the 16th c. subcorpus.

The language *to the right* of 'consideration' within the causal phrase tends to relate to everyday matters, that may typically be the subject of an informal agreement:

- marriage, love, natural affection, personal services: appear immediately after the causal phrase in 58 of the 227 concordance lines (26%) singled out for this category; as opposed to only 14 lines (6%) when these were immediately before;
- payment/debt/sums of money: appear in 72 concordance lines (32%) immediately after the causal phrase, while in merely 30 lines or 13% before;
- references to specific groups of people – *fille, fils/frère/nephew, père/home, femme* – are slightly more balanced in the distribution around the causal phrase: we find these in 36 lines (16%) before and 22 lines (10%) after the causal phrase.

Legal technical terms tend to be more present to the immediate left of the causal phrase. Terms referring to legal instruments or processes immediately precede in 41% of the KWIC lines, whereas they can only be found in 17% to be following the phrase. Nevertheless, the surrounding language cannot be said to be specifically technical nor abstract. So, the phrase 'in consideration of' retains its legal connotation but without necessarily being embedded in highly technical language.

Specialist and Technical Uses

In about 65% or 481 of the 744 concordance lines (Table 31), the word 'consideration' has taken on a specialised and abstract meaning. It appears and 'behaves' as a stand-alone noun with the usual noun-attributes such as adjectives, articles, pronouns and prepositions. The most common accompanying elements are verbs. On 309 occasions in the 481 KWIC lines in this category, a verb is directly related to the term 'consideration', either in its function as grammatical subject (49%) or as a grammatical direct object (51%). The verb mostly associated with the noun 'consideration' is *ester*, in 173 of these concordance lines it can be found before and in 136 lines after the noun. No other verbs stand out as occurring particularly frequently: *faire* and *aver* occur 9 and 10 times respectively before, and 13 and 2 times after the noun 'consideration'.

TABLE 32 Words associated with 'consideration' in the specialist/technical category of the 17th c. corpus

Words accompanying 'consideration'	Occurrences	Left of search term	Right of search term
verbs, e.g. *ester, aver, faire, raiser, paier*	309	56%	44%
adjectives, e.g. *autre, bon, valuable*	275	77%	23%
prepositions, e.g. *pur, sans, sur, de*	255	47%	53%
determiners, e.g. *le, les*	171	96%	4%

All of the 46 different verbs identified indicate material processes (i.e. processes what happens or what X does) and associate the noun 'consideration' with a function of key participant in the clause, rather than on a more peripheral level of circumstances surrounding the process. These grammatical patterns signal that in these concordance lines the word 'consideration' refers to a concept in its own right rather than a mere causal connector as was the case when the word appeared in the phrase 'in consideration of'. In other words, as a unit of meaning and function, it is as that of participant (notion of 'thingness') – at times in the role of actor, at other times in that of goal.

Other frequent accompanying elements in the immediate vicinity of the search term are prepositions. These can be found on 255 occasions, often preceding the term 'consideration', such as *pur, sans, sur, de* etc. The combination with adjectives (275) is also frequent, e.g. 'good', 'effectual', 'false', 'sufficient' etc. These are usually placed to the left of the search term. On 171 occasions we find 'consideration' combined with determiners, such as definite articles, mainly in the singular form: *le(s) consideration(s)* or quantifying determiners such as *nul*.

The various grammatical patterns discussed so far have shown that the term 'consideration' is signposting an abstract concept. The strength of this experiential meaning is further emphasised by the fact that, at times, its use as a single word between two full stops, is sufficient to signify the conceptual meaning. Similarly, we find the term embedded in legal phrases, such as: *Action sur le case. Consideration de marriage* or *Action sur le case in consideration de forbearance* or *Accion sur le case sur assumpsit, le consideration*. On occasions, the term can be found in other strong noun structures, in particular when preceded by a definite article and followed by another noun: *le consideration -del action, -del sanke, -del conveyance.* The meaning here is not in the sense of considering the action, the blood relation or the conveyance. It is rather a reference to the element of legal consideration that is given to make an informal undertaking legally enforceable.

4 Abridgements

For the sake of completeness, other documents, such as Abridgements, were also briefly examined. It must be stressed that abridgements are not as such case reports but collections of cases for easy reference. The terms in which the cases are described and the words used do not necessarily reflect the language actually used in court at the time of the hearings, but express how the author of the abridgement understands, evaluates and categorises the cases. In other words, it reports the law as it is in the mind of a particular abridgment author. Written later than the original report, it still reflects the way these cases were seen at the later time of writing the abridgements.

The *Abridgement of Cases to the End of Henry VI*[88] spans from Edward III until Henry VI (1327–1413). Reading through it, we find that 'assumpsit' is not listed, though we can find 24 entries for action on the case (*accions sur le cas*). Most of them are what was later called trespass on the case, though the word 'trespass' does not appear either. The key words in these actions are *a tort, negligence, vi et armis, gift, bargain conspiration, emprist sur luy*. The actions with *emprist sur luy*, in particular, are what would be later classed as assumpsit actions.

In Fitzherbert's *Le Graunde Abridgement*[89] 52 cases of *accion sur le cas* are listed. These deal with a variety of matters, such as debt, grants, deceit, *vi et armis*, bargain/warranty, covenant. The notion of 'promise' is not mentioned. Assumpsit as such is not discussed in any detail either, though there are two cases that use the phrase *emprist sur luy* and two others with *assuma sur luy/nous*. The Fitzherbert Abridgement further lists one case of 'contract' (discussion on action of contract v. convenant) 31 cases of 'covenant' and 184 cases of 'debt'. In the last category of cases we frequently find key words such as 'payment', 'rent count', 'annuity', 'grant', 'contract'. But the basic concept of a debt action can be found in the notion of 'obligation': *det sur/par obligacion*

88 N. Statham (1490) *Abridgement of Cases to the End of Henry VI*, Rouen: Per me. R. Pynson, www.heinonline.org – Selden Society Publications and the History of Early English Law; Henry VI reigned until 1461.

89 A. Fitzherbert (1577) *Le Graunde Abridgement*, London: In Aedibus Ricardi Tottelli, www.heinonline.org – Selden Society Publications and the History of Early English Law.

In his 1573 Abridgement[90] Brooke lists 123 cases of *action sur le case,* of which 17 deal with situations of assumpsit in the sense of an undertaking. He adopts a greater use of the term 'assumpsit'; in 4 cases the word even figures in the title and in 11 we find it in the description of the case. The verb *emprendre* ('to undertake'), usually in the form of *il emprist*, appears in 7 cases, sometimes alongside 'assumpsit'.

The word 'assumpsit' is used in varying degrees of abstraction. It ranges from more descriptive uses, generally in the verb form, such as *home fait promise ou assumpc de faire chose*[91] and *defend assumps de paier,*[92] to more abstract, usually noun, uses such as *issue sur non assumpsit*[93] and *case sur assumptio,*[94] *action sur case sur Assumps.*[95] It is also interesting to compare how Brooke abridged the cases in his collection of 1573 with the original Year Book reports written earlier. In one of the surgeon's negligence cases,[96] Brooke described that the defendant *emprist de cur le pl dun wounde.* He also used the word *assumpc.* The original Edward III Year Book report for the year 1374 presented this action as a *trespas sur son case.* There was also a discussion of *vi et armis, ne contra pacem,* which in these early days was a prerequisite for engaging an action of trespass.[97] The notion of an undertaking is expressed in extensive use of the verb *emprendre* ('to undertake'), usually in the form of *il emprist*; the word 'assumpsit' does not appear. This comparison is very telling of the evolution that the enforceability of informal contracts has undergone in the two centuries that separate these two reports of the same case. At the time of the original case, the notion of 'assumpsit' had not emerged, and cases were still firmly grounded in the action of trespass, which eventually gave way to the action of assumpsit. But in his report written 200 years later, Brooke reconceptualised the facts of the case using parameters of his own time that were not available at the time the case occurred.

Similarly, a case abridged by Brooke[98] from the time of Henry VIII (1535/36), deals with the question of whether an undertaking to pay a debt is an action on debt. Brooke presents the debate of the case as *aver accion de dett sur le contract*

---

90 R. Brooke (1573) *Le Graunde Abridgement,* London: In Aedibus Ricardi Tottelli, www.heinonline.org – Selden Society Publications and the History of Early English Law.

91 R. Brooke (1573) *Le Graunde Abridgement,* London: In Aedibus Ricardi Tottelli, www.heinonline.org – Selden Society Publications and the History of Early English Law at 4, case 10 (original report 20 Hen.VI 34, or LBEx).

92 Brooke (1573) at 7, case 105 (original report YB 33 Hen. VIII, or LBEx).

93 Brooke (1573) at 4, case 5 (original YB report 27 Hen. VIII 24, 3, or LBEx).

94 Brooke (1573) at 5, case 40 (original YB report 11 Hen. IV 33, or LBEx).

95 Brooke (1573) at 7, case 107 (original YB report 34 Hen. VIII, or LBEx).

96 Brooke (1573) at 4, case 24 (original YB report 48 Edw. III 6, or LBEx).

97 See discussion in Chapter 5.

98 Brooke (1573) at 4, case 5 (original YB report 27 Hen. VIII 24, 3, or LBEx).

ou accion del case sir le promise et issint ceo est in deivers respectes, car sur le promise ne gist acc de dett. His use of the word 'promise' is interesting, introducing a notion absent from the Year Book report fifty years earlier. While both the reports and the abridgement present this case as one about an undertaking through their extensive use of the word 'assumpsit' (and various variants), the concept that such an undertaking is a promise does not appear in the Year Book report, but only in the abridgement. There we find the undertaking (25 uses of 'assumpsit' and variants) described in terms of 'agreement' (22 uses of 'agreement' or the verb form). This reflects the evolution that the action of assumpsit has undergone during the intervening years.[99] And in general, it is striking that in these early assumpsit cases the key words tend to be actions, obligation, duty, conditions, guarantees, undertaking and covenant/contract/debt. The notion that something was promised may appear as inherent in these action to us today, but it was never expressed as such in the use of the vocabulary.

A century later the very comprehensive abridgement of Henry Rolle[100] presents a very different picture. In the section on *Action sur Case* we find a dozen chapters on assumpsit and consideration, which are also headed as such. They date mainly from the mid-16th century to the mid-17th century, though a few cases from either side of the time scale are also included. A manual analysis of the vocabulary in the selected 168 cases shows that 'consideration' is the term that appears by far the most frequently (231 times), followed closely by 'promise' (155 times), then 'assumpsit' (40 times), 'obligation' (39 times) and 'agreement' (11 times). So, by the mid-17th century, not only are assumpsit cases classified as such, but the terminology used reflects that these actions on informal undertakings are discussed in terms of consideration and promise as the elements that make an informal agreement enforceable. This is certainly a very different representation to the abridgements discussed hitherto.

5 Lexicons and Dictionaries

Looking at reference work we would today call lexicons, dictionaries or glossaries – though the works considered here do not use these terms – we also find the evolution of the concept of assumpsit and consideration reflected in the terminology used. Such reference works tend to be thought of as an

99 See discussion in Chapter 5.

100 H. Rolle (1668) *Abridgment des Plusieurs Cases et Resolutions del Common Ley*, London: Printed for A. Crooke [and 12 others], www.heinonline.org – Selden Society Publications and the History of Early English Law.

orderly list of definitions and meanings of relatively reliable and stable units. Yet it can be argued that dictionaries represent much more and that their compilation and use are 'communicative occasions occurring under characteristic circumstances'.[101]

In 1579, Rastell[102] records no separate entries for 'assumpsit' nor 'consideration', though there is one for bare or naked contract, which does not include the word 'consideration', but rather 'recompense'. He defines contract in terms of bargain and covenant (*contracte est vn bargeine ou couenaunt per enter ii. parties*) and the term 'consideration' is used to describe *quid pro quo* or 'one thing given for another' (*vn chose est done pur auter que est appelle quid pro quo* [...] *en consideration de* [...] *que vous dones a moy ceux font bone contractes, pur ceo que il ad vn chose pur auter*). This language of one-thing-for-another still points to the remnants of the proprietary notions that were central in the earlier actions of debt. So does the use of the words *quid pro quo*, which was the standard terminology in debt and clearly expresses a bargain and equivalence of exchange. Yet, by the mid-16th century, the action of assumpsit had evolved to include the concept of promise. And, despite the more proprietary language described above, Rastell mentions promise in the second, more explanatory, half of his entry on contract:

> ...mes si vn home fayt promise a moye que ieo auera xx s. & que il voyle este debtour a moy de ceo...
>
> (but if a man make promise to mee that I shall have twenty shyllinges, and that hee will be debtour to mee thereof)

> ...mes si ascun chose fuyt done pur le xx. s. mesque il ne fuit forsque al value de vn dernier, donques il fuit bone contracte...
>
> (but if any thinge were geuen for the xx. shillinges though it were not but to the value of a peny, then it had ben a good contracte)

Here we have clearly moved on from the idea of basic *quid pro quo*, to one of a more 'symbolic' exchange, of what we would today think of as consideration, in order to 'confirm' the promise and thus make it enforceable. To our 21st

101 R. de Beaugrande (1997) Text Linguistics, Discourse Analysis, and the Discourse of Dictionaries, in: Hermans A. (ed.) *Les dictionnaires specialisés et l'analyse de la valeur*, Louvain-la-Neuve: Peeters, 57–74.

102 W. Rastell (1579) *Exposition of Certaine Difficult and Obscure Wordes and Termes of the Lawes of This Realme, Newly Set Fourth & Augmented, Both in French and English, for the Helpe of Such Younge Studentes as Are Desirous to Attaine the Knowledge for the Same. Whereunto Are Also Added the Olde Tenures,* London: In adibus Richardi Totelli, www.heinonlin.orgw – Selden Society Publications and the History of Early English Law.

century reality and knowledge, this definition may appear paradoxical, as it introduces both the more proprietary concept of *quid pro quo* and the concept of confirming the intention of a promise through an exchange that does not reflect the actual material value of the exchange. It is unlikely to have appeared as such to the lawyers of the mid-16th century, who were still in a transitional phase of evolution and change. The legal concepts at issue were not yet settled in a definite way but were still being developed in the courts.

In Cowell's *Interpreter*[103] over fifty years later, a contract is defined as 'a covenant or agreement with a lawful consideration or cause'. In other words, we move away from notion of bargain towards something more akin to a meeting of minds and the use of word 'lawful' gives to understand that there is a legal definition of 'consideration'. Cowell also includes definitions of 'assumpsit' and 'consideration'. The former describes 'assumpsit' as a

> voluntary promise made by word, whereby a man assumeth, or taketh upon him to performe or pay any thing unto another. This word containeth any verball promise made upon consideration, which the Civilians expresse by divers words, according to the nature of the promise...

Consideration is defined as

> the materiall cause of a contract, without the which, no contract bindeth. This consideration is either expressed [...] or else implyed...

For comparison's sake, it is interesting to leap forward two centuries and consider the entries in Wharton's *Law Lexicon*.[104] The definitions are much more detailed and definite, especially in comparison to the 1579 Rastell entry. A contract is described as "a deliberate engagement between competent parties [...] founded upon the mutual agreement of the parties". A contract must be made

103 J. Cowell (1637) *Interpreter: Or Booke, Containing the Signification of Words*, London: Printed for William Sheares, www.heinonlin.org – Selden Society Publications and the History of Early English Law.

104 J.J.S. Wharton (1848) *Law Lexicon, or Dictionary of Jurisprudence: Explaining All the Technical Words and Phrases Employed in the Several Departments of English Law, including also the Various Legal Terms Used in Commercial Transactions; Together with an Explanatory as well as Literal Translation of the Latin Maxims Contained in the Writings of the Ancient and Modern Commentators (From the London ed.)*, Harrisburg, Pa.: I.G. M'Kinley & J.M.G. Lescure, www.heinonlin.org – Selden Society Publications and the History of Early English Law.

"upon a legal consideration to do, or to abstain from doing, some act". Here, the concept was expanded by notions represented in the use of words such as 'deliberate', 'competent', 'mutual' and the inclusion of non feasance as well as feasance. Wharton also takes the definition of 'consideration' beyond Cowell's 'materiall cause'. He describes consideration as "the price, motive, or matter of inducement of a contract, which must be lawful in itself". This lexicon shows that by the mid-19th centuries, the legal concepts governing contracts have been settled in a broader and more detailed manner.

6 Consideration as Moral Obligation in the Mansfield Corpus

As we fast-forward to the 18th century, we come to an episode in the history of the concept of consideration that lasted a few decades – roughly the second half of the 18th century – and which is of particular interest because it represents a temporary innovation in doctrinal thinking accompanied by a change in terminology. The lawyer at the centre of these attempts to shift the concept of consideration towards a moral obligation, was Lord Mansfield, but there were a number of fellow judges who adopted his approach and this was reflected in their rulings. Consequently, the idea lasted beyond Mansfield's death. As late as 1863, we can find references to the notion of consideration as moral obligation.

The corpus that was constituted for the purpose of the 18th/19th century part of the study was compiled in a very different way to the ones described previously in this chapter. The reason is that the purpose of this part of the study is *not* a continuation of the research done on the 15th, 16th and 17th centuries corpora. Instead it offers some insight into how the use of terminology in particular types of cases was guided by new ideas in the underlying legal thinking. In other words, we are pursuing a specific aspect of the concept of consideration, namely Mansfield's idea of seeing it as a moral obligation. This is also the reason why the study of the Mansfield corpus is presented in a separate section in this chapter, rather than as a continuation of Section 3 above. It is important to stress that in the 18th and 19th century, the language situation is very different to that of the late Middle Ages and Renaissance. The language used was no longer Law French, nor Middle English but Modern English, which had already been the subject of the Great Vowel Shift, inflectional simplification and Johnson's linguistic standardisation. The language is a lot more structured and precise.

So far, the texts for inclusion in the corpora discussed were entire volumes of case reports, independent of legal content. For the compilation of the

Mansfield corpus, the case reports were selected on the basis of their *content* and whether these were a part of the corpus of cases stipulating Mansfield's concept of consideration as moral obligation. Moreover, in order to reveal Mansfield's idea, the corpus was searched with terms that had not figured in relation to the earlier corpora, such as 'obligation', 'duty', 'conscience', all terms that were likely to indicate the context of Mansfield's idea of consideration as a moral obligation. Each search was restricted to the noun form in both singular and plural. This study is more limited compared to the earlier ones described above. It does not attempt to demonstrate the use of the search term(s) in the 18th/19th century law reports in general but only in the specific cases dealing with consideration as moral obligation.

The Mansfield corpus (MC) consists of 56 reported cases, some of which have two references. Most decisions were taken between the 1760s and the 1840s. Two cases before that period were included (1731 & 1759)[105] and two from the mid-19th century (1860 & 1863).[106] A full list of the cases can be found in annex 2 /IV.v. The corpus has 136,788 word tokens and 6,347 word types. A concordance search for the term consideration shows 714 hits, which represents a relative frequency of 522 for every 100,000 words. The language used in the Mansfield corpus is a largely standardised English, with the exception of one KWIC line which is in Law French. This contrasts with the Law French of the earlier subcorpora that were still subject to spelling variations and included sections in Latin and some Middle/Early Modern English.

In comparison to the legal sources of the previous centuries, the MC shows a striking increase of the use of 'consideration'. The concordance and advanced proximity searches provided the results in Table 33. It is interesting to note that the relative frequency for all terms that were also studied in relation to the other subcorpora discussed above, has increased considerably. This may be slightly skewed in view of the fact that the text selection for the MC is content driven. The major exception is 'covenant', which not only has a very low relative frequency but is almost absent in the proximity of 'consideration'. This concept of formal contract-making is no longer relevant to the discourse of Mansfield and his colleagues, who tried to introduced the civil law notion of making promises morally binding.

105 *Hayes v Warren* (1731) 2 Strange 933 or 93 Eng. Rep. 950; *Exeter Corporation v Trimlet* (1759) 2 Wils. K.B. 95 or 95 Eng. Rep. 705.

106 *Shadwell v Shadwell* (1860) 9 C.B. (N.S.) 159 or 142 Eng. Rep. 62; *Flight v Reed* (1863) 1 H. & C. 703 or 158 Eng. Rep. 1067.

TABLE 33 Search terms/proximity to 'consideration' in the Mansfield corpus

Search term	Hits (= N)	Rel. freq. (100,000 words)	Proximity occurrences (= P)	Prox. to 'considera*' (=P/N_0)	Relative proximity (= P/N)
consideration	714 (= N_0)	522	N/A	N/A	N/A
promise	739	540	268	37.5%	36.3%
debt	403	295	63	8.8%	15.6%
contract	320	234	32	4.5%	10%
obligation	160	117	35	4.9%	21.9%
assumpsit	156	114	32	4.5%	20.5%
moral*	111	81	45	6.3%	40.5%
covenant	6	4	1	0.1%	16.7%

TABLE 34 Collocates of 'consideration' in the Mansfield corpus (collocate types: 1,009; collocate tokens: 7,140)

Rank	Freq.	Freq (L)	Freq (R)	Collocate
10	146	26	120	promise
14	97	80	17	sufficient
18	73	70	3	good
46	25	21	4	moral
48	24	13	11	debt
53	22	6	16	assumpsit

These findings are also reflected in the results for the collocate and the clusters functions (Tables 34 and 35). As far as the register of the language is concerned, the same categorisation of language use was applied as for the previous corpora discussed above (Table 36).

TABLE 35 Clusters for 'consideration' in the Mansfield corpus (cluster size min. 2; max. 3)

Rank	Freq.	Range	Cluster (search term on left) 683 cluster types; 1,428 cluster tokens
1	113	29	consideration for
10	17	9	consideration to support
14	11	6	consideration of forbearance
17	9	9	consideration thereof
36	4	4	consideration of assets
Rank	**Freq.**	**Range**	**Cluster (search term on right)** 462 cluster types; 1,428 cluster tokens
1	130	24	the consideration
3	70	18	sufficient consideration
5	54	20	good consideration
12	14	5	legal consideration
17	11	2	executed consideration
19	10	8	moral consideration

TABLE 36 Language register for 'consideration' in the Mansfield corpus (136,788 words)

Language	Matches	% of total
General language use	14	2%
General legal language	106	15%
Technical language	594	83%
Latin	0	0
Total	714	–

6.1 *General Language and Latin*

The general language use is very low (Table 36). In 14 lines we find 'consideration' in the sense of taking into account when forming an opinion. There are no concordance lines in Latin.

6.2 *General Language in Legal Use and Context*

In 106 concordance lines (Table 36), we find 'consideration' used in a general language meaning but in a specific legal context, namely within the causal phrase 'in consideration of' which links the two elements of striking an agreement: something is said/given/paid/done in consideration of something said/given/paid/done. During Mansfield's time and well into the 19th century, these were still the elements required for the formation of a legally binding informal agreement, since the doctrine of offer and acceptance that governs today's contract formation thinking, was not yet established.

The use of the phrase is more stable than had been the case in the previous Law French corpora where we could find any permutation a number of possibilities:

en/in/pur *consideration d'/de/del/do/dun/que*

In the Mansfield corpus, we find

in	consideration	of	(73 times)
in	consideration	that	(20 times)
in	consideration	thereof	(12 times)

and one equivalent Law French phrase *en consideration que.*

The vocabulary surrounding the phrase in the 106 KWIC lines is dominated by the words 'plaintiff' and 'defendant'. In half of these concordance lines, we can find one or both of these words once or several times in a word span of 10 words to the left and right of the phrase. In general, the language is not very technical. In 20% of the lines, we find a legal technical term, such as 'legacy', 'executor', 'assumpsit'. In 24% of the lines, a term relating to financial matters is in the vicinity of the phrase.

6.3 *Specialist and Technical Uses*

In 83% of the concordance lines (Table 36), we find 'consideration' has a specialised legal meaning. In these cases, it appears as a noun with the vested role of full participant in the process, rather than as a part of the layer representing the circumstances surrounding the process. The grammatical and lexical

TABLE 37 Words preceding 'consideration' in the MC

Words immediately preceding 'consideration'	**Occurrence**	**Percentage**
determiner, e.g. *a, the, that, any, no*	284	40%
adjectives, e.g. *good, legal, moral, valuable*	252	35%

TABLE 38 Verbs associated with 'consideration' in the MC

Verb	To left (10 words)	Search term	To right (10 words)	Total
to be	205	consideration	84	289
others	120	consideration	117	237

TABLE 39 Collocates for 'consideration' with 'to be' in the MC (window span: 10L, 10R)

Rank	Freq.	Freq (L)	Freq (R)	Collocate
7	335	184	151	is
9	269	151	118	was
13	189	90	99	be

TABLE 40 Clusters for 'consideration' in the MCc (cluster size: min. 2, max. 3)

Rank	Freq.	Range	Cluster (Search term on left)
7	26	14	consideration was
9	18	10	consideration is

patterning underline this function. In three quarters of the lines the noun is immediately preceded by elements that are typically associated with a full noun, such as determiners and adjectives (Table 37). This is also confirmed by the results from the search for collocates (see Table 34). The first adjectives in the list of collocates sorted by frequency are 'sufficient', 'good', and 'moral'. These tend to be to the left of the search term.

As to processes, it is the verb 'to be' that occurs most frequently and in direct association with 'consideration'. This verb expresses a finite stand – something is or it is not. The language is of a definite nature and rarely moderated by words that express modality of possibility, such as may, might or could (Table 38). The first verbs that figure in the collocate list sorted by frequency are three forms of 'to be' in Table 39. As far as clusters for 'consideration' are concerned, we find 'to be' in the past and present forms high on the list (Table 40).

From the textual evidence collected from the Mansfield corpus, we can observed definite shifts in the use of terminology.

•••

So much for the linguistic study revealing an overall picture of the evolution of the term 'consideration' and its surrounding language. The last chapter will discuss the conclusions that the results from the study show from a diachronic perspective, as well as the concordances that were revealed between the evolution of the term and concept of consideration.

CHAPTER 7

Conclusions

> We may put it, by way of comparison, that whereas the historian of French law has a continuity of language with a discontinuity of law, his English counterpart has a continuity of law with a discontinuity of language.[1]

The aim of this research was to trace the advent and early use of the concept of consideration in English contract law, by studying the doctrinal development in parallel with the corresponding terminological evolution between the 15th and 18th centuries. The question of continuity and discontinuity of law and language is, therefore, at the heart of the research question.

The issue of continuity or discontinuity of law is bound up with that of customary or codified law. English law was never subject to the kind of sweeping *tabula rasa* that was experienced in France during the 18th century. Changes in English law were more of an 'organic' rather than avowed nature and the impetus came from pragmatic considerations relating to getting specific tasks done or succeeding in court actions. The idea of building an overall coherent system was not at the forefront of legal minds. "The life of the law has not been logic: it has been experience".[2] Developments tended to be the result of gently pushing boundaries and then exploiting the wriggle-room obtained. There was continuity, which does not preclude changes, though these were perceived as part of a continuum rather than any radical transformation. The concept of assumpsit and later of consideration is a prime example of changing the law by shifting the categories for legal actions. In the courts there was a need to make agreements legally binding without having to resort to the very complex procedures of deeds (Chapter 5). It is this process of conceptualisation of informal, yet legally enforceable, promises and agreements, that is at the heart of this study.

Whether there was continuity or discontinuity of language in England is more complex to assess, and depends on the extent to which the multilingual landscape of medieval England is perceived as a linguistic continuum. This has been discussed at length in Chapter 4. The fact is that there were continuous

1 *Year Books of 11 Edward II (1317–1318)*, J.P. Collas, W.S. Holdsworth (eds.) 61 Selden Society, at xiii (J.P. Collas).

2 O.W. Holmes (1881) *The Common Law*, www.gutenberg.org, at 1.

 | DOI:10.1163/9789004436169_008

interplay and lexical borrowings, in particular, between continental (Parisian-basin) French, Norman-French, insular Anglo-French and Middle English on English soil. This resulted in substantial absorption of French words into Middle English, the evidence of which can still be found in today's English, as well as in our contemporary legal English. But at a time when both language and the common law were evolving substantially, the use and substantial imports of French vocabulary in England did not go hand in hand with the import of legal concepts. These may or may not have corresponded to the imported terms, except for land law, much of which was brought over by the conquering Normans, together with its specific terminology. An example other than the words discussed in this study is the term *tort*, which came into the 11th century Old French from the Medieval Latin *tortum*,[3] meaning 'wrong, injustice', from *tortus, tortum* ('wrung, twisted'), past participle of Latin *torquere* ('to twist, wring'). It has that sense in the 12th century *Chanson de Roland*[4] and troubadour literature.[5] The law of tort, as we know it today, goes back to the 13th century in the form of actions of trespass and action as on the case and various terms were used to describe concepts of personal remedies. But in the context of legal action for breach of duty, the term *tort* first appeared in English in the 1580s[6] and the action evolved and expanded considerably during the centuries that followed, today covering intentional and negligent infliction of economic loss as well as some emotional, psychological, reputational (etc.) injuries. In other words, the term *tort* has evolved from the Old French general meaning of injustice and wrong (still its modern French meaning) to cover today's very specialised type of wrong. The term must have appeared convenient to use as the action of trespass on the case evolved, but it was not imported into English with any other sense other than the general (French) language meaning. It gradually developed its very specialised legal meaning. While its etymological root is still intact, it describes an autonomous legal concept. We are no doubt dealing with two different sets of language – French (dialects) and English – but this example shows how it is possible to perceive the medieval linguistics landscape in England as a continuum as far as the language of the law is concerned.

3 Compare *tortum facere*, in Art. 20, 23 and 26 of the Edictum Pistense by Charles the Bald of 864, A. Boretius, V. Krause, Capitularia regum francorum, II (Monumenta Germaniae Historica, Legum, II), Hannover, Hahn, 1897, nr. 273, 310–328.

4 Verse 1051: *Paienunt tort e chrestiensuntdreit.*

5 e.g. Guillaume de Cabestaing: *Fis amans deugran tort perdonar* (*Lo jornqu'ie us*).

6 The term was used in Law French well before then in phrases such as *tort e force* and *de son tort demene.*

In this study on the history of the concept of consideration, language was seen as a continuum. The use of Law French continued to flourish and expand while Anglo-French in other registers was declining from the 14th century. Case law reporting was written in French, though this was not necessarily the language spoken in court pleadings. But in many case reports, we find entire passages in English in the middle of the French language report of what appears verbatim transcripts of declarations (written or spoken) made by one of the parties to the case. It is reasonable to conclude that the English language figured alongside French in court proceedings, though we do not know in what proportions. It is likely there was a constant code switching between the two languages without the need for translation, linguistic or conceptual adjustments, nor the danger of anything lost in translation. It is on this basis that the present study considered the original language texts as a language continuum, i.e. as a continuous collection of texts independent of whether the language was Law French, Middle English or early Modern English.

To return to Collas' view of (dis)continuity of law and language, it may be nuanced by suggesting that in both law and language there were changes but within a continuum. In the law, boundaries were nudged, categories extended to let new legal actions in through the back door. The corresponding language, always in need of new terms for emerging legal concepts, did not go as far as introducing neologisms, but relied on everyday vocabulary that gradually evolved into specialised terminology, signposting autonomous legal concepts in concordance with the evolution of legal conceptual thinking.

•••

At the heart of this study was the extent to which the historical and conceptual development of the concept of consideration were matched by changes and shifts in the language, terms and lexical fields used, most notably in relation to the increased abstraction and technicality of both concept and language. This was revealed by undertaking diachronic linguistic and semantic analysis using corpus linguistics methodologies. It is important to stress at this point that the study was not meant either as a full inquiry into the history of the concept of consideration, nor as a complete analysis of the language used in the early Year Books and Law Reports. The research undertaken was of an interdisciplinary nature, using linguistics methodologies of analysis as tools to reveal the evolution of specific legal thinking and ideas, namely in relation to the enforceability of informal contracts.

The underlying premise of the research was that tracing the historical process of legal thought which constituted the concept of consideration, required a wider ambit than just the description and analysis of the content of the case law and legal writings. Though these are essential units of analysis, they must be placed within their diachronic contexts for the conceptual shifts in thought and meaning to be revealed. This approach is akin to the *Begriffsgeschichte* work undertaken in German-speaking academia (Chapter 2). One of the methodological principles they applied was to analyse the semantic fields of political and social language, because language offers a reliable indicator of the thinking and contexts in which concepts are established and shift in meaning. The study of law is, among other things, an enquiry into the abstract entities that make up a legal order. Law is not a collection of physically verifiable 'natural facts', but a phenomenon entirely created by man without existing as such in the physical world. The customary law set-up of the late Middle Ages allowed for the intellectual and doctrinal process involved in the development of a concept to be revealed more readily. Consequently, the language used to describe this phenomenon is intrinsically linked to its specific reality. Studying this language and terminology reveals how legal concepts materialise, evolve and translate into the letter of the law.

We often perceive long-standing, well-established legal concepts and the language used to express them as having been carved in stone as far back as the legal mind can remember. And yet, this is somewhat a post-rationalisation by legal historians, who want to see a linear development of the law, presupposing that the shape legal concepts were to take at the end was aimed at from the start. The doctrine of consideration is a central element to contract formation; it appears so well anchored in contract law and in our legal minds, that we may find it difficult to imagine its development took a tortuous and at times haphazard path, stretching over several centuries (Chapter 5). The forerunners of consideration arose in a medieval legal world with archaic procedures and complex technicalities, where the need was increasingly felt for a tool that could meet growing commercial needs in terms of contracts and quasi-contracts. But various strands from different legal issues came together in the idea that informal promises should be enforceable – the evolution was somewhat haphazard. This is reflected in the terminology, which settled only hesitantly and shows a concordance between the complexity of the concept's evolution and the terminology used to express it. Also relevant in this context is the linguistic landscape of multi-lingual medieval England and the continuous switching between Law French and Middle and later Modern English (Chapter 4).

In this research, language was considered as an act of communication that encodes meanings in the socio-political, cultural and historical contexts in which they are uttered (Chapter 3/1). The language of the law is no exception, as its use, in particular in legal proceedings, is the product and a reliable indicator of these contexts and of how laws are created, practiced and interpreted. The methodology most appropriate to reveal how language and the evolution of legal concepts interact, is to examine the language in question in its textual context. The use of corpus linguistics methods and linguistics/concordance software are ideal for this sort of empirical approach, as they allow for systematic analysis of authentic evidence (Chapter 3/2).

For this research, a diachronic corpus was compiled, which is a collection of naturally occurring texts that vary along the parameter of time. It constituted the empirical basis for carrying out systematic linguistic investigations on authentic evidence. The fact that it is held digitally and searchable electronically offers possibilities that are not otherwise available. The corpus was compiled by continuously revising its design following empirical research carried out on the initial pilot corpus and in order to adjust the design parameters. This was particularly relevant in view of the complexity of working with medieval texts of a specialised but not very uniform register, including two languages neither of which was standardised.

The sources from which the documents were drawn to constitute the corpus can be accessed through the *Anglo-Norman Hub* (www.anglo-norman.net) or the *HeinOnline database for the Year Books and Law Reports* (www.heinonline.org). This textual evidence collected from the corpora that were constituted from the Year Books and Law Reports spanning from the late 14th century to the mid-19th century, was the empirical basis for evaluation. At the centre of the study we find the concept of consideration and its immediate signifier, namely the use of the word 'consideration'. But in order to provide context, the study also included 'consideration' in a general language use, as well as other relevant terms, such as 'assumpsit' and 'promise'. The underlying language theory of functional linguistics was discussed in Chapter 3. The corpus linguistics methodology, the linguistic analysis and all detailed results were described in Chapter 6. In the present chapter we will conclude by considering the results from a diachronic perspective with the information drawn from all subcorpora, to present the findings in a comparative and contrastive way and in order to reveal an overall picture of the evolution of the term and concept of consideration.

The study considered three main search terms associated with the legal enforceability of informal promises: 'assumpsit', 'promise' and 'consideration'. A number of secondary search terms, such as 'covenant', 'debt' and 'contract' were also studied, in particular their contextual proximity to the primary search terms. The presence of the three primary search terms has increased substantially throughout the diachronic subcorpora (Chart 2). For all three terms we can see that the use in the early subcorpora was more tentative. As far as 'assumpsit' was concerned, while the new action was gaining ground, the

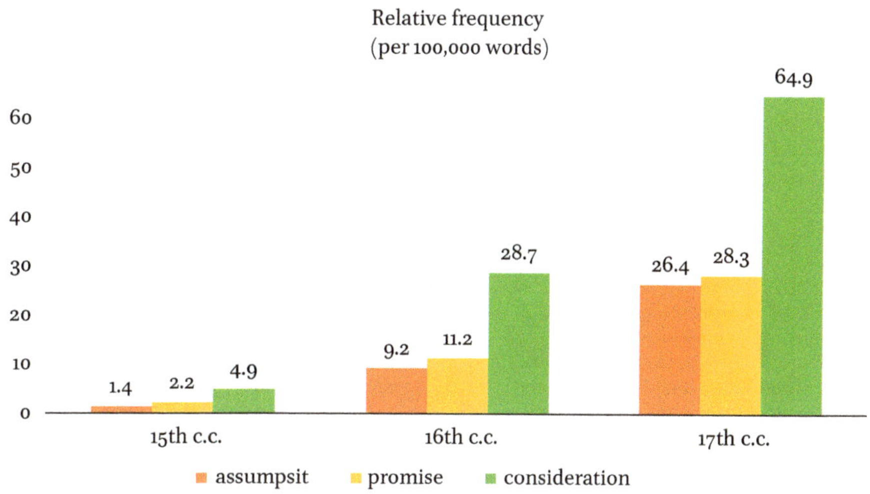

CHART 2 Relative frequencies for primary search terms in the 15th, 16th, 17th subcorpora

vocabulary did not follow at the same speed. In the case of 'promise' it was not used in a strictly contractual sense. Both terms were used increasingly with time, and a look at the relative frequencies in the Mansfield subcorpus show that between the 17th c. and the 18th/19th centuries 'promise' soared exponentially (nineteen fold), while 'assumpsit' levelled out as the action became obsolete (four fold increase).

In this concluding chapter, the Mansfield subcorpus was not systematically included in the comparisons. As pointed out earlier, this particular subcorpus was compiled according to very different selection criteria. Strictly parallel comparisons are, therefore, less appropriate.

The term **'assumpsit'** (Chapter 6/3.1) which we associate today with the newly emerging notion that informal promises could be enforceable, lagged behind in its establishment as a legal technical term. Until the 16th century, the vocabulary used in cases we would see essentially as actions of assumpsit, is not yet settled nor specialised. The language, in particular in the early cases, is descriptive, with relatively little use of nouns that express established concepts and very little specific terminology, except for a few Latin legal phrases. In other words, while the new action of assumpsit was increasingly becoming a legal reality, the textual evidence up to the end of the 15th century did not show the term 'assumpsit' as an established legal technical term or category.

It is only from the latter part of the 16th century, that the use of the term 'assumpsit' became more prominent. By the turn of the century and the early 17th century, the term appears firmly integrated into the Law French language as a

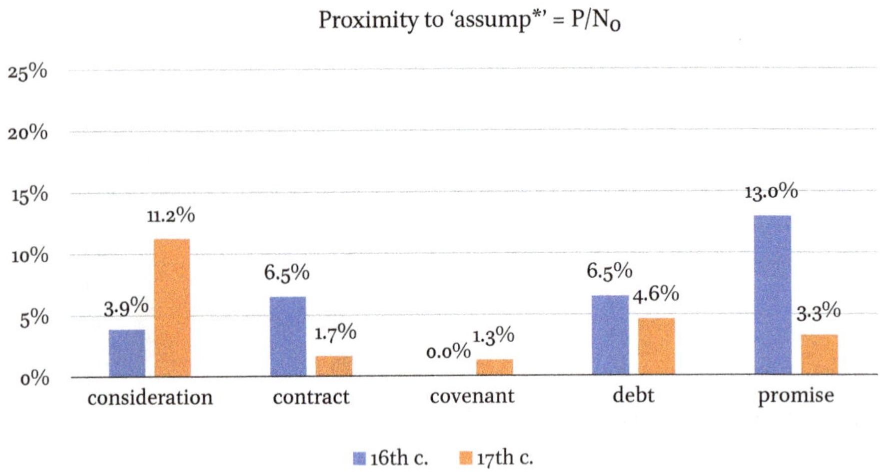

CHART 3 Proximity of secondary terms to 'assumpsit' for 16th and 17th c. (P = absolute proximity frequency of secondary search term to primary search term; N_0 = absolute frequency of primary search term)

word in its own right and no longer needing an accompanying explanation, nor necessarily placed within a Latin context or phrase. It occurs as a term expressing an established concept. It has the grammatical function of a noun accompanied by an article or adjective and thus offers a use more akin to an abstract concept. It has also been found in a definitional use in *conditionell assumption est assumption*. It never appears in a Middle English context. It seems that at this stage, the increased specialisation of the language happened in Anglo-French rather than in the more vernacular Middle English. From the textual evidence that spans from the 14th to the early 17th centuries, we can observed a definite evolution from tentative uses of the term assumpsit to its firm establishment as a term in the legal vocabulary. Thus embedded in the specific terminology of making agreements, it clearly sign posts the concept of enforceability of certain promises.

As explained, the proximity (P) between the primary term and five other secondary terms was calculated in relation to the absolute frequency of the primary search term (P/N_0) and in relation to the absolute frequency of the secondary search term (P/N). Both sets of figures and for both the 16th and 17th centuries can be found in Chart 3.

It is interesting to note that four of the secondary search terms behave in a similar way from one century to the other, whether calculated in terms of absolute or relative proximity. The figures for 'consideration' and 'covenant' rise, though only minimally for the latter. There is a decrease for the values of 'contract' and 'promise', which incidentally correspond almost precisely between the two types of calculation. The exception is the term 'debt'. Not only is there a difference in the figures depending on the whether it represents the absolute or the relative proximity, but there is also a fall for the former and a minimal increase in relation to the latter. A higher value for the absolute proximity of 'debt' to 'assumpsit' in comparison to the relative value, shows that when assumpsit is being discussed in the case law, we are more likely to find issues of debt included. However, in discussions relating to debt, we are less likely to find a issues of assumpsit.

In both sets of figure, a fall can be observed in the values for promise between the 16th and 17th centuries. It appears to suggest that, as time goes on, the promissory element of an informal undertaking is more likely to be described in terms of the more technical term 'assumpsit' than the general language term 'promise'. The opposite applies for 'consideration', which rises from one century to the other, more sharply for the absolute proximity value. In discussions of assumpsit the term 'consideration' appears more frequently and in increasingly technical meanings, as we have been able to established in the discussion on the registers of the language in the relevant concordance lines (Chapter 6/3.1 Table 10, Chart 3 and 4).

The word **'promise'**, discussed in Chapter 6/3.2 above, also struggled to emerge, despite the fact that its corresponding contractual notion was actually at the heart of the new concept. The earlier sources for the 13th and 14th centuries showed very little textual evidence for the use of the term 'promise' in

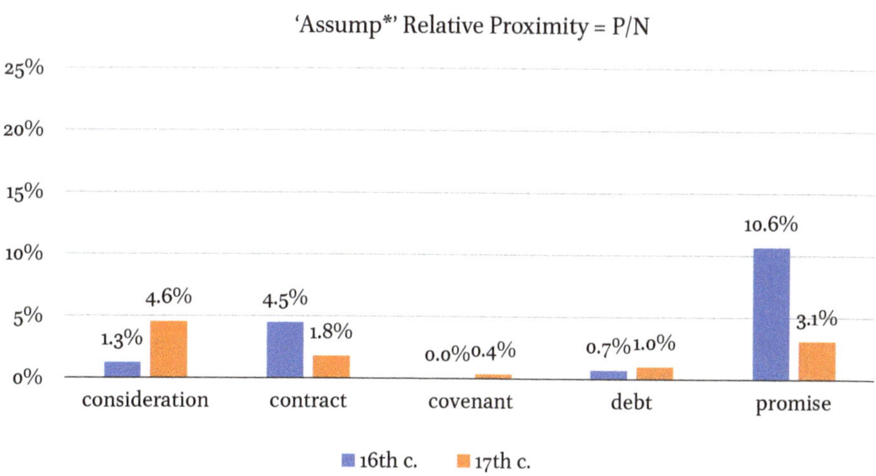

CHART 4 Relative proximity of secondary terms to 'assumpsit' for 16th and 17th c. (P = absolute proximity frequency of secondary search term to primary search term; N = absolute frequency of secondary search term)

the context of making an informal agreement enforceable. Despite the fact that St. German used the term in his writings at the beginning of the 16th century, it only began to feature more prominently in the context of the enforceability of informal agreements later that century. Although the use of the term in a strictly contractual sense was known, it was not necessarily in widespread use. The concept of a promissory rather than proprietary basis for informal agreements was still not reflected in a substantial way in the vocabulary used to describe such cases in the earlier sources, while 'debt' and 'covenant' remained prominent. Broadly, this be the case in the 17th c. subcorpus. 'Debt' and 'covenant' have a strong presence, but the word 'promise' adopted a more specifically legal meaning, as it appeared in restricted contexts of contract formation. This semantic shift towards a contractual meaning can be observed even more so when moving on to the Mansfield subcorpus.

The two methods of proximity calculations show similar upward or downward trends from one century to the other (Charts 5 and 6). The observations made above in relation to the proximity between 'assumpsit' and 'promise' were confirmed in the proximity search for secondary terms to 'promise'. In discussions relating to 'promise', the terms 'assumpsit' is used less frequently in the 17th century. For both 'consideration' and 'debt', the rise is sharper in the case of absolute proximity. In other words, in the 17th century, we find a higher frequency for the terms 'consideration' and 'debt' in discussions relating to

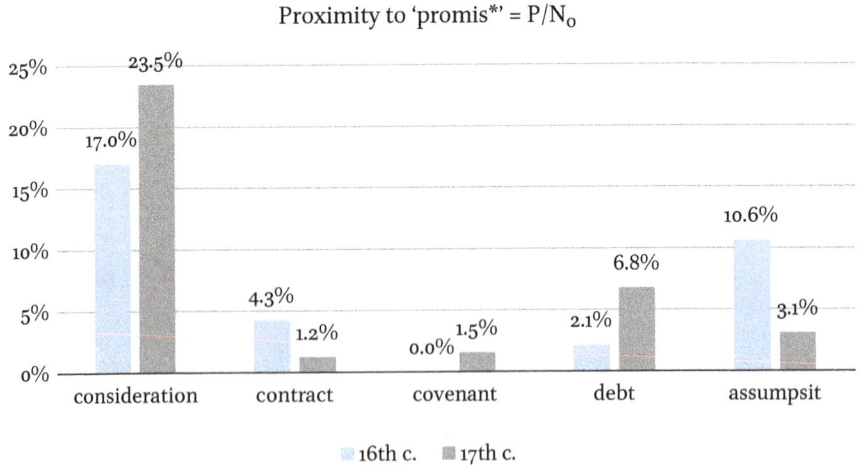

CHART 5 Proximity of secondary terms to 'promise' for 16th and 17th c.

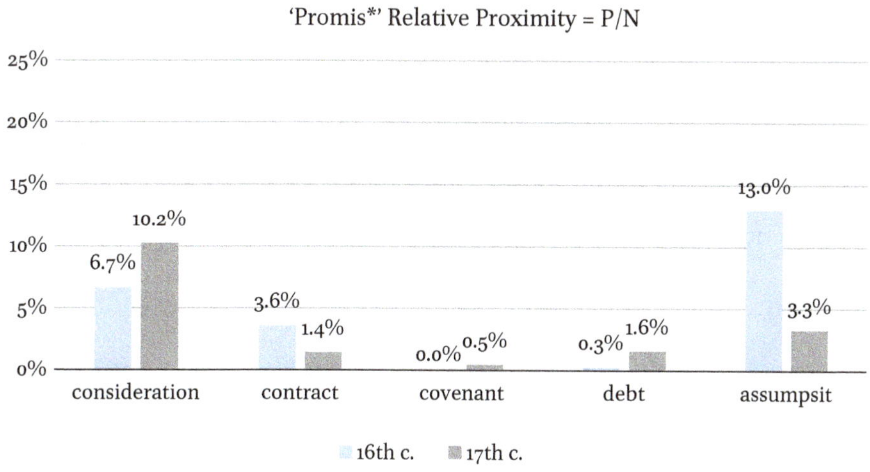

CHART 6 Relative proximity of secondary terms to 'promise' for 16th and 17th c.

promise. Similarly, issues of consideration and debt both raise discussions of promise more frequently during the 17th century.

The main focus of the research centred around the word **'consideration'** (Chapter 6/3.3). From the study of the Anglo-Norman On-line Hub, we can observe that 'consideration' was a term in use in the second half of the 14th century, though it tended to occur in general language meanings, such as examination, reflection, study, contemplation, opinion, conclusion, motive. It could not be found in a general context of making promises or concluding agreement, contracts or covenant, nor in situations of debt or trespass.

The study of the Year Book and Law Reports, spanning from the late 13th to the early 19th centuries, the constitution of a diachronic corpus with four subcorpora, as well as a selection of abridgments and lexicons, have revealed the changes in language and the semantic shifts of the term 'consideration' as the new legal concept of enforcing informal agreements emerged. It is of particular interest to observe the process of increased terminological abstraction alongside the consolidation and development of the concept. In the 13th, 14th and early 15th century law reporting sources, the word 'consideration' is very rarely used and any occurrence has a general language meaning. This is confirmed by a closer examination of the diachronic corpus. The very few occurrences of 'consideration' in the 15th c. subcorpus are all in a general language register and none of the secondary search terms could be found in the proximity of 'consideration'. Moving into the 16th c., there is almost a six fold increase in the relative frequency for 'consideration' and it continues to rise during the

TABLE 41 'Consideration' in the four subcorpora (the relative frequency is calculated on the basis of every 100,000 words)

	15th c.c. (364,743 words)		16th c.c. (836,181 words)		17th c.c. (1,146,827 words)		Mansfield c. (136,788 words)	
Search term (various spellings)	**Hits**	**Relat. freq.**	**Hits**	**Relat. freq.**	**Hits**	**Relat. freq.**	**Hits**	**Relat. freq.**
consideration	18	4.93	240	28.70	744	64.87	714	521.98

following centuries. We also find the term to occur more frequently in a technical legal sense, denoting an abstract concept. This striking increase in the use of the term consideration can be well observed when drawing together the findings for the different subcorpora (Table 41).

It must be stressed that the figures for the Mansfield corpus are slightly skewed as the set of texts was constituted according to different principles of selection, favouring case law that specifically dealt with the consideration as a concept of moral obligation. This content driven approach is bound to yield a higher frequency for the word 'consideration' and other closely related terms. But the inclusion of the figures for the Mansfield subcorpus is of interest in that these confirm the upward trend which had already been revealed through the analysis of the earlier subcorpora.

There is not only a considerable increase in the use of the term 'consideration' with time, but the frequencies for proximity to other key terminology also rise, which suggests greater intensity in the preoccupation with the concept. Between the 16th and 17th centuries all five secondary search terms show an increase in the proximity frequencies, as can be seen in Chart 7.

The term featured most prominently is 'promise', particularly in the relative proximity calculation, which mirrors what was observed above in the study on 'promise'. The proximity figures for 'contract' are surprisingly low, which is also the case for the results in relation to the other primary search terms. In the case of the primary search terms of 'assumpsit' (Charts 3 and 4) and 'promise' (Charts 5 and 6), there is even a fall in the frequency between the 16th and 17th centuries. In view of the fact that today's doctrine of consideration is a central pillar in contract formation, it is interesting to note that historically this does not appear to be reflected in the proximity figures between 'consideration' and 'contract'. Of similar interest is a higher presence of the terms 'covenant', 'debt' and 'assumpsit', especially for the 17th century and in the absolute proximity

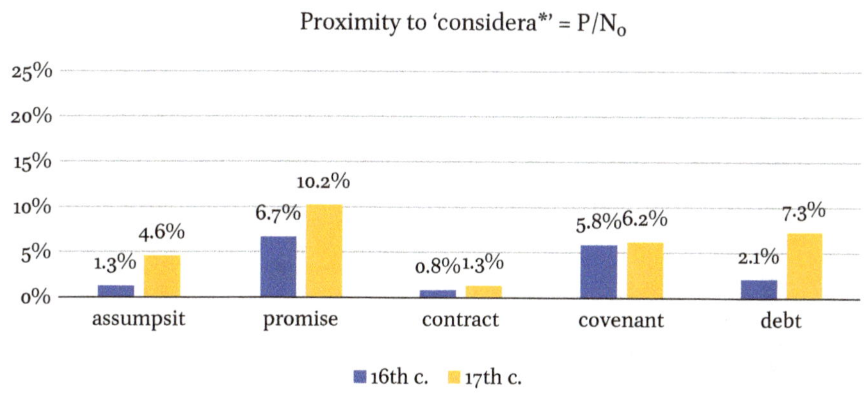

CHART 7 Proximity of secondary terms to 'consideration' for 16th and 17th c.

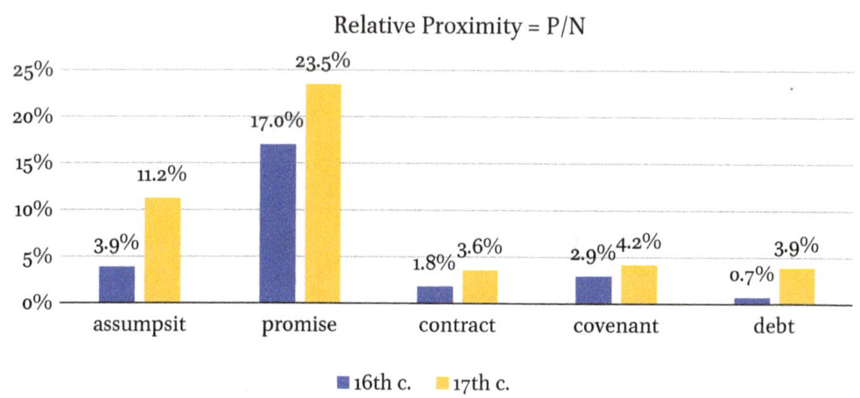

CHART 8 Relative proximity of secondary terms to 'consideration' for 16th and 17th c.

calculation. In view of the fact that in 95% of all the 17th century KWIC lines for consideration, the term is either used in a general but legal context language or with strictly technical meaning (Table 31), we may have expected lower proximity figures for terms standing for actions that the concept of consideration is moving away from, such as 'covenant', 'debt' and 'assumpsit'. Yet, these figures clearly show that when 'consideration' is discussed in the case law, the actions of 'covenant' and 'debt' are also mentioned and more so than 'contract' (Chart 8).

This trend continues in the Mansfield subcorpus (Chart 9). The relative proximity figures (P/N) for 'debt', 'assumpsit' and 'covenant' are higher than those for 'contract'. It means that the term 'consideration' can be found in the proximity of 15.6%, 20.5% and 16.7% respectively of the occurrence of these secondary search terms, while 'contract' is only at 10%. However, the percentages

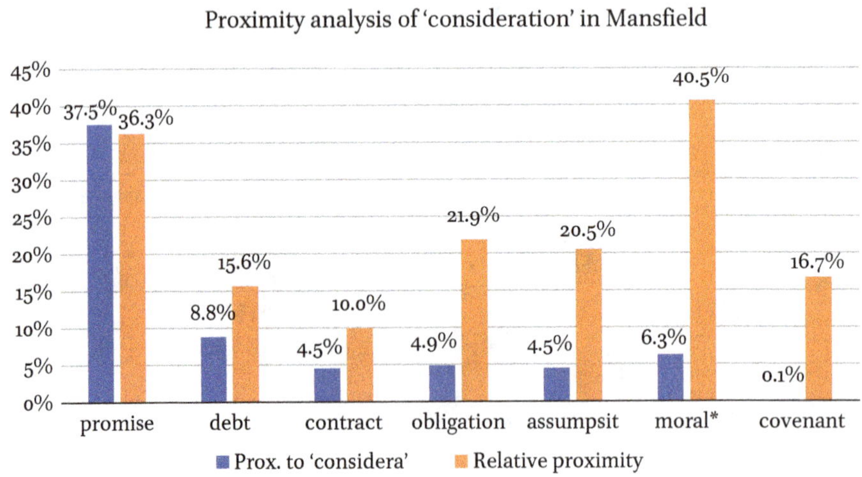

CHART 9 Absolute (P/N_0) and relative proximity (P/N) of secondary terms to 'consideration' in the Mansfield subcorpus

for the absolute proximity (P/N_0) are much smaller, which incidentally is the case for all the secondary search terms used in relation to the Mansfield subcorpus, with the exception of 'promise'. Whether 'promise' or 'consideration' is discussed in the Mansfield cases, you can find a similar percentage of proximity between these terms. The gap between the absolute and relative proximity is particularly striking for the term 'moral' (wildcard search to include variants). In the discussion of 'consideration' we find in 6.3% of the relevant KWIC lines the term 'moral*', whereas in the KWIC lines relating to 'moral*' it is in 40.5% of the concordance lines that we find 'consideration' (Chart 9).

While each set of findings for every search term drawn from the different subcorpora is interesting as such, examining the results diachronically and from a comparative perspective allows for a better understanding of how meanings have evolved over time. In Chart 10 we can find the relative frequency for the six search terms (primary and secondary) examined in this study throughout the four subcorpora.

Considering in the first instance the subcorpora for the 15th to the 17th centuries, probably the most striking feature is that debt consistently shows the highest frequency. Even in the 15th c. subcorpus, the relative frequency is just over 100, when the other terms barely reach 30. Debt continues to remain prominent for the next two centuries. It is reasonable to conclude that this form of action, although among the oldest, remains at the heart of the case law, even when other actions emerged and covered some of the disputes hitherto dealt with through the action of debt. By the 18th/19th centuries, debt still features in cases that discuss consideration, but proportionally less so than other

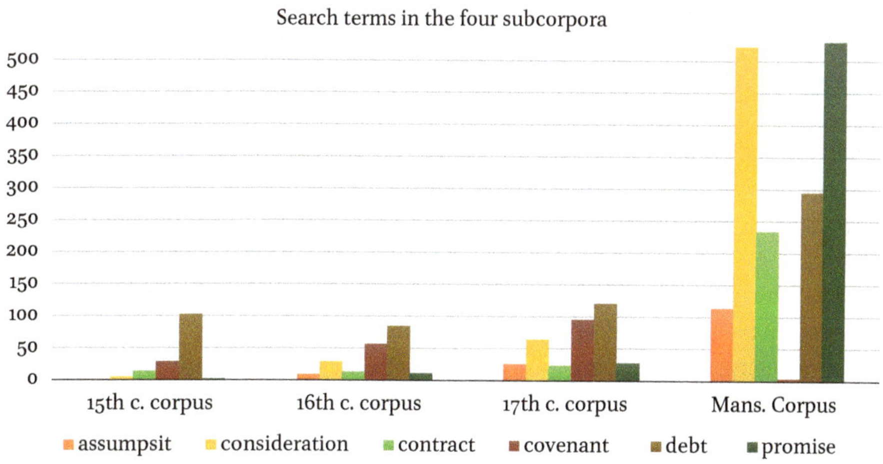

CHART 10 Relative frequency (for every 100,000 words) of search terms in the four subcorpora

issues such as contract and promise. The other instrument that has often been lumped together with debt in the early context of legal enforceability for informal undertakings is covenant. Here, we can observe a steady rise throughout the subcorpora of the 15th to 17th centuries. It gradually catches up with debt, but is far less present in the early case reports. By the time Mansfield sits on the bench covenant is no longer an issue included in the discussions relating to contract and consideration. These figures show that long-established concepts and terminology remained prominent, even when conceptual boundaries shifted. This corresponds to the fact that both the actions of debt and covenant, as forefathers of contractual promises, were not yet seen in terms of contractual agreements or notions of promise but tended to be related to proprietary concepts, rather than promissory ones.

Terms conceptually associated with the enforceability of informal undertakings, such as 'assumpsit', 'consideration', 'contract' and 'promise', all evolve tentatively throughout the first three subcorpora. The term 'consideration' is actually more frequent than 'assumpsit', though it must be stressed that it has a variety of meanings – general and specialised – and the figures include all meanings, while 'assumpsit' can only be found in the legal technical meaning. In the 17th c. subcorpus, where the general language use for 'consideration' is only 3% (Table 31), we also find that term ahead of 'assumpsit'. By that time the concept of consideration was well established and the higher frequency for 'consideration' over 'assumpsit' may well indicate that the former term has begun to displace the latter. This suggestion is certainly borne out by the figures for the Mansfield subcorpus.

There is a striking parallel between the frequencies of the term 'assumpsit' and 'promise'. Conceptually the two are quite close. Both are concerned with making an undertaking and the disputes related to whether this undertaking can be legally enforced. While 'promise' clearly expresses a promissory approach to informal undertakings, 'assumpsit' formed the stepping stone from the previous proprietary notions of executed exchanges. The Mansfield subcorpus clearly shows that 'promise' was at the forefront of his thinking and of that of some of his colleagues during the 18th and 19th centuries. From today's views on the doctrine of contract formation, the term we would expect in the discussion about the enforceability of informal undertakings, is 'contract'. Yet, the term is relatively discreet throughout the 15th to 17th subcorpora. This is also reflected in the proximity figures discussed above.

In the Mansfield subcorpus, the occurrence of both 'consideration' and 'promise' rises exponentially in comparison to earlier corpora. 'Promise' is the first noun to appear in the list of collocates and the list of clusters with 'consideration'. 'Contract' is also more prominent than it had ever been before in the informal agreement/consideration context. It suggests that consideration was discussed in the context of contracts, as we would expect from our 21st century perspective. Finally, the wildcard concordance search for 'moral*' revealed an important presence (relative frequency of 81).

Beside this quantitative data, which shows a general increase, we can also observe a shift in the semantic content of the term 'consideration', while that is less the case for the other two primary search terms. This is best revealed by studying the register of the language, in which the term is embedded. For the sake of this study, four language registers were defined: general language, general legal language, specialised/technical language and Latin, as explained in Chapter 6 under Section 1.3. In the comparative table and charts, we can find the quantitative analysis of the language registers in the concordance lines that featured 'assumpsit', 'promise' and 'consideration' as search terms.

While 'assumpsit' has the general language meaning of an undertaking (OED: 'a taking upon oneself'), it is usually associated with informal contract formation. Three out of the four examples given in the Oxford English Dictionary are directly related to the legal meaning of 'assumpsit'. This is reflected in the 16th and 17th c. subcorpora as can be observed from the Chart 11. While the meaning in 6 % of the KWIC lines can be placed in the registers of general language or general legal language during the 16th century, the subcorpus for the following century shows the term in exclusively legal technical meaning.

A similar scenario can be observed in relation to the term 'promise', although in that case, the dominant language register is general legal language, which figures almost exclusively in the 17th century subcorpus.

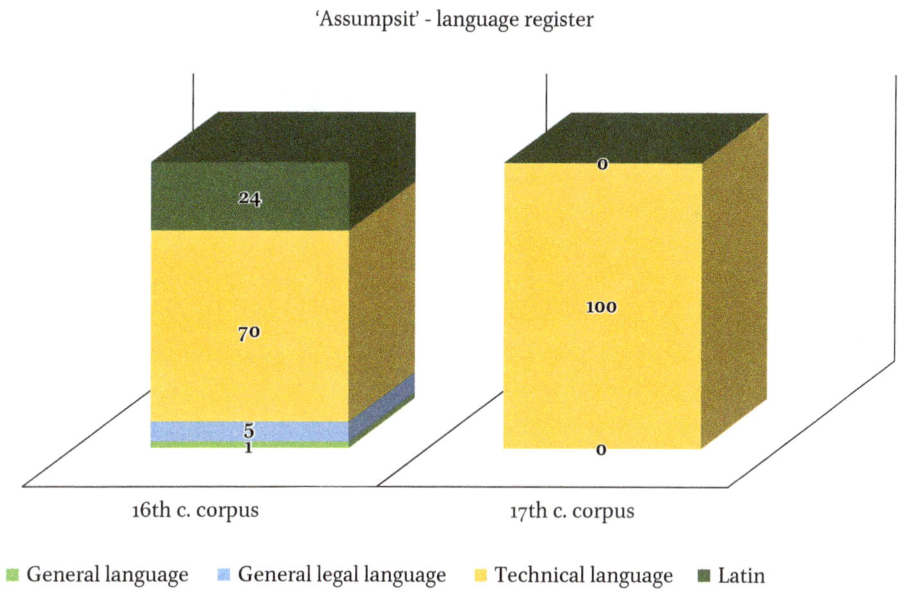

CHART 11 Language register for 'assumpsit' in the 16th and 17th c. subcorpora (%)

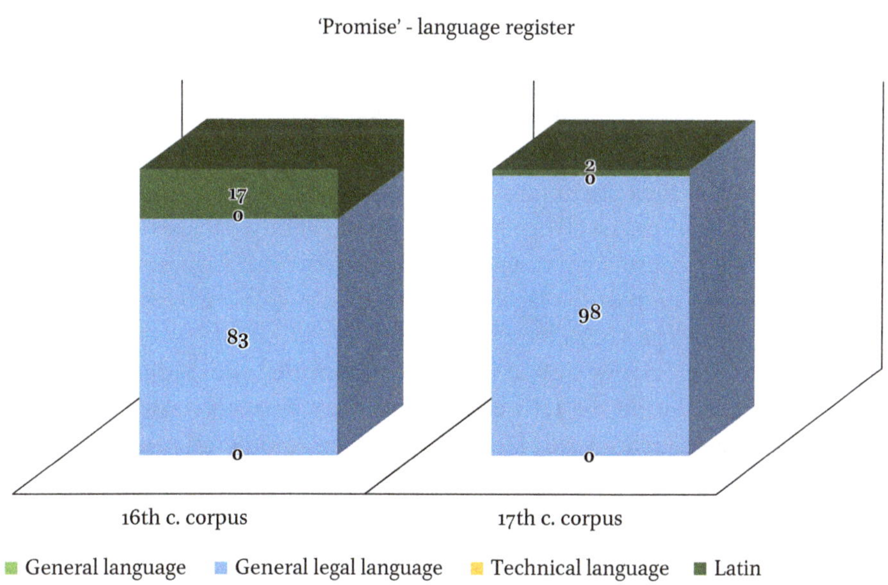

CHART 12 Language register for 'promise' in the 16th and 17th c. subcorpora (%)

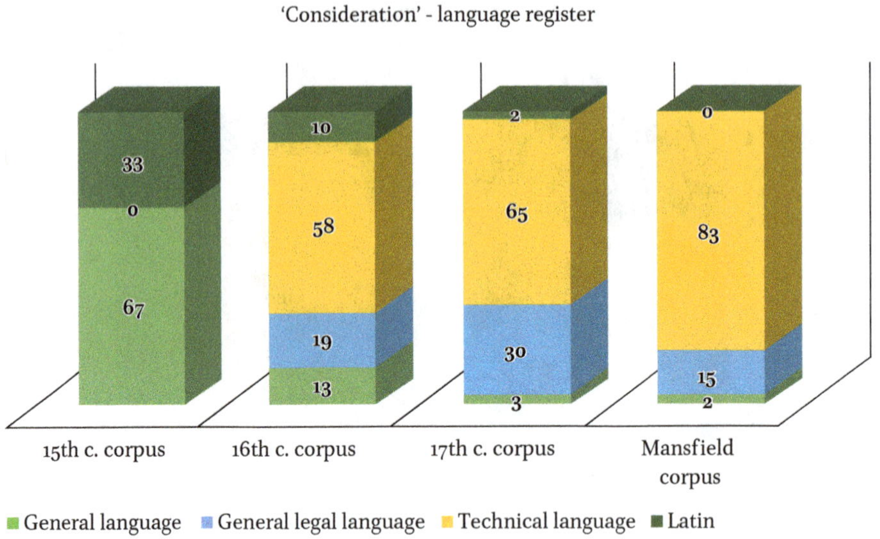

CHART 13 Language register for 'consideration' in the 15th, 16th, 17th c. and Mansfield subcorpora

For 'consideration' as the central term of this study, the concordance lines for all four subcorpora were closely examined.

General language uses of 'consideration', as represented by the light green part of the stacked columns in Chart 13 fall substantially with time. In the earlier sources, it is frequently used in the sense of the court or the judges 'taking (something) into account' when reaching a decision. From the 16th century, this use is less frequent: it falls to a 13% share. It is interesting that the context of these 16th c. general language KWIC lines is almost exclusively in Middle English. It only occurs three times in Anglo-French. This suggests that the increased specialisation of the legal language appears to have happened in Anglo-French rather than Middle English.

The principal semantic shift in the use of the term 'consideration' appears to have happened during the 16th century. We can observe two main changes. First, there is an increased use of the collocation 'in consideration of' as a causal conjunction between the two elements or events necessary for striking a contractual agreement. While this particular collocation could be used in any situation of exchange, the textual context clearly shows that we are dealing with specialist technical matters of the law. It is a relatively restricted set of vocabulary concerned with legal instruments and persons, payments, indenture, estate etc. in exchange of mainly marriage and other family matters. In other words, both the meaning and function of the collocation are in a general language sense but it is the lexical and semantic context that is highly technical.

Second, as we move further into the 16th and towards the 17th centuries, we find 'consideration' in technical uses. The lexical variety of its textual context is relatively poor and semantically restricted. The term 'consideration' tends to be combined with a limited set of words, which is indicative for the use of specialised language. Furthermore, it appears as a full noun in a function of participants, accompanied by adjectives and prepositions, and associated with material processes. The term can also be found as a one-word sentence, where the word is between two full-stops and thus pregnant with conceptual meanings. All these grammatical pointers put the word 'consideration' in prime positions within the clauses, a position where it appears in its own right and as a signpost for a concept, rather than as a mere causal link between two other prime elements. It is in this sense that the word is used in a way akin to a concept.

As we come to the decisions taken by Lord Mansfield and his fellow judges between the mid 18th and the early 19th century, we have a very different language situation (see Chapter 6/6). The language is Modern English and had already been the subject of the Great Vowel Shift, inflectional simplification and Johnson's linguistic standardisation. It means that the use of language and terminology is a lot more structured. Moreover, the selection criteria were different from the other corpora: the corpus compiled for this part of the study was built by selecting cases on the basis of their *content* and whether these were a part of the corpus of cases stipulating Mansfield's concept of consideration as moral obligation.

The shift in the use of the terminology at the time of Mansfield cannot be denied. The quantitative data of the linguistic analysis not only shows a more intensive and precise use of specialised terminology and language, but also bears witness to the new aspects of the concept, namely that informal agreements are seen as contracts and that there is a moral element inherent in the making of a promise, which is a definite, though short-lived, *rapprochement* with the civil law concept of *causa*.

•••

The quantitative analysis has revealed the use and development of the vocabulary associated with the concept of consideration. We have observed a linear evolution showing not only a rising trend in the use of the word 'consideration', but also leading to a more intensive use of the term in a legal-technical context and to describe an autonomous legal concept. As to the development of the idea of enforcing informal agreements from a conceptual point of view, we observe a concordance between the two, yet with a gap in time as the terminology tends to lag behind.

TABLE 42 Terminology in the case law between 1300–1650 and 1750–1850

Date		Terminology	Case law/legal writings
1300–1350	1321	'defaute'	surgeon negligence[a]
	1329	'lui promist de eyder a tort e a droit'	assistance[b]
	1348	'emprist a carier', 'covenant', 'trespass'	*Humber Ferry case*[c] (malfeasance)
1350–1400	1370	'manucepit', 'emprist', 'covenant', 'negligence'	*Waldon v Marshall*[d] (malfeasance)
	1374	'emprist'	Action on the case[e] (surgeon)
1400–1450	1400	'covenant', 'negligence'	*Watton v Brinth*[f] (non-feasance)
	1429	'deceit', 'bargain', 'quid pro quo'	Action on the case[g]
	1431	'deceit', 'bargain'	Action on the case[h]
	1433	'assumpsit' in Latin phrase, 'assumpc', 'assumer', 'assumption'	Action on the case[i]
	1436	'non feasance', 'covenant'	Trespass on the case action[j]
1450–1500	1476	'bargain'	(successful) action of 'deceit on the case'[k]
	1493	'super se assumpsit', 'non assumpsit mode et forma', 'emprist', 'quod non assumpsit'	*Johnson v Baker*[l]
1500–1550	1504	'covenant', 'non fes', 'deceit'	non-feasance recognised[m]
	1518	'promise'	St German[n]
	1522	'jeo done terre en taylle icy est consideration'	replevin[o]
	1535	'det', 'assumpsit', 'assumpc', 'assumption', 'agreemt', 'covenat', 'contract'	Action on the case[p]
1550–1600	1553	'en consideration que son file marier'	uses with/without consideration[q]
	1572	'assumpsit', 'contract', 'det', 'assume'	Action on the case[r]
	1573	'en considerac q', 'assume de payer', 'assumpsit'	*Edwards v Burre*[s]
1600–1650	1602	'assumpsit', 'en consideracin de', 'contract'	*Slade v Morley*[t]
	1623	'le surrender des patents est ben consideration a faire novell grant'	*Seignior Zouch v Sir Edward Moore*[u]
	1629	'le consideration del sanke & amor la pier est continuant'	*Besfich & Coggil*[v]

1750–1850	1765	'whether this be a promise without a consideration'	*Pillans v Van Mierop*[w]
	1782	'to make a consideration to support and assumpsit'	*Hawkes v Saunders*[x]
	1811	'here was a consideration directly moving to the defendant'	*Barrell v Trussell*[y]
	1860	'voluntary courtesy will not have a consideration to uphold an assumpsit'	*Shadwell v Shadwell*[z]

a YB 14 Edw. II.
b 3 & 4 Edw. III or 97 Selden Society, 237.
c *Bukton v Tounesende* (1348) Lib. Ass. 22 Edw III Folio 94a-94b, pl. 41, or LBEx.
d Y.B Mich. 43 Ed. III, 33, 38, or LBEx.
e YB 48 Edw. III, 6, 11, or LBEx.
f Case of 1400 in Y.B. 2 Hen. IV, 3, 9, or in LBEx.
g 7 Hen.VI,1, 3, or LBEx.
h 9 Hen. VI, 53, 37, or LBEx.
i 11 Hen. VI, 18, 24, or LBEx.
j Y.B. 14 Hen. VI, 18, 58, or in LBEx.
k Y.B. 16 Pasch. Edw. IV, 9, 7, or LBEx.
l C.P., Hil. 1493. Record CP 40/914, m. 104 or 115 Selden Society 135.
m Y.B. 20 Mich. Hen. VII, 8, 18, or LBEx.
n Ch. St. German (1518/1974), *Doctor and Student*, Second Dialogue, Chapter 24, edited by T. Plucknett, J. Barton (1974) for the Selden Society, vol. 91.
o *Gervys v Cooke*, (1522) YB 12–14 Hen. VIII, or 119 Selden Society, 108 at 117.
p Y.B. 27 Mich. Hen.VIII, 24, 3, or LBEx.
q Reports of William Dalison, or 124 Selden Society, at 50.
r Dalison 84, 35, or 123 Eng. Rep. 293.
s Dalison 104, 45, or 123 Eng. Rep. 310.
t 4 Co Rep. 92 a.
u 81 Eng. Rep. 795–96.
v 81 Eng. Rep 1219–1221.
w *Pillans and Rose v Van Mierop and Hopkins*, (1765) 3 Burr. 1663, or 97 Eng. Rep. 1035, at 1040.
x *Hawkes v Saunders*, (1782) 1 Cowp. 289, or 98 Eng. Rep. 1091.
y *Barrell v Trussell*, (1811) 4 Taunt. 117, or 128 Eng. Rep. 273, at 274.
z *Shadwell v Shadwell*, (1860) 9 C.B. (N.S.) 159, or 142 Eng. Rep. 62, at 67.

In the Table 42, a selection of relevant cases has been listed with the vocabulary that dominated each case. This is by way of illustration of how the language evolved from the hesitant use of diverse terms to a more settled and structured language.

The idea that failing to honour an undertaking should be actionable emerged in the second half of the 14th century in a number of trespass on the case actions, first for malfeasance then for non feasance, coupled at times with deceit. The action of debt and *indebitatus assumpsit* was also added to the already mixed bag of legal actions (see 1300–1550 in Table 42). The *Slade case* in 1602 clarified the content and ambit of the action of assumpsit. But, while the new action was increasingly becoming a legal reality, the textual evidence towards the end of the 16th century does not show the term 'assumpsit' as an established legal technical term or category, nor does it show the vocabulary in the actions on the case to be very uniform. We can frequently find the verb 'to undertake' (*emprist*), some use of 'assumpsit', though frequently embedded in a Latin phrase, akin to a legal formula. There are repeated references to 'covenant', 'bargain' and 'debt', all notions emanating from older actions but based on proprietary rather than promissory concepts. It appears as though the new legal thinking could not overcome old established categories of proprietary concepts. The terminology used was hesitant and remained on well-trodden paths. The term 'promise' and its underlying notion only figured tentatively in the case law. With today's hindsight, we understand that promise was actually already at the heart of the new legal thinking, in particular in *indebitatus assumpsit* cases. But then it had to be discussed more intensively and for a longer period of time, in particular in the *indebitatus assumpsit* cases, to emerge as a proper concept in its own right. The uncertainty in the use of the vocabulary is a witness to that hesitancy in the legal thinking.

Following the greater clarity that the *Slade case* brought in 1602, we can not only see the rise in the use of the word 'promise', but also that of the causal phrase 'in consideration of' that links one promissory part of the informal agreement to the other. As this concept is tried out, discussed and challenged in the courts, it becomes more established and settled. This can also be observed in the use of the terminology. We have moved from *'consideration'* as a general concept to *'in consideration of'* in a general context, to *'in consideration of'* in a specifically legal context (though still within a general language understanding), to *'consideration'* as the linguistic expression of a legal concept.

As the concept gained in stature, so did its position as an autonomous concept. This was reflected in the use of the term 'consideration', no longer solely in the context of a causal connector but as a stand-alone noun and cover-term for the conceptual thinking of how to make informal agreements enforceable. The term 'consideration' stood hitherto for a legal concept, that has continued to evolve to the present day. But on this path, in particular in the earlier stages, the common law followed its pragmatic driven nose by nudging existing boundaries and thus reaching neighbouring premises. Whether a new rabbit came out of an old hat or whether it was, in fact, a different hat is still somewhat of a moot point.

•••

This research has examined the concept of consideration in the English common law, but to conclude on a more general note, it must be stressed that this type of study need not be restricted to either the Middle Ages/Renaissance or the common law of contract. The approach and methodology adopted are cognitive models that have allowed us to go beyond the conceptual and doctrinal framework of the law and gain a deep level understanding of the origins and evolution of legal thinking and the terminology. Two general concluding remarks should be made here.

First, studying the language of the law from a diachronic terminological angle in combination with the basic premises of the *Begriffsgeschichte* approach, reveals the etymological, semantic and historical aspects of terms. Such knowledge of the emergence and evolution of terminology equips us with a better understanding of how to adapt and use it differently in the present and future. This may be relevant, for example, in the context of legal language reforms. The language of the law has long been criticised as archaic, complex and pompous, thus, excluding large parts of the population from understanding it.[7] And indeed, the language used in law forms a part of the rather grand institutions and practices that have developed due to historical traditions, its normative nature, prescriptive and performative functions and the basic premise that the letter of the law is supreme. The fact that some terms have everyday language meanings, such as 'consideration', only adds to the confusion. Any attempts to reform the legal language, usually with the aim to making it more widely accessible, must start from a deep-level understanding of the significance of terms, including their historical evolution. The kind of linguistic research that was carried out for this study offers essential insights into such deeper understanding.

7 P. Tiersma (1999) Legal Language, Chicago: University of Chicago Press, at 241.

Moreover, diachronic terminological studies may also be relevant in the context of newly emerging bodies of law, such as environmental law that has developed over a relatively short period of time and has thus missed out on the benefits of a more 'organic' evolution in relation to conceptual foundations and the relevant language and terminology.[8] Similarly, corpus linguistics methodologies have also been advocated by members of the US judiciary as a tool for statutory interpretation.[9]

Second, a linguistic and terminological approach also contributes to a better comprehension of the conceptual evolution of the law and of its sociocultural content. This represents an important contribution to the study of the differences or similarities between legal systems. A better grasp of the origins and evolution of specific aspects or elements of the law or a legal system, can contribute to a contextual approach for, among others, comparative law, legal translation or legal harmonisation projects. Moreover, a deep-level understanding of the concepts of law through the study of its language, provides context when tracing the law's "first rudiments among savages, through successive changes, to its highest improvements in a civilised society", as advocated by Lord Kames. To that extent, this is an approach essential for all students of the law to deepen the comprehension of their subject. It is context that renders facts truly informative…

…wodurch doch allein alles Wissen erst Wert bekommt. (Schiller)

8 C. Laske (2021, forthcoming) Environmental Law: Lexical Semantics in the Quest for Conceptual Foundations, in: P. Stoett, S. Lamalle *Representations and Rights of the Environment*, Cambridge: CUP.

9 e.g. Justice Thomas Lee of the Utah Supreme Court, T.R. Lee, S. Mouritsen (2018) Judging Ordinary Meaning, in: *The Yale Law Journal*, 127/4 (2017/2018) 788–1105.

ANNEX 1

Anglo-Norman Sources

A collection of Anglo-Norman source texts can be found on the Anglo-Norman On-Line Hub (www.anglo-norman.net) – Anglo-Norman textbase:

Amys e Amillyoun, ed. by H. Fukui. London: Anglo-Norman Text Society, 1990.

Annales Monasterii de Burton [MS. Cotton. Vespas. E. iii.], ed. by H.R. Luard. London, 1871. French materials only.

Annales Londonienses and Annales Paulini, ed. by W. Stubbs. London: Longman & Co., 1882. French materials only.

The Anonimalle Chronicle 1307–1334 [From Brotherton Collection MS 29], ed. by W.R. Childs and J. Taylor. Leeds: Yorkshire Archaeological Society, 1991. French materials only.

An Anglo-Norman Rhymed Apocalypse, ed. by O. Rhys. Oxford: Anglo-Norman Text Society, 1946.

Guernes de Pont-Sainte-Maxence, La Vie de Saint Thomas Becket, ed. by E. Walberg. Paris, 1935.

Walter de Bibbesworth. Le Tretiz, ed. by W. Rothwell. London: Anglo-Norman Text Society, 1990.

The Black Book of the Admiralty, Vol. 1, ed. by T. Twiss. London, 1871.

Britton, ed. by F.M. Nichols. Oxford 1865.

An Anglo-Norman Brut [MS ROYAL 13.A.xxi], ed. by A. Bell. Oxford: Anglo-Norman Text Society, 1969.

Le livre des psaumes. Ancienne traduction française d'après les manuscrits de Cambridge et de Paris, ed. by F. Michel. Paris, 1876.

Le Livre de Catun, ed. by T. Hunt. London: Anglo-Norman Text Society, 1994.

Phillipe de Thaon, Comput, ed. by I. Short. London: Anglo-Norman Text Society, 1984.

Robert le Chapelain, Corset. A Rhymed Commentary on the Seven Sacraments, ed. by K.V. Sinclair. London: Anglo-Norman Text Society, 1995.

Croniques de London depuis l'an 44 Hen III jusqu'à l'an 17 Edw III, ed. by G.J. Aungier. London: Camden Society, 1844.

La Destructioun de Rome, ed. by L. Formisano. London: Anglo-Norman Text Society, 1990.

The Black Book of the Admiralty, Vol. 2, ed. by T. Twiss. London, 1871.

Les Gius Partiz des Eschez. Two Anglo-Norman Chess Treatises, ed. by T. Hunt. London: Anglo-Norman Text Society, 1985.

 | DOI:10.1163/9789004436169_009

Eighteen Anglo-Norman Fabliaux, ed. by I. Short and R. Pearcy. London: Anglo-Norman Text Society, London, 2000.

Foedera, ed. by T. Rymer and R. Sanderson. Vols 1–4, London 1816–1869. French materials only.

The Anglo-Norman 'Folie Tristan', ed. by I. Short. London: Anglo-Norman Text Society, 1993.

Fouke le Fitz Waryn, ed. by E.J. Hathaway, P.T. Ricketts, C.A. Robson and A.D. Wilshere. Oxford: Anglo-Norman Text Society, 1975.

L'Estoire des Engleis by Geffrei Gaimar, ed. by A. Bell. Oxford: Anglo-Norman Text Society, 1960.

John of Gaunt's Register (1372–76), ed. by S. Armitage-Smith. London: Camden Society, 1911.

The Romance of Horn by Thomas, ed. by M.K. Pope. Oxford: Anglo-Norman Text Society, 1955.

The Hospitallers' Riwle, ed. by K.V. Sinclair. London: Anglo-Norman Text Society, 1984.

A Roll of the Proceedings of the King's Council in Ireland for a Portion of the Sixteenth Year of the Reign of Richard II A.D. 1392–93, ed. by J. Graves. London, 1877. French materials only.

Anglo-Norman Letters and Petitions and Petitions from All Souls MS 182, ed. by M. Dominica Legge. Oxford: Anglo-Norman Text Society, 1941.

Liber Albus [Munimenta Gildhallae Londoniensis, Vol 1], ed. by H.T. Riley. London, 1860. French materials only.

Liber Custumarum, with extracts from Cottonian MS Claudius D. II [Munimenta Gildhallae Londoniensis, Vol 2], ed. by H.T. Riley. London, 1860. French materials only.

Liber Donati. A Fifteenth-Century Manual of French, ed. by B. Merrilees and B. Sitz-Fitzpatrick. London: Anglo-Norman Text Society, 1993.

La Lumere as Lais by Pierre d'Abernon of Fetcham, ed. by G. Hesketh. London: Anglo-Norman Text Society, 1996–2000.

Manières de Langage (1396, 1399, 1415), ed. by A.M. Kristol. London: Anglo-Norman Text Society, 1995.

Mirour de Seinte Eglyse (St Edmund of Abingdon's Speculum Ecclesiae), ed. by A.D. Wilshere. London: Anglo-Norman Text Society, 1982.

Nominale sive Verbale, ed. by W.W. Skeat. Transactions of the Philological Society, 1903–06, pp. 1*–50* 1906.

Northern Petitions illustrative of life in Berwick, Cumbria and Durham in the fourteenth century, ed. by C.M. Fraser. Durham: Surtees Society, 1981. French materials only.

Ancient Petitions relating to Northumberland, ed. by C.M. Fraser. Durham and London: Surtees Society, 1966. French materials only.

The Oak Book of Southampton (c. A.D. 1300), ed. by P. Studer. 2 Vols. Southampton, 1910.

The Oxford Anglo-Norman Psalter [MS Bodleian Douce 320], ed. by F. Michel. Paris, 1876.

The Percy Chartulary, ed. by M.T. Martin. Durham: Surtees Society, 1911. French materials only.

La Petite Philosophie: An Anglo-Norman Poem of the Thirteenth Century, ed. by W.H. Trethewey. Oxford: Anglo-Norman Text Society, 1939.

Le Petit Plet, ed. by B.S. Merrilees. Oxford: Anglo-Norman Text Society, 1970.

Anglo-Norman Political Songs, ed. by I.S.T. Aspin. Oxford: Anglo-Norman Text Society, 1953.

The Port Books of Southampton, 1427–1430, ed. by P. Studer. Southampton, 1913.

Private Indentures for Life Service in Peace and War, 1278–1476, ed. by M. Jones and S. Walker. London: Royal Historical Society, 1994. French materials only.

Hue de Rotelande, Protheselaus, ed. by A.J. Holden. London: Anglo-Norman Text Society, 1991–3.

Rauf de Linham, Kalender, ed. by T. Hunt. London: Anglo-Norman Text Society, 1983.

The Red Book of the Exchequer Part III, ed. by Hubert Hall. London: HMSO, 1896.

Registrum Epistolarum Fratris Johannis Peckham, Archepiscopi Cantuariensis, ed. by C.T. Martin. London, 1882. French materials only.

Le Livere de Reis De Brittanie e Le Livere de Reis de Engletere, ed. by J. Glover. London, 1865.

Li Rei de Engleterre. Ein anglo-normannischer Geschichtsauszug. ed. by J. Koch. Berlin, 1886.

La Seinte Resureccion from the Paris and Canterbury MSS, ed. by T.A. Jenkins, J.M. Manly, M.K. Pope and J.J. Wright. Oxford: Anglo-Norman Text Society, 1943.

The Crusade and Death of Richard I, ed. by R.C. Johnston. Oxford: Anglo-Norman Text Society, 1961.

Memorials of the Church of SS. Peter and Wilfrid, Ripon Vols. 1 and 2, 2 vols. Durham: Surtees Society, 1882, 1886. French materials only.

The Anglo-Norman 'Alexander'. 'Le Roman de toute Chevalerie' by Thomas of Kent, ed. by B. Foster with the assistance of I. Short. London: Anglo-Norman Text Society, 1976–7.

'Le Roman de Philosophie' in: Les Oeuvres de Simund de Freine, ed. by J.E. Matzke. Paris, 1909.

Register of Daniel Rough, Common clerk of Romney 1353–1380, ed. by K.M.E. Murray. Canterbury: Kent Archaeological Society, 1945. French materials only.

Royal and Other Historical Letters Illustrative of the reign of Henry III, ed. by W. Waddington Shirley, London: Longmans, 1866. French materials only.

The Anglo-Norman Voyage of St Brendan, ed. by I. Short and B. Merrilees. Manchester: MUP, 1979.

La Passiun de Seint Edmund, ed. by J. Grant. London: Anglo-Norman Text Society, 1978.

La Estoire de Seint Aedward le Rei, ed. by K.Y. Wallace. London: Anglo-Norman Text Society, 1983.

La Vye de Seynt Fraunceys d'Assise (MS Paris, BNF, Fonds Français 13505), ed. by D.W. Russell, with the collaboration of A.R. Harden and H.S.F. Collins. London: Anglo-Norman Text Society, 2002.

Vie de Saint Georges in: Les oeuvres de Simund de Freine, ed. by J.E. Matzke. Paris, 1909.

St. Modwenna, ed. by A.T. Baker and A. Bell. Oxford: Anglo-Norman Text Society, 1947.

Les Proverbes de Salemon by Sanson de Nantuil, ed. by C.C. Isoz. London: Anglo-Norman Text Society, 1988–94.

Le Secré; de Secrez by Pierre d'Abernun of Fetcham, ed. by O.A. Beckerlegge. Oxford: Anglo-Norman Text Society, 1944.

An Anglo-Norman Rhymed Sermon on Shrift, ed. by Robin F. Jones. Originally published in Modern Philology Volume 79, 1981–2.

The War of Saint-Sardos (1323–1325) Gascon Correspondence and Diplomatic Documents, ed. by P. Chaplais. London: Royal Historical Society, 1954. French materials only.

The Register of Walter de Stapeldon Bishop of Exeter, A.D. 1307–1326, ed. by F.C. Hingeston-Randolph. London, 1892. French materials only.

The Statutes of the Realm Vol. 1, London, 1810. French materials only.

Le livre de seyntz medicines: the unpublished devotional treatise of Henry of Lancaster, ed. by E.J. Arnould. Oxford: Anglo-Norman Text Society, 1940.

Testamentata Eboracensia, ed. by L. Baker and J. Raine. London: Surtees Society, 1836, 1855 & 1864. French materials only.

The Anglo-Norman Pseudo-Turpin Chronicle of Williame de Briane, ed. by I. Short. Oxford: Anglo-Norman Text Society, 1973.

Documents Illustrating the Rule of Walter de Wenlok, Abbot of Westminster, 1283–1307, ed. by Barbara F. Harvey. London: Royal Historical Society, 1965.

The Anglo-Norman Chronicle of Wigmore Abbey, ed. by J.C. Dickinson and P.T. Ricketts. Transactions of The Woolhope Naturalists' Field Club Vol. 39, 1967–9, pp. 413–445.

York Memorandum Book Part I. (1376–1419), ed. by M. Sellers. Durham, London, Berlin: Surtees Society, 1912. French materials only.

ANNEX 2

Legal Sources

The case law used for this research has been drawn from the Year Books, the *Selden Society* (Annual) series, the *Ames Foundation* publications or the *English Reports, Full Reprint*. All documents can be accessed electronically through www.heinonline.org. The first three are listed under the title of 'Selden Society Publications and the History of Early English Law', the last one can be found under 'English Reports'. A detailed description of each is given below. All reported cases mentioned are usually listed with their name and two references: one relating to the name of the original report and one to the compilation in which they can be found on HeinOnline.

Examples of case references:

Watton v Brinth (1400) Y.B. 2 Hen. IV, 3, 9, or Lawbook Exchange (sometimes abbreviated as LBEx):

- first the name of the case and the date it was reported (between brackets), N.B. many early cases do not have a name;
- followed by the reference of the original report: here it can be found in the Year Book (Y.B.) during the second year of the reign of Henry IV, sometimes the legal term is also included (Michaelmas: Oct.-Dec., Hilary: Jan.-Apr., Easter: Apr.-May, Trinity: June-July);
- followed by two numbers signposting the section within the Year Book;
- followed by 'or' and the reference for finding it on HeinOnline: here it is in the Year Books (Lawbook Exchange).

Cleymon v Vyncent (1535) Y.B. Trin. 27 Hen. VIII, 23, 21 or 119 Selden Society at 46–47:

- case dated 1535;
- originally reported in the Year Book of the Trinity term of the 27th year of the reign of Henry VIII;
- two numbers to signpost the specific section;
- 'or' in the 119th volume of the Selden Society (Annual) series at pp. 46–47 on the HeinOnline database.

Norwood v Reed (1558) 1 Plowd. 180 or 75 Eng. Rep. 277:

- cases dated 1558;
- originally reported in the first volumes of the Plowden Reports in section 180;
- 'or' in volume 75 of the English Reports, Full Reprint, on page 277 on the HeinOnline database.

 | DOI:10.1163/9789004436169_010

A table of cases can be found in Annex 3. The table is subdivided into one sorted by date and one in alphabetical order. It lists the cases mentioned in the theoretical discussion of the concept of consideration, that is in Chapter 5.

•••

All sources listed here are electronically accessible via the database of HeinOnline (www.heinonline.org). Beside every title below is listed each click to access the documents in question.

I Selden Society Publications and the History of Early English Law – All Titles – Alphabetical Search

I.i *Year Books* (*Lawbook Exchange*)

- 1–10 Edward III 1327–1337
- 17–39 Edward III 1343–1366
- 40–50 Edward III 1366–1377
- Liber Assisarum 1327–1377
- Henry IV & Henry V 1399–1422
- 1–20 Henry VI 1422–1442
- 21–39 Henry VI 1442–1461
- Edward IV 1461–1483
- 5 Edward IV 1465–1466
- Edward V, Richard III, Henry VII & Henry VIII 1483–1535

I.ii *Year Books of the Reign of King Edward the First*

- 1 (Years XX–XXI)
- 2 (Years XXI–XXII)
- 3 (Years XXII–XXXII)
- 4 (Years XXXII–XXXIII)
- 5 (Years XXXIII–XXV)

II Selden Society Publications and the History of Early English Law – Ames Foundation Publications

Year Books of Richard II:

- 2 Richard II 1378–79
- 6 Richard II 1382–83

- 7 Richard II 1383–84
- 8–10 Richard II 1385–87
- 11 Richard II 1387–88
- 12 Richard II 1388–89
- 13 Richard II 1389–90

III Selden Society Publications and the History of Early English Law – Selden Society Publications – Selden Society (Annual) Series

- Earliest English Law Reports Vol. I & II (111 & 112 Selden Society)
- Earliest English Law Reports Vol. III & IV (122 & 123 Selden Society)
- Year Books of Edward II & III:
  - 1 and 2 Edward II 1307–1308 and 1308–1309 (Year Book Series I or 17 Selden Society)
  - 2 and 3 Edward II 1308–1309 and 1309–1310 (Year Book Series II or 19 Selden Society)
  - 3 Edward II 1309–1310 (Year Book Series III or 20 Selden Society)
  - 3 and 4 Edward II 1310 (Year Book Series IV or 22 Selden Society)
  - 4 Edward II 1310–1311 (Year Book Series V or 24 Selden Society)
  - 4 Edward II 1311 (Year Book Series VI or 26 Selden Society)
  - 4 Edward II 1311 (Year Book Series X or 63 Selden Society)
  - 5 Edward II 1311 (Year Book Series XXI or 54 Selden Society)
  - 5 Edward II 1311–1312 (Year Book Series XI or 31 Selden Society)
  - 5 Edward II 1312 (Year Book Series XII or 33 Selden Society)
  - 6 Edward II 1312–1313 (Year Book Series XIII or 34 Selden Society)
  - 6 Edward II 1312–1313 (Year Book Series XIV or 38 Selden Society)
  - 6 Edward II 1313 (Year Book Series XIV or 43 Selden Society)
  - 6 and 7 Edward II 1313 (Year Book Series XV or 36 Selden Society)
  - 6 and 7 Edward II 1313–1314 (Year Book Series VII or 27 Selden Society)
  - Eyre of Kent, 6 and 7 Edward II 1313–1314 (Year Book Series VIII or 29 Selden Society)
  - 7 Edward II 1313–1314 (Year Book Series XVI or 39 Selden Society)
  - 8 Edward II 1314–1315 (Year Book Series XVII or 41 Selden Society)
  - 8 Edward II 1315 (Year Book Series XVIII or 37 Selden Society)
  - 9 Edward II 1315–1316 (Year Book Series XIX or 45 Selden Society)
  - 10 Edward II 1316–1317 (Year Book Series XX or 52 Selden Society)
  - 10 Edward ii 1316–1317 (Year Book Series xxi or 54 Selden Society)
  - 11 Edward ii 1317–1318 (Year Book Series xxii or 61 Selden Society)
  - 12 Edward ii 1318 (Year Book Series XXIII or 65 Selden Society)

  - 12 Edward II 1319 (Year Book Series XXIV or 70 Selden Society)
  - 12 Edward II 1319 (Year Book Series XXV or 81 Selden Society)
  - 14 Edward II 1320 (Year Book Series XXVII or 104 Selden Society)
  - The Eyre of London, 14 Edward II 1321 (Year Book Series XXVI Part i or 85 Selden Society)
  - The Eyre of London, 14 Edward II 1321 (Year Book Series XXVI Part ii or 86 Selden Society)
  - The Eyre of Northhamptonshire, 3 and 4 Edward III 1329–1330 (Year Book Series or 97 & 98 Selden Society)
- Select Cases before the King's Council, 1243–1482 (35 Selden Society)
- Select Cases in the Exchequer Chamber before all the Justices of England, 1377–1461 (51 Selden Society)
- Year Books of Henry VI, 1 Henry VI A.D. 1422 (50 Selden Society)
- Year Books of 10 Edward IV and 49 Henry VI A.D. 1470 (47 Selden Society)
- Reports of Cases by John Caryll, Part I, A.D. 1485–1499 (115 Selden Society)
- Reports of Cases by John Caryll, Part II, A.D. 1501–1522 (116 Selden Society)
- Select Cases in the Council of Henry VII (1485–1509) (75 Selden Society)
- Select Cases Before The King's Council in The Star Chamber, vol. I, A.D. 1477–1509 (16 Selden Society)
- Select Cases Before The King's Council in The Star Chamber, vol. II, A.D. 1509–1544 (25 Selden Society)
- The Reports of Sir John Spelman, vol. I, 1502–1540 (93 Selden Society)
- Year Books of Henry VIII, 12–14 Henry VIII, A.D. 1520–1523 (119 Selden Society)
- The Reports of William Dalison, A.D. 1552–1558 (124 Selden Society)
- Reports from the Lost Notebooks of Sir James Dyer, vol. 1 & 2 (109 & 110 Selden Society)

IV English Reports – English Reports, Full Reprint

IV.i *Eng. Rep. vol. 72*

The English Reports – King's Bench Division containing:
- Bellewe (1585):

> LES ANS DU ROY RICHARD LE SECOND. Collect' Ensembl' Hors les Abridgments De Statham, Fitzherbert et Brooke. Per RICHARD BELLEWE, de Lincolns Inne. 1585

– Keilwey (1688):

REPORTS d'ascuns CASES (qui ont evenus aux temps dy Roy Henry le Septieme de tres heureuse memoire, & du tres illustre Roy Henry le huitiesme, & ne sont comprises deins les livres des Terms & Ans demesmes les Roys.) Seliges hors des papiers de ROBERT KEILWEY, Esp.; par JEAN CROKE, Sergeant al Ley, Jades Recorder del City de Londres & Prolocuteur del meason des Communes es derniers jour du rege de la Royne Elisabeth. 1688.

Ovesque les Reports d'ascuns Cases prises per le Reverend Juge *Guilleaume Dallison* un des Justices del Bank le Roy, au temps de la Reyne *Elisabeth* & per *Guilleaume Bendloe* Serjeant al Ley au temps de la mesme Royne; touchants la construction de divers Acts de Parliament par equitè.

La tierce Edition embellie de pluis que deux milles References aux autres livres cybien Ancient que Moderne de la ley, *Jamais* uncore imprimès.

– Moore (1688):

CASES Collect and Report per Sir Fra. Moore, Chevalier, Serjeant del Ley. Imprime and Publie per l'Original jadis remainent en les maines de Sir GEFREY PALMER, Chevalier and Bar., Attorney-General a son Tres-Excellent Majesty le Roy Charles le Seond. Le Seco Edition. 1688

IV.ii ***Eng. Rep. vol. 73***

The English Reports – King's Bench Division containing:

– Benloe (1661):

Les REPORTS de GULIELME BENDLOES Serjeant de la Lay: Des Divers Resolutions et Judgments donne par les Reverendes Judges de la Ley: De certeine Matieres en la Ley en le Temps del Raigne de Roys et Roignes Hen. VIII., Edw. VI., Phil et Mar. et Elisab. Avec que Autres Select Cases en la Ley adjudges et resolves en le Temps del Regne de Tresillustres Roys Jaques et Charles le premier: Jammais par cy devant imprimee. Publies en le XIII au de Treshaut et Renosmes Charles le Second Par le Grace de Deiu Roy d'Angleterre, Scoce, Fr. et Irel. Le Restituteur et Conservateur de la Ley. 1661

– also containing in English translation:
Dyer, volumes 1, 2 and 3; Brook's new cases; these were disregarded.

IV.iii ***Eng. Rep. vol. 123***
The English Reports – Common Pleas containing:
– Benloe (1689):

> Les REPORTS de GULIELME BENLOE, Serjeant del Ley, Des divers PLEADINGS et CASES en le COURT del COMON-BANK, en le several Roignes de les tres Hault & Excellent Princes, le ROY HENRY VII., HENRY VIII., EDW. VI., & le ROIGNES MARY & EIZABETH. 1689

– Dalison (1689):

> Les REPORTS des divers SPEICAL CASES Adjudge en le COURT del COMON BANK en les Reignes de les tres hault & Excellent Princes HEN. VIII. EDW. VI. et les Reignes MAR. & ELIZ. Colligees par GULIELME DALISON un des JUSTICES Del BANK le ROY. London, 1689.

– Anderson, vols. 1 and 2 (1664):

> Les REPORTS du Treserudite EDMUND ANDERSON, Chivalier, Nadgairs, Seigniour CHIEF JUSTICE del COMMON-BANK. Des mults principals CASES ARGUES & AGJUGES en le temps del jadis ROIGN ELIZABETH cibien en le COMMON-BANK come devant touts les Juges de cest Poialme, colligees & escries per luy mesme & imprimees per l'Original ore remaneant en les maines des Imprimeur. London, 1664.

– Savile (1688):

> Les REPORTS de Sir JOHN SAVILE, Chevalier, Nadgairis Baron de l'Exchequer, de Divers SPEICAL CASES cybien en le COURT de COMMON Bank, come L'EXCHEQUER en le Temps de ROYNE ELIZABETH. London, MDCLXXXVIII

– also containing in English translation:
Brownlow and Goldesborough, vols. & and 2; Hutton; Bridgman; these were disregarded.

IV.iv ***Eng. Rep. vol. 81***

The English Reports – King's Bench Division containing:

– Rolle (1675):

> Les REPORTS de HENRY ROLLE Searjeant del' Ley, de divers CASES en le COURT del' BANKE le ROY. En le Temps del' REIGN de ROY JAQUES. Colligees par luy mesme & Imprimees par L'Original. 1675.

– Palmer (1721):

> The REPORTS of SIR JEFFREY PALMER, Knight and Baront; ATTORNEY GENERAL to His Most Excellent Majesty, KING CHARLES the SECOND; The Second Edition. 1721

– also containing in English translation:
Bulstrode; this was disregarded.

IV.v Mansfield Cases (in alphabetical order)

Atkins v Banwell
(1802) 2 East 505, or 102 Eng. Rep. 462
(1802) 3 Easr 92, or 102 Eng. Rep. 531

Atkins v Hill
(1775) 1 Cowp. 284, or 98 Eng. Rep. 1088

Barnes v Hedley
(1809) 2 Taunt. 184, or 127 Eng. Rep. 1047

Barrell v Trussell
(1811) 4 Taunt. 117, or 128 Eng. Rep. 273

Brooks v Haigh
(1840) 10 Ad & E. 323, or 113 Eng. Rep. 124

Clarke v Shee
(1774) 1 Cowp. 197, or 98 Eng. Rep. 1041

Cooper v Martin
(1803) 4 East 77, or 102 Eng. Rep. 759

Exeter Corporation v Trimlet
(1759) 2 Wils. K.B. 95, or 95 Eng. Rep. 705

Earle v Oliver
(1848) 2 Ex. 71, or 154 Eng. Rep. 410

Eastwood v Kenyon
(1840) 11 Ad. & E. 438, or 113 Eng. Rep. 482

Farmer v Arundel
2 Black. 824, or 96 Eng. Rep. 485
Flight v Reed
(1863) 1 H. & C. 703, or 158 Eng. Rep. 1067
Floyer v Edwards
(1774) Lofft, 595, or 98 Eng. Rep. 817
(1774) 1 Cowp., 112, or 98 Eng. Rep. 995
Grenville v Da Costa
(1797) Peake Add Cas. 113, or 170 Eng. Rep. 213
Haigh v Brooks
(1839) 10 Ad & E. 309, or 113 Eng. Rep. 119
Hawkes v Saunders
(1782) 1 Cowp. 289, or 98 Eng. Rep. 1091
Hayes v Warren
(1731) 2 Strange 933, or 93 Eng. Rep. 950
Holliday v Atkinson
(1826) 5 B. & C. 501, or 108 Eng. Rep. 187
Jestons v Brooke
(1778) 2 Cowp. 793, or 98 Eng. Rep. 1365
Lee v Muggeridge
(1813) 5 Taunt. 36, or 128 Eng. Rep. 599
Lindon v Hooper
(1776) 1 Cowp. 414, or 98 Eng. Rep. 1160
Littlefield v Shee
(1831) 2 B. & Ad. 811, or 109 Eng. Rep. 1343
Longchamp v Kenny
(1779) 1 Dougl. 138, or 99 Eng. Rep. 91
Marriot v Hampton
(1797) 7 T.R. 269, or 101 Eng. Rep. 969
Martyn v Hind
(1776) 2 Cowp. 437, or 98 Eng. Rep. 1174
(1776) 1 Dougl. 142, or 99 Eng. Rep. 94
Mawson v Stock
(1801) 6 Ves. Jun. 300, or 31 Eng. Rep. 1062
Mayor Yarmouth v Eaton
(1763) 3 Burr. 1402, or 97 Eng. Rep. 896
Meyer v Haworth
(1763) 8 Ad. & E. 467, or 112 Eng. Rep. 916
Montefiori v Montefiori
(1762) 1 Black. 363, or 96 Eng. Rep. 203
Moses v Macferlan
(1760) 2 Burr. 1005, or 97 Eng. Rep. 676

Munt v Stokes
(1792) 4 T.R. 561, or 100 Eng. Rep. 1176
Nightingal v Devisme
(1770) 5 Burr. 2589, or 98 Eng. Rep. 361
Paynter v Williams
(1833) 1 C. & M. 810, or 149 Eng. Rep. 626
Pillans and Rose v Van Mierop and Hopkins
(1765) 3 Burr. 1663, or 97 Eng. Rep. 1035
Power v Wells
(1778) 2 Cowp. 818, or 98 Eng. Rep. 1379
Price v Neal
(1762) 1 Black. 390, or 96 Eng. Rep. 221
Randall v Morgan
(1805) 12 Ves; Jun. 66, or 33 Eng. Rep. 26
Rann v Hughes 1778
(1778) 4 Bro. P.C. 27, or 2 Eng. Rep. 18
7 T.R. 350, or 101 Eng. Rep. 1014
Reech v Kennegal
(1748) 1 VEs. Sen. 123, or 27 Eng. Rep. 932
Roberts v Hartley
(1780) 1 Dougl. 312, or 99 Eng. Rep. 201
Shadwell v Shadwell
(1860) 9 C.B. (N.S.) 159, or 142 Eng. Rep. 62
Smith v Bromley
(1760) 2 Dougl. 696, or 99 Eng. Rep. 441
Stock v Mawson
(1798) 1 Bos. & Pul. 286, or 126 Eng. Rep. 907
Tate v Hilbert
(1793) 2 Ves. Jun. 111, or 30 Eng. Rep. 548
Thomas v Thomas
(1842) 2 Q.B. 851, or 114 Eng. rep. 330
Thornton v Illingworth
(1824) 2 B. & C. 824, or 107 Eng. Rep. 589
Trueman v Fenton
(1777) 2 Cowp. 544, or 98 Eng. Rep. 1232
Wells v Horton
(1826) 2 Car. & P. 383, or 172 Eng. Rep. 173
Wendall v Adney
(1803) 3 Bos. & P., 247 at 250, or 127 Eng. Rep. 137
Weston v Downes
(1778) 1 Dougl. 23, or 99 Eng. Rep. 19

Willliams v Moor
(1843) 11 M. & W. 256, or 152 Eng. Rep. 798
Wing v Mill
(1817) 1 B. & Ald. 104, or 106 Eng. Rep. 39

V Abridgements. *Selden Society Publications and the History of Early English Law – All Titles* – Alphabetical Search

N. Statham (1490), *Abridgement of Cases to the End of Henry VI* (original title page lacking), N.B. Henry VI reigned until 1461, Rouen: Per me. R. Pynson.

R. Brooke (1573): *Le Graunde Abridgement,* London: In Aedibus Ricardi Tottelli.

Fitzherbert (1577): *Le Graunde Abridgement, Collecte par le Iudge tresreuerend monsieur Anthony Fitzherbert, dernierment Conferre ouesque la Copye escript et per ceo correcte, ouesque le nombre del feuil, per quell facilement poies trouer les cases cy Abrydges en les Liuers dans, nouelment annote: iammais deuaunt imprimes. Auxi vous troueres les residuums de lauter liuer places icy in ceo liuer en le fine de lour apte titles,* London: In Aedibus Ricardi Tottelli.

H. Rolle (1668): *Un Abridgment des Plusieurs Cases et Resolutions del Common Ley,* London: Printed for A. Crooke [and 12 others].

VI Lexicons and Dictionaries. *Selden Society Publications and the History of Early English Law – All Titles* – Alphabetical Search

W. Rastell (1579), *Exposition of Certaine Difficult and Obscure Wordes and Termes of the Lawes of This Realme, Newly Set Fourth & Augmented, Both in French and English, for the Helpe of Such Younge Studentes as Are Desirous to Attaine the Knowledge for the Same. Whereunto Are Also Added the Olde Tenures,* London: In adibus Richardi Totelli.

J. Cowell (1637), *Interpreter: Or Booke, Containing the Signification of Words,* London: Printed for William Sheares.

J.J.S. Wharton (1848), *Law Lexicon, or Dictionary of Jurisprudence: Explaining All the Technical Words and Phrases Employed in the Several Departments of English Law, including also the Various Legal Terms Used in Commercial Transactions; Together with an Explanatory as well as Literal Translation of the Latin Maxims Contained in the Writings of the Ancient and Modern Commentators (From the London ed.),* Harrisburg, Pa.: I.G. M'Kinley & J.M.G. Lescure.

ANNEX 3

Table of Key Cases

The tables of cases (one sorted by date and one in alphabetical order) list the cases mentioned in the theoretical discussion of the concept of consideration in Chapter 5. All listed cases can be found on the HeinOnline database. The reference 'SS/YBEdw I' refers to the Year Books of the Reign of King Edward the First (A. Horwood, 5 v. London: Longmans Green, Reader and Dyer, 1866-1879). References such as '20 Selden Society 191' refer to the 20th volume of the Selden Society (Annual) Series, page 191. The reference 'Lawbook Exchange' refers to the Year Books (N.J. Clark, 11 v., Lawbook Exchange, 2007, 1678). All three can be found in the Selden Society Publications and the History of Early English Law. The English Reports references can all be found with volume and page references in English Reports, Full Reprint (1220-1867).

1 Sorted by Date

Date	Case name	Original report references	Report reference	Page
1294	*Anon.*	2 Y.B. Mich. 22 Edw. I	SS/YBEdw I, at 499	84
1294	*Anon.*	2 Y.B. Mich. 22 Edw. I	SS/YBEdw I, at 349	84
1303	*Anon.*	3 Y.B. Mich. 31 Edw. I	SS/YBEdw I, at 389	84
1304	*Anon.*	4 Y.B. Hil. 32 Edw. I	SS/YBEdw I, at 37	84
1304	*Anon.*	4 Y.B. Mich. 32 Edw. I	SS/YBEdw I, at 341	84
1305	*Anon.*	5 Y.B. Mich. 33 Edw. I	SS/YBEdw I, at 39	84
1306	*Anon.*	5 Y.B. Hil. 34 Edw. I	SS/YBEdw I, at 153	84
1307	*Anon.*	5 Y.B. Mich. 35 Edw. I	SS/YBEdw I, at 439	84
1310	*Loveday v Ormesby*	Y.B. 3 Edw. II, 25	20 Selden Society 191	65
1312	*Anon.*	Y.B. 5 Edw. II	33 Selden Society 2	87
1313	*Anon.*	Y.B. 6, 7 Edw. II 83	36 Selden Society 83	87
1321	*Anon.*	Y.B. 14 Edward II	86 Selden Society 353	69, 127, 140, 192–193
1329	*Anon.*	3 & 4 Edw. III	97 Selden Society 237	69, 127, 192–193

 | DOI:10.1163/9789004436169_011

Date	Case name	Original report references	Report reference	Page
1348	*Bukton v Tounesende*	Lib. Ass. 22 Edw. III, 94a-94b, 41	Lawbook Exchange	70, 71, 127, 128, 192–193
1370	*Waldon v Marshall*	Y.B. Mich. 43 Edw. III, 33, 38	Lawbook Exchange	72, 128, 192–193
1400	*Watton v Brinth*	Y.B. 2 Hen. IV, 3, 9	Lawbook Exchange	74, 192–193
1428	*Anon.*	Y.B. Hen. VI, 1, 3	Lawbook Exchange	74, 129, 192–193
1433	*Somerton's Case – writ*	Y.B. 11 Pasch. Hen. VI, 1, 25	Lawbook Exchange	74
1433	*Somerton's Case – legal arguments*	Y.B. 11 Hen. VI Trin., 55, 26;	Lawbook Exchange	74
1433	*Somerton's Case – legal arguments*	ibid. Hil., 18, 10; ibid., Pasch., 24, 1	Lawbook Exchange	74, 75
1436	*Anon.*	Y.B. 14 Hen. VI, 18, 58	Lawbook Exchange	73, 74, 129, 192–193
1442	*Doige's Case*	Y.B. 20 Trin. Hen. VI, 34, 4	Lawbook Exchange	75
1458	*Anon.*	Y.B. 37 Mich. Hen. VI, 8, 18	Lawbook Exchange	66, 85, 129
1476	*Anon.*	Y.B. 16 Pasch. Edw. IV, 9, 7	Lawbook Exchange	75, 192–193
1504	*Anon.*	Y.B. 20 Mich. Hen. VII, 8, 18	Lawbook Exchange	75, 192–193
1516	*Assaby v Lady Manners*	Dyer 335a	73 Eng Rep. 520	102
1520	*Anon.*	Y.B. 12 Mich. Hen. VIII, 11, 3	Lawbook Exchange	76
1535	*Jordan's or Tatam's Case*	Y.B. 27 Mich. Hen. VIII, 24, 3	Lawbook Exchange	77, 99, 163, 192–193
1539	*Marler v Wilmer*	KB 27/1111, m. 64	in Baker (2013) at 1180	86
1549	*Newman v Gybbe*	KB 27/1152, m. 135	in Baker (2013) at 1182	87

Date	Case name	Original report references	Report reference	Page
1556	*Pecke v Redman*	2 Dyer 113a	73 Eng. Rep. 248	94
1557	*Joscelin v Shelton*	3 Leonard 4	74 Eng. Rep. 503	88, 94
1558	*Norwood v Reed*	1 Plowden 180	75 Eng. Rep. 277	76
1564	*Sharington v Strotton*	1 Plowden 298	75 Eng. Rep. 454	88, 95, 100, 103–104
1567	*Lord Grey's Case*		in Baker & Milsom at 492	99, 100
1568	*Hunt v Bate*	Dyer 272	73 Eng. Rep. 605	93, 100, 102
1572	*Anon.*	Dalison 84, 35	123 Eng. Rep. 293	77, 192–193
1572	*Rogers v Snow*	Dalison 94	123 Eng. Rep. 301	96
1573	*Edwards v Burre*	Dalison 104, 45	123 Eng. Rep. 310	78, 192–193
1574	*Calthorpe's Case*	3 Dyer 334b	73 Eng. Rep. 756	81, 87, 88, 91
1574	*Moore v Williams*	Moore K.B. 220	72 Eng. Rep. 542	93, 94
1577	*West v Stowell*	2 Leonard 154	74 Eng. Rep. 437	94, 96
1577	*Onely v Earl of Kent*	Dyer 355b	73 Eng Rep. 797	96
1577	*Webb's Case*	4 Leonard 110	74 Eng. Rep. 763	96
1584	*Richards v Bartlett*	1 Leonard 19	74 Eng. Rep. 17	92, 96
1585	*Sidenham v Worlington*	2 Leonard, 224	74 Eng. Rep. 497	89, 91, 93, 102
1586	*Fuller's Case*	Godbolt 95	78 Eng. Rep. 58	94
1586	*Golding's Case*	2 Leonard 72	74 Eng. Rep. 367	95
1586	*Gill v Harewood*	1 Leonard 61	74 Eng. Rep. 57	96
1586	*Fooly v Preston*	1 Leonard 297	74 Eng. Rep. 270	96
1587	*Whorwood v Gybbons*	Gouldsborough 48	75 Eng. Rep. 986	88
1587	*Manwood v Burston*	2 Leonard 203	74 Eng. Rep. 479	89
1587	*Sturlyn v Albany*	Cro. Eliza. 67	78 Eng. Rep. 327	91

Date	Case name	Original report references	Report reference	Page
1587	*Marsh v Kavenford (Rainsford)*	Cro. Eliz. 59	78 Eng. Rep. 319	93
1587	*Foster v Scarlett*	Cro. Eliz. 70	78 Eng. Rep. 330	96
1587	*Browne v Garborough*	Cro. Eliz. 64	78 Eng. Rep. 324	102
1587	*Pearle v Unger*	Cro Eliz. 94	78 Eng. Rep. 353	93
1587	*Preston v Tooley*	Cro. Eliz. 74	78 Eng. Rep. 334	96
1588	*Marsh and Rainsford's Case*	2 Leonard 111	74 Eng. Rep. 400	93, 102
1588	*Simmes v Westcott*	1 Leonard 299	74 Eng. Rep. 273	94
1588	*Stone v Wythipol*	1 Leonard 113	78 Eng. Rep. 106	96, 97
1588	*Harford and Gardiner's Case*	2 Leonard 30	74 Eng. Rep. 332	101
1589	*Strangeborough v Warner*	4 Leonard 3	74 Eng. Rep. 686	76
1590	*Applethwait and Nertleys Case*	4 Leonard 56	74 Eng. Rep. 727	94
1590	*Byne v Playne*	1 Leonard 220	74 Eng. Rep. 202	96
1593	*Stone v Wythipol*	Cro. Eliz. 126	78 Eng. Rep. 383	96, 97
1593	*Sackford v Phillips*	Moore K.B. 690	72 Eng. Rep. 842	95
1594	*Jeremy v Goochman*	Cro. Eliz. 442	78 Eng. Rep. 683	93
1595	*Reynolds v Pinhowe*	Cro. Eliz. 429,	78 Eng. Rep. 669	98
1596	*Gower v Capper*	Cro Eliz. 543	78 Eng. Rep. 790	95
1597	*Metcalfe's Case*	Moore K.B. 549	72 Eng. Rep. 750	95
1598	*Rigges v Bullingham*	Cro. Eliz 714	78 Eng. Rep. 949	93
1599	*Wichals v Johns*	Cro Eliz. 703	78 Eng. Rep. 938	95, 96
1599	*Barker v Halifax*	Cro. Eliz 741	78 Eng. Rep. 974	102
1600	*Bret v J.S. and his Wife*	Cro. Eliz 755	78 Eng. Rep. 987	85, 103
1600	*Sherwood v Woodward*	Cro. Eliz. 700	78 Eng Rep. 935	98

Date	Case name	Original report references	Report reference	Page
1602	*Slade v Morley*	4 Co. Rep. 92 a.	76 Eng. Rep. 1074	78, 108, 192–193, 194
1602	*Riches v Briggs*	Yelverton 4	80 Eng. Rep. 4	96
1602	*Riches v Briggs*	Cro. Eliz 883	78 Eng. Rep. 1108	96
1602	*Pinnel's Case*	5 Co. Rep. 117a	77 Eng. Rep. 237	97
1602	*Lea v Exelby*	Cro Eliz. 888	78 Eng. Rep 1112	95
1603	*Bosden v Thinne*	Yelverton 40	80 Eng. Rep. 29	93
1604	*Game v Harvie*	Yelverton 50	80 Eng. Rep. 36	96
1608	*Pickas v Guile*	Yelverton 128	80 Eng. Rep. 86	96
1609	*Bettisworth v Campion*	Yelverton 133	80 Eng. Rep 90	95
1610	*Warbrook v Griffin*	2 Brownl. & Golds. 254	123 Eng. Rep. 927	79
1613	*Bagge v Slade*	3 Bulstrode 162	81 Eng. Rep. 137	98
1613	*Jones v Clarke*	3 Bulstode 73	80 Eng. Rep 969	93
1615	*Nichols v Raynbred*	Hob. 88	80 Eng. Rep. 238	95
1616	*Hodge v Vavisour*	3 Bulstrode 222	81 Eng. Rep. 188	93
1616	*Lampleigh v Braithwaite*	Hob 105	80 Eng. Rep. 255	94, 95, 97
1616	*Cotton v Westcott*	1 Rolle 381	81 Eng. Rep. 549	93
1616	*Spanish Ambassador v Gifford*	1 Rolle 336	81 Eng. Rep. 526	95
1618	*Winter v Foweracres*	2 Rolle 39	81 Eng. Rep. 645	104
1620	*Browne v Downing*	2 Rolle 194	81 Eng. Rep. 745	95
1623	*Wheatley v Low*	Cro Jac. 668	79 Eng. Rep. 578	96
1625	*Flight v Crasden*	Cro. Car. 8	79 Eng. Rep. 612	98
1628	*Bibble v Cunningham*	Hetley 89	124 Eng. Rep. 365	95
1635	*Townsend v Hunt*	Cro. Car. 408	79 Eng. Rep. 955	93, 103
1651	*Shann v Bilby*	Style 280	82 Eng. Rep. 710	95
1660	*Bennett v Astell*	1 Lev. 20	83 Eng. Rep. 276	95

Date	Case name	Original report references	Report reference	Page
1655	*Ernly v Lord Falkland*	Hard. 103	145 Eng. Rep. 349	95
1662	*Anon.*	1 Lev. 87	83 Eng. Rep. 311	95
1667	*Johnson v Astell*	1 Lev. 198	83 Eng. Rep. 367	98
1670	*Edgcomb v Dee*	Vaughan, 101	124 Eng. Rep. 984	79
1671	*Peters v Opie*	1 Vent. 177	86 Eng. Rep. 120	95
1697	*Ball v Hesketh*	Comb. 381	90 Eng. Rep. 541	108, 109
1699	*Hyleing v Hastings*	1 Ld. Raym. 389		108, 109
1731	*Hayes v Warren*	2 Strange 933	93 Eng. Rep. 950	168
1759	*Exeter Corporation v Trimlet*	2 Wils. K.B. 95	95 Eng. Rep. 705	168
1760	*Moses v Macferlan*	2 Burr. 1005	97 Eng. Rep. 676	106
1765	*Pillans and Rose v Van Mierop & Hopkins*	3 Burr. 1663	97 Eng. Rep. 1035	107, 192–193
1775	*Atkins v Hill*	1 Cowp. 284	98 Eng. Rep. 1088	109
1777	*Trueman v Fenton*	2 Cowp. 544	98 Eng. Rep. 1232	109
1778	*Rann v Hughes – pleadings/ arguments*	4 Brown, P.C. 27	2 Eng. Rep. 18	80, 107–108
1778	*Rann v Hughes – judgement of Skynner*	L.C.B. in 7 T.R. 350		80, 107–108
1782	*Hawkes v Saunders*	1 Cowp. 289	98 Eng. Rep. 1091	108, 192–193
1802	*Atkins v Banwell*	2 East 505	102 Eng. Rep. 462	110
1803	*Wendall v Adney*	3 Bos. & P., 247	127 Eng. Rep. 137	110
1813	*Lee v Muggeridge*	5 Taunt. 36	128 Eng. Rep. 599	110, 111
1817	*Wing v Mill*	1 B. & Ald. 104	106 Eng. Rep. 39	110
1840	*Eastwood v Kenyon*	11 Ad. & E. 438	113 Eng. Rep. 482	111
1860	*Shadwell v Shadwell*	9 C.B. (N.S) 159	142 Eng. Rep. 62	168, 192–193
1863	*Flight v Reed*	1 H. & C. 703	158 Eng. Rep. 1067	110, 168

Date	Case name	Original report references	Report reference	Page
1870	*Callisher v Bischoffsheim*	L.R.5. Q.B.449		97
1884	*Foakes v Beer*	9 A.C. 605		98

2 Sorted Alphabetically

Date	Case name	Original report references	Report reference	Page
1294	*Anon.*	2 Y.B. Mich. 22 Edw. I	SS/YBEdw I, at 499	84
1294	*Anon.*	2 Y.B. Mich. 22 Edw. I	SS/YBEdw I, at 349	84
1303	*Anon.*	3 Y.B. Mich. 31 Edw. I	SS/YBEdw I, at 389	84
1304	*Anon.*	4 Y.B. Hil. 32 Edw. I	SS/YBEdw I, at 37	84
1304	*Anon.*	4 Y.B. Mich. 32 Edw. I	SS/YBEdw I, at 341	84
1305	*Anon.*	5 Y.B. Mich. 33 Edw. I	SS/YBEdw I, at 39	84
1306	*Anon.*	5 Y.B. Hil. 34 Edw. I	SS/YBEdw I, at 153	85
1307	*Anon.*	5 Y.B. Mich. 35 Edw. I	SS/YBEdw I, at 439	84
1313	*Anon.*	Y.B. 6, 7 Edw. II 83	36 Selden Society 83	87
1321	*Anon.*	Y.B. 14 Edward II	86 Selden Society 353	69, 127, 140, 192–193
1329	*Anon.*	3 & 4 Edw. III	97 Selden Society 237	69, 127, 192–193
1428	*Anon.*	Y.B. Hen. VI, 1, 3	Lawbook Exchange	74, 129, 192–193
1436	*Anon.*	Y.B. 14 Hen. VI, 18, 58	Lawbook Exchange	73, 74, 129, 192–193
1458	*Anon.*	Y.B. 37 Mich. Hen. VI, 8, 18	Lawbook Exchange	66, 85, 129
1476	*Anon.*	Y.B. 16 Pasch. Edw. IV, 9, 7	Lawbook Exchange	75, 192–193
1504	*Anon.*	Y.B. 20 Mich. Hen. VII, 8, 18	Lawbook Exchange	75, 192–193
1520	*Anon.*	Y.B. 12 Mich. Hen. VIII, 11, 3	Lawbook Exchange	76
1662	*Anon.*	1 Lev. 87	83 Eng. Rep. 311	95
1312	*Anon.*	Y.B. 5 Edw. II	33 Selden Society 2	87

Date	Case name	Original report references	Report reference	Page
1572	*Anon.*	Dalison 84, 35	123 Eng. Rep. 293	77, 192–193
1590	*Applethwait and Nertleys Case*	4 Leonard 56	74 Eng. Rep. 727	94
1516	*Assaby v Lady Manners*	Dyer 335a	73 Eng Rep. 520	102
1802	*Atkins v Banwell*	2 East 505	102 Eng. Rep. 462	110
1775	*Atkins v Hill*	1 Cowp. 284	98 Eng. Rep. 1088	109
1613	*Bagge v Slade*	3 Bulstrode 162	81 Eng. Rep. 137	98
1697	*Ball v Hesketh*	Comb. 381	90 Eng. Rep. 541	108, 109
1599	*Barker v Halifax*	Cro. Eliz 741	78 Eng. Rep. 974	102
1660	*Bennett v Astell*	1 Lev. 20	83 Eng. Rep. 276	95
1609	*Bettisworth v Campion*	Yelverton 133	80 Eng. Rep 90	95
1628	*Bibble v Cunningham*	Hetley 89	124 Eng. Rep. 365	95
1603	*Bosden v Thinne*	Yelverton 40	80 Eng. Rep. 29	93
1600	*Bret v J.S. and his Wife*	Cro. Eliz 755	78 Eng. Rep. 987	85, 103
1620	*Browne v Downing*	2 Rolle 194	81 Eng. Rep. 745	95
1587	*Browne v Garborough*	Cro. Eliz. 64	78 Eng. Rep. 324	102
1348	*Bukton v Tounesende*	Lib. Ass. 22 Edw. III, 94a-94b, 41	Lawbook Exchange	70, 71, 127, 128, 192–193, 193
1590	*Byne v Playne*	1 Leonard 220	74 Eng. Rep. 202	96
1870	*Callisher v Bischoffsheim*	L.R.5. Q.B.449		97
1574	*Calthorpe's Case*	3 Dyer 334b	73 Eng. Rep. 756	81, 87–88, 91
1616	*Cotton v Westcott*	1 Rolle 381	81 Eng. Rep. 549	93
1442	*Doige's Case*	Y.B. 20 Trin. Hen. VI, 34, 4	Lawbook Exchange	75
1840	*Eastwood v Kenyon*	11 Ad. & E. 438	113 Eng. Rep. 482	111
1670	*Edgcomb v Dee*	Vaughan, 101	124 Eng. Rep. 984	79
1573	*Edwards v Burre*	Dalison 104, 45	123 Eng. Rep. 310	78, 192–193

Date	Case name	Original report references	Report reference	Page
1655	*Ernly v Lord Falkland*	Hard. 103	145 Eng. Rep. 349	95
1759	*Exeter Corporation v Trimlet*	2 Wils. K.B. 95	95 Eng. Rep. 705	168
1863	*Flight v Reed*	1 H. & C. 703	158 Eng. Rep. 1067	110, 168
1625	*Flight v Crasden*	Cro. Car. 8	79 Eng. Rep. 612	98
1884	*Foakes v Beer*	9 A.C. 605		98
1586	*Fooly v Preston*	1 Leonard 297	74 Eng. Rep. 270	96
1587	*Foster v Scarlett*	Cro. Eliz. 70	78 Eng. Rep. 330	96
1586	*Fuller's Case*	Godbolt 95	78 Eng. Rep. 58	94
1604	*Game v Harvie*	Yelverton 50	80 Eng. Rep. 36	96
1586	*Gill v Harewood*	1 Leonard 61	74 Eng. Rep. 57	96
1586	*Golding's Case*	2 Leonard 72	74 Eng. Rep. 367	95
1596	*Gower v Capper*	Cro Eliz. 543	78 Eng. Rep. 790	95
1588	*Harford and Gardiner's Case*	2 Leonard 30	74 Eng. Rep. 332	101
1782	*Hawkes v Saunders*	1 Cowp. 289	98 Eng. Rep. 1091	108, 192–193
1731	*Hayes v Warren*	2 Strange 933	93 Eng. Rep. 950	168
1616	*Hodge v Vavisour*	3 Bulstrode 222	81 Eng. Rep. 188	93
1568	*Hunt v Bate*	Dyer 272	73 Eng. Rep. 605	93, 100, 102
1699	*Hyleing v Hastings*	1 Ld. Raym. 389		108, 109
1594	*Jeremy v Goochman*	Cro. Eliz. 442	78 Eng. Rep. 683	93
1667	*Johnson v. Astell*	1 Lev. 198	83 Eng. Rep. 367	98
1613	*Jones v Clarke*	3 Bulstode 73	80 Eng. Rep 969	93
1535	*Jordan's or Tatam's Case*	Y.B. 27 Mich. Hen. VIII, 24, 3	Lawbook Exchange	77, 99, 163, 192–193
1557	*Joscelin v Shelton*	3 Leonard 4	74 Eng. Rep. 503	84, 94
1616	*Lampleigh v Braithwaite*	Hob 105	80 Eng. Rep. 255	94, 95, 97
1602	*Lea v Exelby*	Cro Eliz. 888	78 Eng. Rep 1112	95
1813	*Lee v Muggeridge*	5 Taunt. 36	128 Eng. Rep. 599	110, 111
1567	*Lord Grey's Case*		in Baker & Milsom at 492	99, 100
1310	*Loveday v Ormesby*	Y.B. 3 Edw. II, 25	20 Selden Society 191	65
1587	*Manwood v Burston*	2 Leonard 203	74 Eng. Rep. 479	89
1539	*Marler v Wilmer*	KB 27/1111, m. 64	in Baker (2013) at 1180	86

Date	Case name	Original report references	Report reference	Page
1588	*Marsh and Rainsford's Case*	2 Leonard 111	74 Eng. Rep. 400	93, 102
1587	*Marsh v Kavenford (Rainsford)*	Cro. Eliz. 59	78 Eng. Rep. 319	93
1597	*Metcalfe's Case*	Moore K.B. 549	72 Eng. Rep. 750	95
1574	*Moore v Williams*	Moore K.B. 220	72 Eng. Rep. 542	93, 94
1760	*Moses v Macferlan*	2 Burr. 1005	97 Eng. Rep. 676	106
1549	*Newman v Gybbe*	KB 27/1152, m. 135	in Baker (2013) at 1182	87
1615	*Nichols v Raynbred*	Hob. 88	80 Eng. Rep. 238	95
1558	*Norwood v Reed*	1 Plowden 180	75 Eng. Rep. 277	76
1577	*Onely v Earl of Kent*	Dyer 355b	73 Eng Rep. 797	96
1587	*Pearle v Unger*	Cro Eliz. 94	78 Eng. Rep. 353	93
1556	*Pecke v Redman*	2 Dyer 113a	73 Eng. Rep. 248	94
1671	*Peters v Opie*	1 Vent. 177	86 Eng. Rep. 120	95
1608	*Pickas v Guile*	Yelverton 128	80 Eng. Rep. 86	96
1765	*Pillans and Rose v Van Mierop & Hopkins*	3 Burr. 1663	97 Eng. Rep. 1035	107, 192–193
1602	*Pinnel's Case*	5 Co. Rep. 117a	77 Eng. Rep. 237	97
1587	*Preston v Tooley*	Cro. Eliz 74	78 Eng. Rep. 334	96
1778	*Rann v Hughes – judgement of Skynner*	L.C.B. in 7 T.R. 350		80, 107–108
1778	*Rann v Hughes – pleadings/ arguments*	4 Brown, P.C. 27	2 Eng. Rep. 18	80, 107–108
1595	*Reynolds v Pinhowe*	Cro. Eliz. 429,	78 Eng. Rep. 669	98
1584	*Richards v Bartlet*	1 Leonard 19	74 Eng. Rep. 17	92, 96
1602	*Riches v Briggs*	Yelverton 4	80 Eng. Rep. 4	96
1602	*Riches v Briggs*	Cro. Eliz 883	78 Eng. Rep. 1108	96
1598	*Rigges v Bullingham*	Cro. Eliz 714	78 Eng. Rep. 949	93
1572	*Rogers v Snow*	Dalison 94	123 Eng. Rep. 301	96
1593	*Sackford v Phillips*	Moore K.B. 690	72 Eng. Rep. 842	95
1860	*Shadwell v Shadwell*	9 C.B. (N.S) 159	142 Eng. Rep. 62	168, 192–193
1651	*Shann v Bilby*	Style 280	82 Eng. Rep. 710	95

Date	Case name	Original report references	Report reference	Page
1564	*Sharington v Strotton*	1 Plowden 298	75 Eng. Rep. 454	88, 95, 100, 13–104
1600	*Sherwood v Woodward*	Cro. Eliz. 700	78 Eng Rep. 935	98
1585	*Sidenham v Worlington*	2 Leonard, 224	74 Eng. Rep. 497	89, 91, 93, 102
1588	*Simmes v Westcott*	1 Leonard 299	74 Eng. Rep. 273	94
1602	*Slade v Morley*	4 Co. Rep. 92 a.	76 Eng. Rep. 1704	78, 108, 192–193, 194
1433	*Somerton's Case – legal arguments*	Y.B. 11 Hen. VI Trin., 55, 26;	Lawbook Exchange	74
1433	*Somerton's Case – legal arguments*	ibid. Hil., 18, 10; ibid., Pasch., 24, 1	Lawbook Exchange	74–75
1433	*Somerton's Case – writ*	Y.B. 11 Pasch. Hen. VI, 1, 25	Lawbook Exchange	74
1616	*Spanish Ambassador v Gifford*	1 Rolle 336	81 Eng. Rep. 526	95
1588	*Stone v Wythipol*	1 Leonard 113	78 Eng. Rep. 106	96, 97
1593	*Stone v Wythipol*	Cro. Eliz. 126	78 Eng. Rep. 383	96, 97
1589	*Strangeborough v Warner*	4 Leonard 3	74 Eng. Rep. 686	76
1587	*Sturlyn v Albany*	Cro. Eliza. 67	78 Eng. Rep. 327	91
1635	*Townsend v Hunt*	Cro. Car. 408	79 Eng. Rep. 955	93, 100
1777	*Trueman v Fenton*	2 Cowp. 544	98 Eng. Rep. 1232	
1370	*Waldon v Marshall*	Y.B. Mich. 43 Edw. III, 33, 38	Lawbook Exchange	72, 128, 192–193
1610	*Warbrook v Griffin*	2 Brownl. & Golds. 254	123 Eng. Rep. 927	79
1400	*Watton v Brinth*	Y.B. 2 Hen. IV, 3, 9	Lawbook Exchange	74, 192–193
1577	*Webb's Case*	4 Leonard 110	74 Eng. Rep. 763	96
1803	*Wendall v Adney*	3 Bos. & P., 247	127 Eng. Rep. 137	110
1577	*West v Stowell*	2 Leonard 154	74 Eng. Rep. 437	94, 96
1623	*Wheatley v Low*	Cro Jac. 668	79 Eng. Rep. 578	96

Date	Case name	Original report references	Report reference	Page
1587	*Whorwood v Gybbons*	Gouldsborough 48	75 Eng. Rep. 986	88
1599	*Wichals v Johns*	Cro Eliz. 703	78 Eng. Rep. 938	95, 96
1817	*Wing v Mill*	1 B. & Ald. 104	106 Eng. Rep. 39	110
1618	*Winter v Foweracres*	2 Rolle 39	81 Eng. Rep. 645	104

ANNEX 4

Reigns of Kings and Queens between 1066 and 1900

House of Normandy

William I	25 Dec. 1066–1087
William II	26 Sept. 1087–1100
Henry I	5 Aug. 1100–1135
Stephen	26 Dec. 1135–1154

Angevins (House of Plantagenet)

Henry II	19 Dec. 1154–1189
Richard I	3 Sept. 1189–1199
John	27 May 1199–1216

Plantagenets

Henry III	28 Oct. 1216–1272
Edward I	20 Nov. 1272–1307
Edward II	8 July 1307–1327
Edward III	25 Jan. 1327–1377
Richard II	22 June 1377–1399

House of Lancaster

Henry IV	30 Sept. 1399–1413
Henry V	21 March 1413–1422
Henry VI	1 Sept. 1422–1461

House of York

Edward IV	4 March 1461–1483
Edward V	9 April 1483
Richard III	26 June 1483–1485

 | DOI:10.1163/9789004436169_012

House of Tudor

Henry VII	22 Aug. 1485–1509
Henry VIII	22 April 1509–1547
Edward VI	28 Jan. 1547–1553
Mary I (alone)	19 July 1553–1554
Philip & Mary	25 July 1554–1558
Elisabeth I	17 Nov. 1558–1603

House of Stuart

James I	24 March 1603–1625
Charles I	27 March 1625–1649
[Interregnum	1649–1660]
Charles II	30 Jan. 1649 (*de jure*); restored 29 May 1660–1685
James II	6 Feb. 1685–1688
William & Mary	13 Feb. 1689–1694
William III (alone)	28 Dec. 1694–1702
Anne	8 March 1702–1714

House of Hannover

George I	1 Aug. 1714–1727
George II	11 June 1727–1760
George III	25 Oct. 1760–1820
George IV	29 Jan. 1820–1830
William IV	26 June 1830–1837
Victoria	20 June 1837–1901

King James VI of Scotland was proclaimed King of England in 1603 following Elisabeth I, who died without a direct heir. James styled himself 'King of Great Britain'. However, the kingdoms of England and Scotland were united as the United Kingdom of Great Britain only in 1707 during the reign of the last Stuart ruler, Queen Anne.

As far as Ireland is concerned, Henry VIII assumed the style 'King of Ireland' in 1541. But the two kingdoms remained distinct until the Act of Union of 1800, when the Kingdom of Ireland became part of the 'United Kingdom of Great Britain and Ireland'. Following the partition of Ireland in 1922, the kingdom was described as 'United Kingdom of Great Britain and Northern Ireland'.

Bibliography

Albaric, M. (2004) Hugues de Saint-Cher et les concordances bibliques latines (XIII–XVIII siècles), in: L-J. Bataillon, G. Dahan, P.-M. Gy (eds.) *Hugues de Saint-Cher (†1263), bibliste et théologien: Etudes réunies*, 467–479.

Ames, A. (1913) *Lectures on Legal History and Miscellaneous Legal Essays*, Cambridge: Harvard University Press.

Baker, J. (1971) New Light on *Slade's Case*, Part I, in: *Cambridge Law Journal* 29 (1), 51–67, Part II in: *Cambridge Law Journal* 29 (2), 213–236.

Baker, J., S.F.C. Milsom (1986) *Sources of English Legal History. Private Law to 1750*, London: Butterworth.

Baker, J. (1990) *Manual of Law French*, Aldershot: Scolar Press.

Baker, J. (1998) The Three Languages of the Common Law, in: 43 *McGill Law Journal* 5–24.

Baker, J., S.F.C. Milsom (1999) *Sources of English Legal History: Private Law to 1750*, London: Butterworth.

Baker, J. (2007) *An Introduction to English Legal History*, Oxford: OUP.

Baker, J. (2013) Origins of the doctrine of consideration 1535–1585, in: J. Baker, *Collected Papers on English Legal History*, vol III. Cambridge: CUP.

Baker, J. (2012) Deeds Speak Louder Than Words: Covenants and the Law of Proof, 1290–1321, in: S. Jenks, J. Rose, Ch. Whittick (eds.) *Laws, Lawyers and Texts: Studies in Medieval Legal History in Honour of Paul Brand*, Leiden: Brill, 177–200.

Baker, M. (1993) Corpus Linguistics and Translation Studies: Implication and Applications, in: M. Baker, G. Francis, E. Tognini-Bonelli (eds.) *Text and Technology: in Honour of John Sinclair*, Amsterdam and Philadelphia: John Benjamins, 233–250.

Barbour, W.T. (1914) The History of Contract in Early English Equity, in: P. Vinogradoff (ed.) *Oxford Studies in Social and Legal History*, vol. IV, Oxford: Clarendon Press.

Barlow, H. (1793) *Treatise on Equity*, vol. I, Dublin: Byrne, Moore, Jones, Lynch and Watts.

Barton, J.L. (1969) The Early History of Consideration, in: 85 *Law Quarterly Review*, 382–383.

Baugh, A. (1935) *A History of the English Language*, New York: Appleton-Century.

Becket, A. (1787) *Concordance to Shakespeare*, London: G.G.J. and J. Robinson.

Bell, J., D. Ibbetson (2012) *European Legal Development. The Case of Tort*. Volume 9, Cambridge: CUP.

Bell, J. (2014) The Importance of Institutions, in: M. Adams, D. Heirbaut (eds.) *The Method and Culture of Comparative Law*, Oxford: Hart Publishing, 207–219.

Bentham, J. (1823) *A Fragment on Government, Or, A Comment on the Commentaries*, London: E. Wilson.

de Beaugrande, R. (1997) Text Linguistics, Discourse Analysis, and the Discourse of Dictionaries, in: A. Hermans (ed.) *Les dictionnaires specialisés et l'analyse de la valeur*, Louvain-la-Neuve: Peeters, 57–74.

Biber, D. (1993) Representativeness in Corpus Design, in: *Literary and Linguistic Computing*, Vol. 8, No. 4, 243–257.

Biber, D., J. Burges (2000) Historical change in the language use of women and men. Gender differences in dramatic dialogue, in: *Journal of English Linguistics*, 28(1), 21–37.

Blackstone, W. (1765) *Commentaries on the Laws of England*, Introduction, Oxford: Clarendon Press.

Bracton (attributed to Henry of Bracton, c. 1210–1268) *De Legibus Et Consuetudinibud Angliae* (Bracton on the Laws and Customs of England), edited and translated by S. Thorne (1968–77), Online edition: www.bracton.law.harvard.edu.

Brand, P. (1992) *The Making of the Common Law*, London: Hambledon Press.

Brand, P. (2000) The Languages of the Law in Later Medieval England, in: D. Trotter (ed.) *Multilingualism in Later Medieval Britain*, Cambridge: Brewer, 63–76.

Brand, P. (2004) Petitions and Parliament in the Reign of Edward I, in: *Parchment and People: Parliament in the Middle Ages*, Linda Clark (ed.) 14–38.

Brand, P. (2010) The Language of the English Legal Profession: The Emergence of a Distinctive Legal Lexicon on Insular French, in: R. Ingham (ed.) *The Anglo-Norman Language and its Contexts*, York: York Medieval Press, 94–101.

Brand, P. (2012) Editing law reports and doing legal history: compatible or incompatible projects?, in: A. Musson, C. Stebbings (eds.) *Making Legal History. Approaches and Methodology*, Cambridge: CUP, 18–29.

Brand, P. (2015) The Languages of the Courtroom in England, c. 1300, in: M. Carruthers (ed.) *Language in Medieval Britain: Networks and Exchanges: Proceedings of the 2013 Harlaxton Symposium*, Donington, 48–58.

Brooke, R. (1573) *Le Graunde Abridgement*, London: In Aedibus Ricardi Tottelli, www.heinonline.org – Selden Society Publications and the History of Early English Law.

Brunner, H. (1907) The Sources of English Law, in: Committee of the Association of American Law Schools, *Select Essays in Anglo-American Legal History*, vol. 2.

Brunner, O., W. Conze, R. Koselleck (2004) *Geschichtliche Grundbegriffe. Historisches Lexikon zur Politisch-sozialen Sprache in Deutschland*, Stuttgart: Klett-Cotta, 9 volumes.

Butt, D., R. Fahey, S. Feez, S. Spinks, C. Yallop, (2000) *Using Functional Grammar. An Explorer's Guide*, Sydney: Macquarie University.

Collas, J.P., W.S. Holdsworth (eds.) *Year Books of 11 Edward II (1317–1318), Introduction,* 61 Selden Society.

Chang, P. (2002) Who's behind the personal pronouns in talk radio? Cartalk: a case study, in: A. Sanchez-Macarro (ed.) *Widows on the World: Media Discourse in English*, Valencia: University of Valencia Press.

Chomsky, N. (1965) *Aspects of the Theory of Syntax*. MIT Press.

Chomsky, N. (2000) *The Architecture of Language*, New Delhi: OUP (India).

Chomsky, N. (2007) Approaching UG from Below, in: H.-M. Gärtner, U. Sauerland (eds.) *Interfaces + Recursion = Language? Chomsky's Minimalism and the View from Syntax-Semantics*. Studies in Generative Grammar. Berlin: Mouton de Gruyter.

Coke, E. (1703 – 10th ed.) *Commentary upon Littleton.*

Cornu, G. (2005) *Linguistique Juridique*, Paris: Montchrestien.

Cornu, G. (2007) *Vocabulaire juridique*, Paris: PUF.

Cowell, J. *Interpreter: Or Booke, Containing the Signification of Words*, 1 v., London: Printed for William Sheares, 1637, www.heinonline.org – Selden Society Publications and the History of Early English Law.

Crespo, B. (2000) Historical Background of Multilingualism and its Impact on English, in: D. Trotter (ed.) *Multilingualism in Later Medieval Britain*, Cambridge: Brewer, 23–35.

Crystal, D. (2004) *The Stories of English*, London: Penguin Books.

de Saussure, F. (1916/2005) *Cours de linguistique générale,* Paris: Payot & Rivages.

Douglas, D.C. (1953) 'Edward the Confessor, Duke William of Normandy, and the English succession', in: English Historical Review LXVIII, 526–545.

Dury, P. (2005) Terminology and Specialized Translation: the Relevance of the Diachronic Approach, in: *LSP & Professional Communication*, vol. 5, nr. 1, 31–40.

Fairclough, N. (1992) *Discourse and Social Change*, Cambridge: Polity.

Felber, H. (2001) *Allgemeine Terminologielehre, Wissenslehre und Wissenstechnik. Theoretische Grundlagen und philosophische Betrachtungen*, Wien: Termnet.

Ferguson, C. (1959) Diglossia, in: *Word* 15: 325–340.

Fifoot, C.H.S. (1977/reprint of 1936 edition) *Lord Mansfield*, Aalen: Scientia Verlag.

Fifoot, C.H.S. (1949) *History and Sources of the Common Law: Tort and Contract*, London: Stevens.

Firth, J.R. (1957) A synopsis of linguistics theory 1930–1955, in: Studies in Linguistic Analysis, Oxford: Philological Society, 1–32.

Fishman, J. (1967) Bilingualism with and without diglossia; diglossia with and without bilingualism, in: *Journal of Social Issues* 23 (2): 29–38.

Fitzherbert, A. (1577) *Le Graunde Abridgement, Collecte par le Iudge tresreuerend monsieur Anthony Fitzherbert, derniermment Conferre ouesque la Copye escript et per ceo correcte, ouesque le nombre del feuil, per quell facilement poies trouer les cases cy*

Abrydges en les Liuers dans, nouelment annote: iammais deuaunt imprimes. Auxi vous troueres les residuums de lauter liuer places icy in ceo liuer en le fine de lour apte titles, London: In Aedibus Ricardi Tottelli, www.heinonline.org – Selden Society Publications and the History of Early English Law.

Fleta. seu Commentarius juris Anglicani (c. 1290), edited and translated by H. Richardson, G. Sayles for the Selden Society, www.heinonline.com, Selden Society Publications: 72 Selden Society (1953) Vol. II: Prologue, Books 1 and 2, 89 Selden Society (1972) Vol. III: Books 3 and 4, 99 Selden Society (1983) Vol. IV: Books 5 and 6.

Fortescue, J. (1741 – 2nd ed.) *De Laudibus Legum Angliae.*

Friedman, L.M. (1964) Law and its Language, in: 33 *George Washington Law Review*, 563–579.

Gerber, D.J. (1998) System Dynamics: Towards a Language of Comparative Law?, in: 46 *American Journal of Comparative Law* 719–734.

Gémar, J-C. (1995) *Traduire ou l'art d'interpréter, Langue, droit et société: éléments de jurilinguistique,* tome 2: *Application – Traduire le texte juridique*, Saint-Nicolas: Presses de l'Université du Québec.

St. German, Ch. (1518/1974), *Doctor and Student,* Second Dialogue, edited by T. Plucknett, J. Barton (1974) for the Selden Society, vol. 91.

de Glanvil, R. (1187–89) *Tractatus de legibus et consuetudinibus regni Anglie* (The treatise on the laws and customs of the realm of England commonly called Glanvil), edited and translated by G. Hall, M. Clanchy (2002), Oxford: Clarendon Press.

Goldberg, A. (1995) *Constructions: A Construction Grammar Approach to Argument Structure,* Chicago: University of Chicago Press.

Gordley, J. (1993) *The Philosophical Origins of Modern Contract Doctrine*, Oxford: OUP/ Clarendon Law Series.

Gries, S., M. Hilpert (2008) The identification of stages in diachronic data: variability-based neighbour clustering; in: *Corpora*, 1: 59–81.

Halliday, M. (1985/1994), *An Introduction to Functional Grammar,* London: Edward Arnold.

Halliday, M., R. Hasan, eds. (1985) *Language, context and texts: Aspects of language in a social semiotic perspective,* Geelong: Deaking University Press.

Hart, H.L.A. (1961) Positivism and the separation of law and morals, in: *Harvard Law Review* 71/4, 593–629.

Heirbaut, D. (2012) The spokesmen in medieval courts: the unknown leading judges of the customary law and makers of the first continental law reports, in: P. Brand, J. Getzler (eds.) *Judges and judging in the history of the common law and civil law: from antiquity to modern times*, Cambridge: CUP, 192–208.

Heirbaut, D. (2012) Exploring the law in medieval minds: the duty of the legal historian to write the books of non-written law, in: A. Musson, C. Stebbings (eds.) *Making Legal History. Approaches and Methodology*, Cambridge: CUP, pp. 118–130.

Helmholz, R. (1975) Assumpsit and *Fideo Laesio*, in: *The Law Quarterly Review*, 91, 406–432.

Hilbert, M. (2006) Distinctive collexeme analysis and diachrony; in: *Corpus Linguistics and Linguistic Theory*, 2(2): 243–257.

Hilbert, M., S. Gries (2009) Assessing frequency changes in multistage diachronic corpora: Applications for historical corpus linguistics and the study of language acquisition, in: *Literary and Linguistic Computing*, vol 24, No. 4, 385–401.

Hinneburg, A., H. Mannila, S. Kaislaniemi, T. Nevalainen, H. Raumolin-Brunberg (2007) How to handle small samples: bootstrap and Bayesian methods in the analysis of linguistic change, in: *Literary and Linguistic Computing*, 22: 137–150.

Hobbes, Th. (1651/1996) *Leviathan*, Oxford: OUP.

Hohfeld, W.N. (1913–1914) Some Fundamental Legal Conceptions as Applied in Judicial Reasoning, in: 23 *Yale Law Journal*, 16–59.

Holdsworth, W.S. (1903–1966) *A History of English Law*, London: Methuen.

Holdsworth, W.S. (1923) *A History of English Law*, vol. II, London: Methuen.

Holdsworth, W.S. (1923) *A History of English Law*, vol. III, London: Methuen.

Holdsworth, W.S. (1924) *A History of English Law*, vol. VI, London: Methuen.

Holdsworth, W.S. (1925) *A History of English Law*, vol. VIII, London: Methuen.

Holdsworth, W. (1938/1966 reprint) *Some Makers of English Law*, Cambridge: CUP.

Holmes, O.W. (1881) *The Common Law*, www.gutenberg.org.

Holmes, O.W. (1885) Early English Equity, in: *Law Quarterly Review*, 162–174.

Home, H. (Lord Kames) (1761) *Historical Law Tracts*, 2nd edition, Edinburgh: Kincaid.

Hudson, J. (2012) *The Oxford History of the Laws of England*, Volume II, 871–1216, Oxford: Oxford University Press.

Hunston, S., G. Francis (1998) Verbs Observed: A Corpus-driven Pedagogic Grammar, in: *Applied Linguistics*, 19/1, 45–72.

Ibbetson, D. (1982) Assumpsit and Debt in the Early Sixteenth Century: The Origins of the Indebitatus Count, in: *Cambridge Law Journal*, 41, 1, 142–161.

Ibbetson, D. (1984) Sixteenth Century Contract Law: *Slade's Case* in context, in: *Oxford Journal of Legal Studies* 4 (3), 295–317.

Ibbetson, D. (1986) Words and Deeds: the Action of Covenant in the Reign of Edward I, in: *Law and History Review*, 4, 71–94.

Ibbestson, D. (2001) *A Historical Introduction to the Law of Obligations*, Oxford: OUP.

Ibbetson, D. (2012) Comparative legal history: a methodology, in: A. Musson, C. Stebbings (eds.) *Making Legal History. Approaches and Methodology*, Cambridge: CUP, 131–145.

Ingham, R. (2010) Later Anglo-Norman as a Contact Variety of French?, in: R. Ingham (ed.) *The Anglo-Norman Language and its Contexts*, York: York Medieval Press, 3–25.

Ingham, R. (2010) The Transmission of Later Anglo-Norman: Some Syntactic Evidence, in: R. Ingham (ed.) *The Anglo-Norman Language and its Contexts*, York: York Medieval Press, 164–182.

Ingham, R. (2016) Investigating language change using Anglo-Norman spoken and written data, in: *Linguistics*, 54(2), 381–410.

Jespersen, O. (1955 reprint/1935) *Growth and Structure of the English Language*, Garden City: Doubleday.

Johnson, S. (1755) *Dictionary of the English Language: in which The Words are deduced from their Originals, and Illustrated in their Different Significations by Examples from the best Writers*; Ancestor of the OED (first published in 1884 as unbound fascicles) *A New English Dictionary on Historical Principles; Founded Mainly on the Materials Collected by The Philological Society.*

Joseph, J.E. (1995) Indeterminacy, Translation and the Law, in: M. Morris (ed.) *Translation and the Law*, Amsterdam/Philadelphia: John Benjamins Publishing Company, 13–36.

Kelsen, H. (1967) *The Pure Theory of Law*, Berkeley: University of California Press.

Kiralfy, A.K.R. (1951) *The Action on the Case*, London: Sweet & Maxwell.

Koselleck, R. (1979) Begriffsgeschichte und Sozialgeschichte, in: *Vergangene Zukunft. Zur Semantik geschichtlicher Zeiten*, Frankfurt am Main: Suhrkamp.

Koselleck, R. (2006) *Begriffsgeschichten*, Frankfurt am Main: Suhrkamp.

Kristeva, J. (1986) Word, dialogue and novel, in: T. Moi (ed.) *The Kristeva Reader*, Oxford: Basil Blackwell, 34–61.

Lambley, K. (1920) *The teaching and cultivation of the French language in England*, Manchester: The University Press.

Laske, C. (2012) Translating the Law, in: *Rechtgeleerd Magazijn Themis*, 267–278.

Laske, C. (2013) Translators and Legal Comparatists as Objective Mediators between Cultures? in: J. Husa, M. Van Hoecke (eds.) *Objectivity in Law and Legal Reasoning*, Oxford: Hart Publishing, 213–227.

Laske, C. (2016) Losing Touch with the Common Tongues – the story of Law French, in: *International Journal of Legal Discourse*, 2(2), 169–192.

Laske, C. (2021, forthcoming) Environmental Law: Lexical Semantics in the Quest for Conceptual Foundations, in: P. Stoett, S. Lamalle (eds.) *Representations and Rights of the Environment*, Cambridge: CUP.

Laviosa, S. (1998) The corpus-based approach: a new paradigm in translation studies, in: *Meta* XLIII, 4, 478–479

Lee T.R., S. Mouritsen (2018) Judging Ordinary Meaning, in: The Yale Law Journal, 127/4 (2017/2018) 788–1105.

Leech, G. (1991) The state of the art in corpus linguistics, in: K. Aijmer, B. Altenberg (eds.) *English Corpus Linguistics*, London: Longman, 8–29.

Legge, M. (1963) *Anglo-Norman Literature and Its Background*, Oxford: Clarendon Press.

Liebermann, F. (1903) *Die Gesetze der Angelsachsen: hrsg. im Auftrage der Savigny-Stiftung*, Halle an der Saale: Niemeyer.

Lobban, M. (2010) Contract, in: W. Cornish, S. Anderson, R. Cocks, M. Lobban, P. Polden, K. Smith (eds.) *The Oxford History of the Laws of England*, vol. XII (1820–1914), Oxford: OUP.

Locke, H. (1965/1966) *Slade's Case* and the Origin of the Common Counts, in: 81 *Law Quarterly Review,* Part I: 422–538, Part II: 539–561, Part III in: 82 *Law Quarterly Review* 81–96.

Lorenzen, E. (1919) Causa and consideration in the law of contracts, in: 28 *Yale Law Journal*, 621–646.

Louw, B. (1997) The Role of Corpora in Critical Literary Appreciation, in: A. Wichmann, S. Fligelstone, T. McEnery, G. Knowles (eds.) *Teaching and Language Corpora*, London and New York: Longman, 240–251.

Lusignan, S. (2009) French Language in Contact with English: Social Context and Linguistic Change, in: J. Wogan-Browne (ed.) *Language and Culture in Medieval Britain*, York: York Medieval Press, 19–30.

MacCormick, D.N. (1974) Law as Institutional Fact, in: *Law Quarterly Review*, 90.

MacCormick, D.N., O. Weinberger (1986) *An Institutional Theory of Law*, Dordrecht: Kluwer.

MacMahon, M.S. (1994) *Understanding Language Change*, Cambridge: CUP.

Macmillan, H.P. (1932) Scots Law as a subject of comparative study, in: 48 *Law Quarterly Review*, 477–487.

Maitland, F.W. (1903) Of the Anglo-French Language in the Early Year Books, in: Introduction to *Year Books of Edward II*, 17 Selden Society, at xiii.

Malinowski, A. (2006) *Polski jezyk prawny. Wybrane zagadnienia*, Warszawa: Wydawnictwo Prawnicze LexisNexis.

Marsh, G. (1862) *The Origin and History of the English Language*, New York: Scribner.

Mattila, H. (2013) *Comparative Legal Linguistics. Language of Law, Latin and Modern Lingua Francas*, Surrey: Ashgate.

Mattila, H. (2012) Legal Vocabulary, in: P. Tiersma, L. Solan (eds.) *The Oxford Handbook of Language and Law*, 27–51.

McGovern, W. (1969) Contract in Medieval England: The Necessity for Quid Pro Quo And a Sum Certain, in: 13 *American Journal of Legal History*, 173–201.

Mellinkoff, D. (1963) *The Language of the Law*, Boston: Little, Brown & Co.

Meyer, I., K. Macintosh (2000) When Terms Move into our Everyday Lives: An Overview of De-terminologization, in *Terminology* 6(1), 111–118.

Meyer, P., L. Toulmin-Smith (1889) *Les contes moralisés de Nicole Bonzon*; Paris: Société des anciens textes français.

Miller, G. (2002) The Death of French in Medieval England, in: C. Wiltshire, J. Camps (eds.) *Romance Phonology and Variation,* Amsterdam/Piladelphia: John Benjamins Publishing, 145–160.

Milroy, J. (1992) *Linguistic Variation and Change*, Oxford: Blackwell.
Milsom, S.F.C (1961) Sale of Goods in the Fifteenth Century, in: 77 *Law Quarterly Review*, 257–284.
Milsom, S.F.C. (1981) *Historical Foundations of the Common Law*, London: Butterworth.
Milsom, S.F.C. (1985) *Studies in the History of the Common Law,* London: The Hambledon Press.
Mitchell, P. (2012) *The Impact of Institutions and Professions on Legal Development.* Volume 8, Cambridge: CUP.
Munday, J. (1998) A computer-assisted approach to the analysis of translation studies, in: *Meta* XLIII, 4, 542–556.
Musson, A., C. Stebbings (2012) *Making Legal History. Approaches and Methodology*, Cambridge: CUP.
Nevalainen, T., H. Raumolin-Brunberg, (1996) *Sociolinguistics and Language History. Studies based on Corpus of Early English Correspondence*, Amsterdam: Rodopi.
Nevalainen, T. (2000) Gender differences in the evolution of standard English. Evidence from the corpus of the early English correspondence; in: *Journal of English Linguistics*, 28(1), 38–59.
Nevalainen, T., R. Reppen, S. Fitzmaurice, D. Biber (2002) *Using Corpora to Explore Linguistic Variation*, Amsterdam: Benjamins.
O'Halloran, K. (2010) How to use corpus linguistics in the study of media discourse, in: A. O'Keeffe, M. McCarthy (eds.) *The Routledge Handbook of Corpus Linguistics*, London: Routledge, 563–576.
O'Halloran, K. (2011) Critical discourse analysis, in: J. Simpson (ed.) *The Routledge Handbook of Applied Linguistics*, London and New York: Routledge, 109–125.
O'Keeffe, A. (2006) *Investigating Media Discourse*, London: Routledge.
Oleson, T.J. (1957) 'Edward the Confessor's promise of the throne to Duke William of Normandy', in: *English Historical Review* LXXII, 221–228.
Ormrod, W.M. (2003) The Use of English: Language, Law and Political Culture in Fourteenth-Century England, in: *Speculum* 73/3, 750–787.
Orr, J. (1948) *The Impact of French on English*, The Taylorian Lecture, Oxford: Clarendon Press.
The Oxford History of the Laws of England, Vol. VI 1483–1558, J. Baker (ed.) Oxford: OUP, 2003.
The Oxford History of the Laws of England, Vol. XII 1820–1914, W. Cornish, S. Anderson, R. Cocks, M. Lobban, P. Polden, K. Smith (eds.) Oxford: OUP, 2010.
Palmer, R. (1993) *English Law in the Age of the Black Death, 1348–1381*, Chapel Hill & London: The University of North Carolina Press.
Plucknett, T. (1956) *A Concise History of the Common Law*, London: Butterworth.
Pollock, F., F.W. Maitland (1895/1968) *The History of English Law before the Time of Edward I*, vol. I & II, Cambridge: CUP.

Pope, M. (1934) *From Latin to Modern French*, Manchester: Manchester University Press.

Poser, N. (2013) *Lord Mansfield. Justice in the Age of Reason*, Montreal & Kingston: McGill-Queen's University Press.

Pothier, R.J. (1761/2011) *Traité des obligations*, Paris: Dalloz.

Pothier, R.J. (1802) *A Treatise on Obligations considered in a Moral and Legal View*, translation: F.X. Martin, Newburn, NC: Martin & Ogden.

Pothier, R.J. (1806): *A Treatise on the Law of Obligations, Or Contracts*, translation: Sir William Evans (republished in Philadelphia in 1826, 1839 and 1853).

Price, G. (1984) Anglo-Norman, in: G. Price (ed.) *The Languages of Britain*, London: Edward Arnold.

Rastell, W. (1579) *Exposition of Certaine Difficult and Obscure Wordes and Termes of the Lawes of This Realme, Newly Set Fourth & Augmented, Both in French and English, for the Helpe of Such Younge Studentes as Are Desirous to Attaine the Knowledge for the Same. Whereunto Are Also Added the Olde Tenures*, 1 v., London: In adibus Richardi Totelli, www.heinonline.org – Selden Society Publications and the History of Early English Law.

Raumolin-Brunberg, H. (2003) *Historical Socio-Linguistics: Language Change in Tudor and Stuart England*, London: Pearson Education.

Reichardt, R., E. Schmitt, H.J. Lüsebrink, J. Leonard (1985-) *Handbuch politisch-sozialer Grundbegriffe in Frankreich 1680–1820*, München: Oldenbourg Wissenschaftverlag.

Reynolds, S. (1994) *Fiefs and Vassals: The Medieval Evidence Reinterpreted*, Oxford: OUP.

Richter, M. (1987) *Begriffsgeschichte* and the History of Ideas, in: *Journal of the History of Ideas*, vol. 48(2), 247–263.

Ritter, J., K. Gründer, G. Gabriel (1971–2007) *Historisches Wörterbuch der Philosophie*, Basel: Schwabe.

Rolle, H. (1668) *Abridgment des Plusieurs Cases et Resolutions del Common Ley*, 1 v., London: Printed for A. Crooke [and 12 others], www.heinonline.org – Selden Society Publications and the History of Early English Law.

Roszkowski, S. (1999) The language of law as sublanguage, in: J. Tomaszczyk (ed.) *Aspects of Legal Language and Legal Translation*, Lodz: Lodz University Press, 7–16.

Rothwell, W. (1975) The Role of French in Thirteenth-Century England, in: 58 *Bulletin, John Rylands Library*, 445–466.

Rothwell, W. (1991) The missing link in English etymology: Anglo-Norman, in: *Medium Ævum*, LX, 173–196.

Rothwell, W. (1992) The Problem of Law French, in: *French Studies*, XLVI, 3, 259–271.

Rothwell, W. (1993a) From Latin to Anglo-French and Middle English: the Role of the Multilingual Gloss, in: 88 *Modern Language Review*, 582–599.

Rothwell, W. (1993b) Language and government in medieval England, in: 93 *Zeitschrift für französische Sprache und Literatur*, 258–270.

Rothwell, W. (1996) Adding Insult to Injury: The English Who Curse in Borrowed French, in: H-F. Nielsen, L. Schosler (eds.) *The Origins and Development of Emigrant Languages*, Odense: Odense University Press, 41–54.

Rothwell, W. (1998) Arrivals and Departures: The Adoption of French Terminology into Middle English, in: 79 *English Studies*, 144–165.

Rothwell, W. (2001) English and French in England after 1362, in: *English Studies* 82, 539–559.

Salmond, J. (1887) The History of Contract, in: *Law Quarterly Review*, 3, 166–178.

Searle, J.R. (1995) *The Social Construction of Reality*, London: Allen Lane.

Shelly, P. (1921) *English and French in England: 1066–1100*, Philadelphia: University of Pennsylvania.

Simpson, A.W.B. (1958) The place of *Slade's Case* in the history of contract, in: 74 *Law Quarterly Review*, 381–396.

Simpson, A.W.B. (1975a) *A History of the Common Law of Contract: The Rise of the Action of Assumpsit*, Oxford: Clarendon Press.

Simpson, A.W.B. (1975b) Innovation in nineteenth century contract law, in: *Law Quarterly Review*, 91, 247–278.

Simpson, A.W.B. (1979) The Horwitz Thesis and the History of Contracts, in: *The University of Chicago Law Review*, 46, 533–601.

Sinclair, J. (1991) *Corpus Concordance Collocation*, Oxford: OUP.

Statham, N. (1490) *Abridgement of Cases to the End of Henry VI*, Rouen: Per me. R. Pynson, www.heinonline.org – Selden Society Publications and the History of Early English Law.

Stoljar, S. (1954) A Common Lawyer's French, in: 47 *Law Library Journal*, 119–224.

Stoljar, S. (1975) *A History of Contract at Common Law*, Canberra: Australian National University Press.

Stubbs, W. (1913) *Select charters and other illustrations of English constitutional history*, Oxford: The Clarendon Press.

Style, W. (1658) *Narrationes Modernae*, London: Lee, Pakemen, Bedel, Adams.

Suggett, H. (1946/1968) The Use of French in England in the Late Middle Ages, in: R. Southern, *Essays in Medieval History: selected from the transactions of the Royal Historical Society on the occasion of its centenary*, London: Macmillan, 213–239.

Teubner, G. (1993) *Law as an Autopoietic System*, Oxford: Blackwells Publishers.

Tognini-Bonelli, E. (2001) *Corpus Linguistics at Work*, Amsterdam and Philadelphia: John Benjamins.

Trotter, D. (2003) Not as eccentric as it looks: Anglo-French and French French, in: *Forum for Modern Language Studies* 39, 427–428.

Tymoczko, M. (1998) Computerized corpora and the future of translation studies, in: *Meta* XLIII, 4, 652–660.

van Caenegem, R. (1991) *Legal History: A European Perspective*, London: The Hambledon Press.

Van Hoecke, M., M. Warrington (1998/2010) Legal Cultures, Legal Paradigms and Legal Doctrine: Towards a New Model for Comparative Law' (first published 1998) reprinted in M. Del Mar, W. Twining, M. Giudice (eds), *Legal Theory and the Legal Academy*, The Library of Essays in Contemporary Legal Theory, vol III (Farnham, Ashgate, 2010) 291–332.

Van Hoecke, M. (2002) *Law as Communication*, Oxford: Hart Publishing.

Vising, J. (1923) *Anglo-Norman language & literature*, London: OUP.

Warr, J. (1650/1810) 6 *The Harleian Miscellany*, London: Dutton.

Weinreich, U., W. Labov, M. Herzog (1968) Empirical foundations for a theory of language change, in: W.P. Lehmann, Y. Malkiel (eds.) *Directions for Historical Linguistics: A Symposium*, Austin: University of Texas Press, 95–195.

Wharton, J.J.S. (1848) *Law Lexicon, or Dictionary of Jurisprudence: Explaining All the Technical Words and Phrases Employed in the Several Departments of English Law, including also the Various Legal Terms Used in Commercial Transactions; Together with an Explanatory as well as Literal Translation of the Latin Maxims Contained in the Writings of the Ancient and Modern Commentators (From the London ed.)*, Harrisburg, Pa.: I.G. M'Kinley & J.M.G. Lescure, www.heinonline.org – Selden Society Publications and the History of Early English Law.

Wilson, R. (1943) English and French in England 1100–1300, in: *History*, 28, 107, 37–60.

Wogan-Browne, J. (2009) General Introduction: What's in a Name: The 'French' of 'England', in: Wogan-Browne (ed.), *Language and Culture in Medieval Britain*, York: York Medieval Press, 1–13.

Wright, R. (1936) Ought the doctrine of consideration to be abolished from the Common Law? in: 49 *Harvard Law Review*, 1225–1253.

Woodbine, G. (1943) *The Language of English Law*, in: 18 Speculum, 395–436.

Zimmermann, R. (1993) Der europäischer Character des englishen Rechts, in: *Zeitschrift für Europäisches Privatrecht*, 4–50.

Zimmermann, R. (1996) *The Law of Obligations. Roman Foundations of the Civilian Tradition*, Oxford: OUP.

Zimmermann, R. (2001) *Roman Law, Contemporary Law, European Law: The Civilian Tradition Today*, Oxford: OUP.

Zimmermann, R. (2011) Roman Law and the Harmonization of Private Law in Europe, in: A. Hartkamp, M. Hesselink, E Mondius (eds.) *Towards a European Civil Code*, Alphen aan den Rijn: Kluwer.

Index of Names

Index of Subjects

www.ingramcontent.com/pod-product-compliance
Lightning Source LLC
Chambersburg PA
CBHW071323230926
51849CB00002B/301
9789004428485